Women World Leaders Presents

COURAGEOUS
STEPS OF FAITH

WITH GOD ALL THINGS ARE POSSIBLE

*God has a plan for your
your life. May C S O F inspire
you to walk out your
beautiful purpose in Him!
Praying for you dear friend.*

*Exceedingly
Abundantly
Beyond*

*Kimberly Hobbs
Eph. 3:20*

VISIONARY AUTHORS
KIMBERLY ANN HOBBS & JULIE T. JENKINS

For information regarding special discounts for bulk purchases, please contact the publisher:
LaBoo Publishing Enterprise, LLC
staff@laboopublishing.com
www.laboopublishing.com

Table of Contents

Introduction

God has a role to be birthed in you! He is bringing forward the greatest overturning of injustice in your life and he is removing chains that are holding you back. You will change history!

Examples of courage are scattered throughout this book in hopes of inspiring you. What is courage? The quality of mind or spirit that enables a person to face difficulty, danger, pain etc., without fear; bravery.

What is Biblical courage? The ability to do something brave out of a motivation of the heart. What is Faith? The Bible says, "Now faith is the substance of things hoped for, the evidence of things not seen" (Hebrews 11:1 KJV).

Now is the time to speak out a declaration over your life. What has been will be no more and you will echo this declaration out of your mouth: "God is changing history and shaping it through my obedience."

God will change history through your life, but you must be obedient, taking the first courageous step of faith to get there. Walk by faith into your God-given destiny.

Seek God to receive divine wisdom and authority from Him. As you read each story of courage and faith within this book, may you begin to release anything that may be holding you back. May God impart wisdom to spark renewed "hope" into your life. May you be fully awake and completely alert to what God is speaking to you throughout the pages and stories inside *Courageous Steps of Faith*.

The authors in this book have prayed over you. Our ongoing prayer is that courage will be embedded deep within your hearts as you read throughout this book. May you have strength in the face of grief and never give up hope. May you always remain faithful to God and press forward into your calling by Him. May you take Courageous steps of faith forward, realizing, "With God ALL things are possible."

Kimberly Ann Hobbs is an International Bestselling Author. Her most recent book "Fuel for Life" is a 90-day spiritual coaching guide into abundant living.

She is a Speaker, Teacher, Leader and Life Coach.

She has been a guest speaker on Moody Bible radio's God at work, as well as other television appearances encouraging others. She is Co-Founder of Women World Leaders, a worldwide ministry that empowers women to find their purpose which God has designed for them.

Kimberly is an established artist with much of her work reaching around the country and across the world. Through Kerus Global in South Africa, she helps raise support for her mission passion projects and over 100 orphaned children whom she loves. Kimberly sits on the advisory board for Kerus Global Education.

Kimberly is married and lives in South Florida with her husband Ken, they have children and grandchildren. Together they own and operate a successful financial coaching business.

My Pain ~ His Purpose

Kimberly Ann Hobbs

One of the most painful times in my life led me to my calling, my beautiful purpose today. It did not just perfectly appear with bright lights and clarity on the horizon; it took courage and faith to find it amidst the darkness of tragedy and pain.

Inside our hearts, we carry measures of grief from regrets, hurts, mistakes and disappointments. What we do with these measures of grief will determine our future of living and how we function throughout our lives; if we can be free to serve Christ moving forward or if we choose to live in bondage to our past or what is present in our lives today.

Sometimes making difficult decisions about releasing pain can require motivation of the heart. For me, overcoming past wounds of rejection, bitterness and unforgiveness toward me required a courageous step of faith. Feeling unworthy to lead held me in a captive state for many years and prevented me from living out my dream of becoming a leader. If the enemy of my life could keep me detained in my mind with the feelings of rejection, hurt and unworthiness, if he were to succeed, he could prevent the dream of a lifetime from coming to fruition. Being a structured person and a strong, encouraging motivator, I always felt I had the capability to become a great leader, but the enemy knew that if he controlled my thoughts, my actions would follow, and he could then persuade me to "give up" on God's purpose for my life.

My Story…

I believe the most excruciating pain a parent can feel is the loss of a child. When physical death strikes out of nowhere, it is final – it is over; however, this is not my story. Knowing my daughters are still alive today and having absolutely no communication with them is an ongoing, raging pain that has shredded my heart indescribably. If only I could get clarity from my daughters as to why they suddenly abandoned our relationship, I believed in my heart I would be able to fix it.

The torment in my mind raged as I tried to figure out the "why" of the reality. I attempted to connect, to open the door to painful truths, and to apologize if necessary. Unanswered phone calls, ignored text messages, letters sent with no response, unacknowledged gifts left on doorsteps – a deafening silence of rejection.

Past wounds of my own guilt and shame resurfaced as sadness in my heart allowed grief to escalate. I had asked and received forgiveness for past wrongs and nothing in the present seemed to justify the sudden and dramatic change in our relationship; my mind became nothing but a whirlwind of confusion. Their current behaviors were not in my control and the enemy used our division to drain the life from my soul. Days turned into months, and months into years. Unanswered questions and no responses.

One of my greatest joys was being a mother and a grandmother. The wicked spirits haunted and tormented me through countless, sleepless nights of questioning why. The raging battle in my mind was fierce and relentless.

As I watched all my friends on Facebook celebrating the joys of motherhood and grandparenting, I cried my eyes out to God, asking Him, "Why?" I begged Him to help me understand if there was anything I had personally done to cause this division and the break in relationship. I prayed and I searched my heart. I did everything I could possibly do, but God remained silent.

In the depths of my faith I trusted that one day God would bring my daughters back to me, but the fear of the present made my unworthy feelings escalate. Suffering a severe broken heart left me feeling that I could die at any moment; that is, until a sudden shift in perspective came and shed some light, bringing comfort from my Father in heaven.

A "shift" came when this question arose in my spirit: "Was my desperation of wanting a relationship with my estranged children becoming an obstacle to my service to God somehow?" Feelings of rejection from my children were consuming my thoughts and holding me captive day by day and week by week. I had to gather up courage to take steps of faith to emerge from that place of pain and rejection that I no longer wanted to live in. I would only be able to do this with God's strength and the power of His Word.

I began to lay down my mothering life to God. In laying down my life, I surrendered my desires in my own flesh of what I wanted so desperately (a relationship with my children). I had to trust God in the silence for His plan that I could not see with my eyes taking place in the lives of my children.

Proverbs 3:5 (NIV) – Trust in the Lord with all your heart and lean not to your own understanding.

God began showing me through His Word that something was happening. "I" was learning to release the hurts to God so I could love my children more despite the current status of our relationship. God allowed me to see that He had a plan for their lives, despite the fact that I could not see it.

Every person has choices to make throughout their lives, and my children's choices belong to them, not me. I was the one in fear over what I felt was being stolen from me, my relationship with my children and grandchildren. I felt tremendous fear of not having influence in their lives. Through my "shift" in perspective, Scripture reminded me that all of it, EVERYTHING, belonged to God – especially my kids. I needed to begin to trust God and not contaminate His ultimate plan for their lives.

We all have a calling on our lives, a purpose that God planned for us long ago. The enemy will attack us with whatever tactics he can, including attaching fear to an area where we are being called to serve, in order to distract us. My feelings of unworthiness were heightened as the enemy tried to damage my soul with this belief: "You are not worthy to lead anyone; your own children rejected you." He spoke this lie to me and tormented me with past mistakes that became giants in my mind. How would I ever know that beyond these enormous giants lay my life's destiny?

Through my state of hopelessness, I gathered courage to step forward in faith and begin slaying the giants of fear, rejection, and unworthiness. I needed to operate out of the courage God commands versus the fear the enemy dictates.

Joshua 1:9 (NIV) – Have I not commanded you? Be strong and courageous. Do not be afraid; do not be discouraged for the Lord your God will be with you wherever you go.

God expects us to be courageous – but our courage must not be in ourselves. We must draw our strength from God, but how? Often, we do not realize how strong we really are until being strong is all we have left. God provides strength for us when we ask. We need to let go of whatever it is that holds us back and allow God to take over.

This was not easy for me. Oh, how I needed more strength.

I realized time and again, through trying to reach my kids, that this was simply not in my control. The magnitude of this situation was something only God could resolve.

Any of us may realize, when we are in a situation that involves others who may be hindering or hurting us, that if we've done everything God's Word says to do to make things right, we must release both the individuals involved and the situation to God – completely. I had to realize that my children "belong to God." I raised them as best as I could at the time. God knows that – because He is God.

Proverbs 22:6 (KJV) – Train up a child in the way he should go: and when he is old, he will not depart from it.

This verse has been on my table since my girls were babies. It is my promise-scripture from God. I have no control over our relationship now as they are adults with children of their own, having their own choices to make.

Relinquishing control of this situation and handing it over to God has not been easy for me, but it allowed me to take my first faith steps and rely on God even though I felt I had to know the "whys" of the situation. It was and continues to be a learning process; I learned how to release and trust God.

Isaiah 41:10 (ESV) – Fear not for I am with you – be not dismayed for I am your God – I will strengthen you. I will uphold you with my righteous right hand.

The only safe place for my vulnerable, hurting heart was now at the feet of Jesus, surrendering the entire situation to Him.

1 Peter 5:6 (KJV) – Humble yourselves therefore under the mighty hand of God, that he may exalt you in due time.

God will appear in the silence when we are ready!

James 1:3 – For you know that when your faith is tested, it stirs up power within you to endure all things and then as your endurance grows even stronger it will release perfection to every part of your being until there is nothing missing and nothing lacking.

Nothing I did on my own worked, so by surrendering this situation of my life and the lives of my children to God, I could begin to see other things that God wanted me to see. My heart still yearns to have reconciliation with my girls, but I began to be able to see past my own needs and wants. God's timing for my pain of rejection will one day turn to a joy of healing for all of us and a reconciliation of our family; it will be perfect. Until then, my life still has great meaning and purpose; it is infused with helping others. I became proactive.

I began a "Faith, Food and Finance" online coaching group on Facebook which grew rapidly. I wrote daily encouragements and godly inspirations to help others get healthy in these three areas of life. My writing skills began to manifest, and people were drawn to what I was writing concerning different topics of faith, food and finance. What seemed to draw the most attention, and what I loved writing about the most, was the faith portion. I could write about the Lord all day long, and how He helped me through my trials. Lives were being touched and I saw it; people reached out and I could help them.

As I picked up my sword and shook the dust from my feet, I began to face the battle of my life in serving God. I became His vessel by mentoring others in the area of faith, but the devil was not happy with me.

As the chains that so tightly bound me started breaking away, the thoughts of unworthiness began to dissipate, allowing my confidence to rise. I realized the enemy was coming at me stronger now. It did not matter to me because God gave me eyes to begin seeing it. God's Word is true, and I saw it come alive with POWER at a time I truly needed it.

Ephesians 2:10 TPT – "We have become his poetry, a re-created people that will fulfill the destiny he has given each of us, for we are joined to Jesus, the Anointed One. Even before we were born God planned in advance our destiny and the good works we would do to fulfill it!"

This liberating verse showed me that God planned on using me long before I knew it. People were moved to action by the encouraging words I wrote and the power of God working in them. This fueled me as I began seeing miracles happening around me and the power of faith through prayer making a difference in the lives God was touching. I wrote daily and loved it.

The Facebook group I started led me to a publisher who had become part of the group. The publisher noticed my work and I was encouraged to write my first book. That book is *Fuel for Life: Abundant Living Through Daily Coaching.* This book is a 90-day, faith-based coaching book that helped me to heal as I wrote it. This book was also dedicated to the Lord to touch millions for His purpose. As I wrote, the enemy came back at me strong and hard as thoughts of unworthiness were resurfacing: "How can I lead others with coaching if my own family is rejecting me?" Although I was taunted through writing, the "voice of truth" was progressively louder. Through my writing, I had to be saturated in the Word daily; it was where I gathered all my information and all my strength. Knowing the Word of God and the truth within silenced the voice of the devil. The demonic forces that tried to come at me already knew this book would be a glory for our Lord and wanted to cripple me before my purpose ever began.

Even in my excruciating motherly pain, God built my confidence in an area that would house my purpose and allow me to lead through writing and encouraging. By sharing my vulnerable life stories and relating it all back to Scriptures, God allowed me to step into my destiny with great awakening.

I could not move one step without seeking God first. He became my lead and my lean. Daily I asked God for His wisdom and eyes to see and ears to hear from Him. I wrote only what the Holy Spirit led me to write each day.

Although it seemed I was worthless to some, God allowed me to feel priceless when it came to serving Him. The more I wrote, the more people were drawn in for encouragement. While I was helping others find healing in their souls, God was also healing mine. The battle of this mother's broken heart belongs solely to God, and He was covering my hurts.

During my obedience of writing my first book, *Fuel for Life*, God planted a vision in my soul. This was a firm, clear vision completely from God, and it was the glimpse of what would soon become Women World Leaders, a group of women gathering from around the world to serve Jesus.

There were weeks and weeks of preparation. I planned the very first meeting of Women World Leaders in my family room with some friends who God showed me would be leaders, a help for this huge vision. The devil came at me with a vengeance. It was in the time frame of our first meeting that I received a late-night call asking if I had looked at Facebook. Feeling as though something were wrong, I looked on my phone from bed. My heart was beyond shattered! I saw the post that another grandchild had arrived. The saddest thing was I had no advance notice that he was even on his way. I cannot even write enough descriptive words to adequately explain the pain I felt that night when I saw the post, because it is just too hurtful to even reflect on. I will say this: That night I was as close to death from a broken heart as a mother ever could be. But God and a loving husband, who both held me in their arms, allowed me to grieve!

God had been building my strength muscles, so with thankfulness in my heart as I reflect, I was able to endure the pain and live, hearing the "voice of God" through it all. My husband cried out and sang out the repeated Name of Jesus with me all night long.

Through my writing, God told me to be expectant. Have faith for a double portion.

Hebrews 11:6 (NIV) – And without faith it is impossible to please God.

God had given me a voice through writing. I was hearing His voice to write the words out on paper that were locked up inside me.

God specifically told me, "Your shame is leaving you. You are my forgiven daughter and your life will become an open book. You will minister to the hearts of women everywhere, showing them where true freedom and deliverance begins. They will experience healing through Me and My scriptures, and you will be My messenger, a leader in My Name." Remembering God rewards the faith of those who passionately seek Him, a deluge of peace came over me.

Despite the distractions the enemy threw at me yet again in trying to start a ministry, I am a true testimony of what God says in his Word: "With God all things are possible."

With God's strength, a mighty miracle work began in me. I had a mission! The vision God gave me was that of a massive movement, a women's group that was taking form. The women I gathered in Jesus' Name began serving the Lord, and Women World Leaders began to sprout and grow. This group, now a worldwide organization, all took form as I was leading during my worst personal storm. It is still incomprehensible as I reflect on it. But God again...

As passions of service in my life unfolded, they were packaged in difficulties as the enemy constantly sought my demise. I have great news! The enemy's ferocious roar no longer echoed in my ears because God's voice became the piercing sound of thunder that came to penetrate my entire being. Through the power of His Holy Word and the word of my testimony, God was teaching me by showing me how to slay the giants that were in my way.

As woman after woman came to me, I would love and encourage them, pointing them to Jesus; and God grew Women World Leaders one person at a time. God brought me women, the same age as my own precious daughters, from around the world, who needed love and empowerment through our Lord Jesus Christ. As I helped each of them, God continued to heal my hurting heart, and tremendous blessings flowed and are still flowing each day.

I believe with all my heart that one day God will restore my relationship with my children and grandchildren, and I pray that it will be this side of heaven, but that's up to God, for it is all in His timing, and I am totally OK with that now. I believe He is taking my children through their own journeys and, in His timing, their stories will become our family testimony of God's amazing restoration and forgiveness.

God creates new opportunities with each passing day in our lives – some that correspond with hurts and pains, some with joys and triumphs. We must be aware and be prepared to seize every opportunity that comes our way, realizing that they do not always come to us packaged with a "pretty pink bow" or standing out with beauty.

Are you willing to allow God the opportunity to use you and share your stories to help others? This is what this book is about – stories of women taking courageous steps of faith in hope that sharing their stories will inspire others to do the same.

God uses situations in our lives to show us our need to rely on Him and strengthen our faith. If my life were going merrily along, would I ever have reached out to God when nothing else I did was working? By crying out to God and embracing his Words of Truth each day, I was drawn so close to Him. He strengthened me by identifying with my pain through His Word, and He delivered me by allowing me to share my testimony and to encourage others. Through my pain, others have hope.

I think of the apostle Paul – while he was hurting (thorn in the flesh), he begged God, "Please fix it, please take it away." I too asked God, "Please bring my children back." In fact, I begged Him, "Please, please stop their pain, and mine too!"

God said, "My grace is sufficient for you; for my power is made perfect in weakness."

The apostle Paul said, "I will boast all the more gladly in my weaknesses, so that Christ's power may rest on me" (2 Corinthians 12:9 NIV).

I had to release everything to God and not contaminate His divine plan with my controlling agenda. I needed to remind myself that it is not about the pain; it is about the purpose. God can use my pain for His purpose. I am His and He has authority.

God is healing my mind from inadequacies that haunted me, and now He is teaching me to become a passionate leader, identifying with the hearts of others. God's teaching is truly a treasured gift to me. Having the ability to lead and coach others is a humbling experience. To do so, I must remain humble and be saturated in His Holy Word daily. This is what draws me so intimately close to Him. I can now realize my pain of rejection is NOTHING compared to the rejection Christ felt as He bore my sin and shame nailed to the cross. I can now overcome rejection and unworthiness by the power of my testimony as God says in Revelation 12:11. God covers me, empowers me and protects me whether I am up for the battle or not. He is always there. He will NEVER leave me or forsake me.

The miracle in sharing this story with you is that it allows me to walk out my courageous steps of faith, sharing my stories while overcoming obstacles with thousands of women. My goal is to see millions of women transformed through the blood of the Lamb and have them come beside me to serve our King together – in all their beauty and the capacity that God provides.

…With God all things are possible (Matthew 19:26).

God is waiting and He will do great and mighty things through you. You are loved, you are called, and you can be chosen and fully equipped by God to live out the powerful Ephesians 3:20 life that He has assigned to you. But it is a choice. It is YOUR choice.

Where I once walked in brokenness, feeling unworthy to lead an ant to an anthill, God taught me to walk boldly and courageously with passion, holding convictions and leading souls to heaven for eternity.

I now realize that the pain I went through led me to this purpose, leading Women World Leaders. God is doing the gathering, and you can share your story here for Him, for His honor and glory. God has a place for you.

What will you do through your pain, your fear, or whatever you are facing right now?

Isaiah 43:1 NIV – Do not fear, for I have redeemed you; I have summoned you by name; you are mine.

IT IS TIME TO REDEEM YOUR TIME.

We are on this earth for an incredibly short while. Do not wait for tragedy to remind you to look to the heavens. You have a purpose. Fulfill your God-given calling wherever you are placed in this moment of time.

Be bold and courageous. I cannot emphasize this enough. God wants to empower you to do what is absolutely His best for you. He wants you to believe the powerful truth about your worth and position in Jesus Christ and your gifted calling on this earth.

Ephesians 3:20 NIV – Unto him who is able to do exceedingly abundantly above all we could ask or imagine; according to the power that is at work within us.

My prayer to you: May your eyes be open to see God at work everywhere you go and through everything you live out in the remainder of your life on this planet. May God do the impossible through you and through your obedience; with a humbled heart may you be willing to step out with courage and faith. May this book empower you to take that courageous first step.

I triumph because I do not cling to my own life anymore. I released it, and I did so in its entirety to God. It is the only way that my life is working now, fully surrendered. By the power of my testimony,

HIS Word goes out to the world as I serve Him.

Your story will look different than mine or any of the other women in this book because it will be yours, delivered by God, if you say yes to Him.

I said, "Yes Lord, here I am, send me" … Will you say "yes" to God and allow Him to pen your story of courage on your heart? Will you take it one step further and share it?

He will absolutely use you if you are willing – but being willing requires action. You must trust God and take your first courageous step of faith, and when you do, hold this verse in your heart and mind …

… "WITH GOD ALL THINGS ARE POSSIBLE!"

. . . .

Courage to overcome
UNWORTHINESS
Kimberly Ann Hobbs

Romans 8:39 NIV – Neither height nor depth, nor anything else in all creation, will ever be able to separate us from the love of God that is in Jesus our Lord.

You are so loved … Even in your weakest moments where you feel unworthy and inadequate, you are loved and seen in fullness and greatness. Often, we fall into brokenness and let our weakness and insecurities overtake us. We allow them to define us because we focus on that which comes out of the mouths of others about us instead of believing the truth that pours from our Lord to us.

It takes tremendous courage to talk down lies from the enemy and listen to the Voice of Truth. The voice of truth from God's Word will speak to you and strengthen you to combat the lies you believe. The truth from God will propel you to true freedom. We need to recognize any issue that can harm us and release it to God through prayer. Feelings of inadequacy sometimes cause you to feel that you don't have the qualities and abilities necessary to do something or cope with life in general. We all have hope. Our hope lies in Jesus Christ.

When we are feeling unworthy, we need to muster up courage from truth – not lies. We must identify the lies. Ask God to help you. He will give you courage. Courage that says, "because God's love is perfect and unconditional and pure, he will help you."

Trust God and understand the core of your being He created is in your soul. God created you and he thinks you are worthy! He will show you in his Word that you will no longer need to depend on the fleeting approval of others because your worth will be built on the solid foundation of an unchanging God. But you must trust His love for you.

God talks to you through the Bible. It's his love letter to you. God believes you are worthy. So worthy that He engraved you on the palm of His hands. He says that in Psalm 49:15-16. He also sees you as a masterpiece (Ephesians 2:10) and He calls you His own (1 John 3:1).

Despite your past mistakes, God's gift to you is Jesus Christ; and by trusting Him as your Savior, viewing your life's inadequacies can become something of the past. Why? You are now worthy because you belong to the King. You now are His child, and God makes NO MISTAKES. He created you with His purpose in mind.

· ·

 **Julie Jenkins** is the Teaching and Curriculum Leader for Women World Leaders. As an author, speaker, teacher and leader of Biblical Truth, Julie walks in response to her calling from the Lord. She grew up in Ohio, earned her Bachelor of Communications at The University of Tulsa, and her Master of Biblical Exposition from Moody Bible College.

Events that have shaped Julie's worldview include growing up in a small midwestern town; traveling with Up With People, an international leadership program where she performed on stage, participated in community involvement, and lived with host families in several countries; being a long-time leader in several different capacities for Bible Study Fellowship and other ministries and churches; and participating in various Biblical and leadership training programs.

Julie, her husband Michael, and their children currently live in Jupiter Florida where she enjoys the beach, her family, and working with her husband at J29 Marketing, their digital marketing company. She can be contacted at julie@womenworldleaders.com

Stepping into the Shadows
Julie Jenkins

I remember the moment it happened. The moment I was called to step into the shadows. Most Courageous Steps of Faith involve stepping OUT of the shadows in some form or fashion. My moment was different. God was calling me to let go of my pride, to let go of the control I thought I had on my life – to surrender it all. And to let God be God.

I was raised to be a strong, independent woman. I was the youngest of seven, and my parents encouraged each of us to fly our own paths. I went to college 900 miles from home, learned leadership early on, and knew how to get my way and make a path for myself. I graduated from college, began to work in the career of my choice, and made a name for myself. I traveled, made good money, married the man of my dreams, and we bought our first house early in our marriage. I was involved in our church, but only when it suited me and when I could fit it in around my busy schedule. And a busy schedule it was! I was the coordinating producer for Major League Soccer, having worked on a very small team as we built the television platform for the newly formed national league. I worked with the league, the teams, the owners, the sponsors, the television networks, and the talented players who flocked to the United States from around the world.

A couple of years into marriage and several years into the career I loved seemed to be the right time to have children. My husband and I knew how many children we wanted, and exactly how we would space their births. I talked to my employers, told them my plan, and boldly announced that within a year I would need to be taken off the travel schedule, and if they couldn't do that, I would have to quit. They obliged. Within a year, my job no longer required me to travel from our main office, and I was pregnant with our first child.

Sarah was born on March 11, 2000 – which gave me time to take maternity leave and still gear up for the upcoming MLS season. We found a great daycare just down the street from my office – and I fell into the routine of dropping Sarah off when the doors opened at 7:30am and picking her up at 6:00pm when they closed. I was ALWAYS one to get my money's worth! Each day at lunch I took a break to go feed her. My husband and I took turns taking our newborn to her doctor's appointments, and we marveled at the fact that people said that having a child would change your life, because it hadn't changed ours at all. We were just a little more tired.

And then it happened. You are probably waiting to hear the story of a tragic accident, illness, or life-altering event. But that wasn't what happened at all. It was a still, small voice that rocked my world.

Throughout Scripture we read stories of God speaking in a still, small voice. Elijah was a prophet whose life, although filled with wonder and words from the Lord, was not an easy one. At one point, Elijah was running for his life, and the Lord came to him and said, *Go out and stand on the mountain in the presence of the Lord, for the Lord is about to pass by* 1 Kings 19:11 (NIV). Elijah did – and he experienced a great wind, followed by an earthquake, followed by a fire. With each event, I'm sure that Elijah was looking for God's presence. But Scripture tells us that the Lord was NOT in the wind. He was NOT in the earthquake. And He was NOT in the fire. And then came a gentle whisper. A still small voice. The voice, the Lord, asked, *What are you doing here, Elijah* (v. 13)? Elijah poured out his heart, and God graciously gave him a list of instructions – where to go and who to anoint, reassuring Elijah that He was in control.

The day that I heard the still small voice I had picked up Sarah from daycare at 6:00pm, and we went back to the office so that I could finish my work. Truth be told, I was never really done with my work, but only survived from one deadline to the next.

Sarah was five months old – too young to recognize that she spent more time at daycare and in her car seat than in her own home. Too unaware to realize that she lived on my schedule. Too sweet to make my life difficult over the fact that I acted like I loved my job more than I loved her. And I was too focused on my idol of work to notice.

Praise God for the still, small voice.

For that day I picked her up at 6:00pm, we drove back to the office, and I put her down in her car seat carrier right by my feet at my desk. And as I typed, she smiled up at me. And that's when my world changed. That's when I heard God say, *What are you doing here, Julie?*

I knew. I knew that God wanted something different for her than to sit at my feet while I worked. God had a plan for her – to grow, and thrive, and become. He had an anointing for her life, and it was my job, my honor, to be part of that anointing. God graciously gave me His instructions in a whisper, telling me that I had a responsibility, to Him and to the family that He had given me. It was no longer about me, my job, or my title. For years I had been in the spotlight, and I knew that it was time for me to step into the shadows. Little did I know that, as God works all things together for the good of those who love Him (Rom 8:28), His whisper to me was as much for my benefit as it was for the benefit of my family.

I'd love to say that the transition to being a stay-at-home mom was easy, but it took courage to follow the path that God made so clear. My life was not in danger, as Elijah's was, but my pride sure was.

Shortly after that fateful day, God orchestrated a move for our family to a new community hundreds of miles away. We also took a step back socio-economically, as we had given up my income and had moved to an area where it was more expensive to live. That was hard. But God provided everything that we needed, and I was so busy with the move and the baby and our dogs that I didn't really notice the change. As soon as things slowed down, however, I was hit with my own strong wind and earthquake and fire – and it didn't feel like God was anywhere to be found.

I grieved. I grieved the fact that I was no longer "somebody." Nobody in our new community knew my name, and I didn't have an answer when people asked me what my job was. I grieved that I could no longer go to the mall and shop for expensive clothes – we didn't have the money and I didn't have anywhere to wear them. I grieved my busy lifestyle – I was bored! I spent countless hours painting the house trying to make it a home, but also trying to numb my mind.

And I fought jealousy. My husband's career was thriving. My daughter was growing and happy and well-adjusted. My parents were traveling, living their best life. And everyone at church seemed content, and they all walked with purpose.

So I started looking for a purpose – and there were just two requirements: My purpose couldn't cost any money, and it couldn't interfere with our family time. Let me make it clear that these were nobody's requirements but my own. My husband was wonderful and would have moved the moon for me, but I was serious about my calling, and I was pridefully determined to serve and not be served (Mark 10:45).

Growing up, there was a handmade sign that hung on the wall of our home that said, "I am third." I can remember asking my mom what that meant, and she explained to me that it meant that God is first, others are second, and I am third. During this time of stepping into the shadows, those words kept returning to the forefront of my mind. I understood quite well what "I am third" meant, and I knew what it meant to make my family "second," but what did it mean to make God "first?"

As I strived to understand my purpose during this time in my life, church became the center of our family. I am ashamed to say that it wasn't because I wanted to put God first, but because church fit in with the criteria that I had devised to find my purpose: It was free and it didn't interfere with our family life. But thankfully, God works *all* things together for the good of those who love Him (Romans 8:28).

You know the scripture that says, "Whether you turn to the right or to the left you will hear a voice saying, 'This is the way, walk in it'" (Isaiah 30:21)? There can be no better way to describe the next 20 years of my life. There was NEVER a question of what God wanted for my life or that He was orchestrating it perfectly. And although He was leading me, I often felt like I was just walking down a dark hallway looking for an open door.

My husband and I had three wonderful children. Emily was born two years after Sarah, and Matthew was born four years later. Our move to Florida after I quit my career was the first of many moves. My husband's job was thriving, and my job was to support him and the kids. We bought and sold houses like many people buy and sell cars – another new one every one to three years. That meant new schools, new sporting venues, new veterinarians, and new churches. Routinely, things would get settled, and I would begin looking for my purpose again. Then the process would start over.

But in the in-between, before it would start over, God kept calling me and teaching me, whether I turned to the right or to the left.

If you have been involved in more than one church, or even know someone who goes to a different church than you, you likely know that every church approaches discipleship a bit differently. Discipleship in the Christian church is following after Jesus Christ – maturing and growing in His image, as He has called. It is putting God first, others second, and yourself third. Most churches offer classes or small groups or service opportunities. Some offer schools of leadership, programs committed to the service of the sick, or Sunday schools. And the thing about these offerings is that they are generally free of charge and provide a free companion class for children – so a young mom can drop off her kids and, for a short period of time while they learn and are nurtured, she can spend time learning and growing herself.

Do you see God's plan coming together here? I didn't. But in retrospect it is as clear as a freshly cleaned window.

As I courageously put myself in the shadows to serve my family, as we moved from church to church, as I put myself third and my family second, God graciously taught me how to put Him first. And it was when I put Him first that everything else lined up correctly.

You see, in that dark hallway, I tried EVERY DOOR. I took every class I could, I read every book that was presented, I listened to every pastor teach me, and I got involved in every ministry available. I sang in choirs, led a Wednesday night worship team, directed a children's choir, taught children's Sunday school and adult Sunday school, and led Vacation Bible School. I attended leadership conferences, did online studies learning about different denominations, taught Bible classes, and attended retreats. I worked as a preschool teacher, a pastor's administrative assistant, a ministry coordinator, and was a leader and teacher in a renowned Bible study program. I attended a leadership college and got my Master's in teaching the Bible. And I did it all with prayer – that God would set my foot on the right stone, that He would lead me in the right direction, that He would open the right door to serve Him.

Oh, I courageously walked away from my career in an effort to put my family second, but what I didn't know was that God was orchestrating my life so that I would put Him first. What started out as a selfish pursuit – I was bored, I was purposeless, I was seeking something I could afford and that would not interfere with my family – God used for His glory. Changing me along the way. Teaching me the joy of putting Him first.

There are so many instances of God's provision, protection and guidance that I can point to throughout my life. When I took the steps to attend Leadership College and to get my Master's, God provided financially through other people and by blessing both my and my husband's work. He continually put mentors and friends in my life to encourage and support me, and He has graciously protected us financially and in His perfect timing as He has moved us from place to place, buying and selling homes.

After I finished Leadership College, God kept giving me the scripture from Revelation 3, *These are the words of him who is holy and true, who holds the key of David. What he opens no one can shut, and what he shuts, no one can open. I know your deeds. See, I have placed before you an open door that no one can shut. I know that you have little strength, yet you have kept my word and have not denied my name* (Revelation 3:7-8 NIV). Even as I felt like I was walking down a dark hall, some days with *little strength*, and that none of the doors were opening, God assured me that He had the key to the right door, and that what He opens, no one can shut. And that, I believe, was the beginning of my courageous step *out* of the shadows.

My kids are now 20, 18, and 14 years old. And they are magnificent! I have not done everything perfectly as a mom – far from it! And they are not perfect people. But our God is gracious and giving and He honors our heart. Going back to that day in my office, with my infant sitting at my feet, I am so thankful that I heard and heeded God's still small voice saying, *What are you doing here, Julie?* If I hadn't, I don't know what door I would have walked through, but it wouldn't have been the right one. And I don't know what our family would look like right now, but without intentionally seeking to put my feet where God wanted them, I never would have learned the joy it is to have Him first in my life. I may have enjoyed greater financial wealth, pride the size of a Macy's Thanksgiving Day parade balloon, and a very busy life. But I would not have found my true purpose – as a disciple of Christ.

I am old enough to say that I have come full circle. I stepped into the shadows at God's calling, and now He is calling me out of the shadows, and that is requiring courage beyond my wildest imaginings.

Last year, Kimberly Hobbs and I struck up a God-given connection, and God melded our hearts together, opening the door to lead Women World Leaders to the place He has ordained for this ministry. He has given us a vision together to unite women in service – to empower them, edify them, and support them in faith and with love, and to develop other passionate leaders with purpose.

We at Women World Leaders strengthen each other to follow God's call and lean on each other to take Courageous Steps of Faith. I will always give God the glory for closing the door to my selfish pride over 20 years ago – for calling me INTO the shadows. And I give Him the glory for opening the door to serve Him in this ministry today – for calling me OUT of the shadows. And I will forever be grateful to Him for giving me the courage to step through both doors.

. . . .

Courage to Overcome Pride

Julie Jenkins

> *For who makes you different from anyone else? What do you have that you did not receive? And if you did receive it, why boast as though you did not? 1 Cor 4:7 (NIV)*

We are taught as children to achieve, to accomplish, and to control our destiny by making a plan. We fight for the good grades, practice to get the big trophy, and fill our resume, even in high school, to get into the best college. And we revel in our achievements.

But there is a difference between confidence and pride, and that difference comes from our very roots.

Pride, as warned about in Proverbs 8:13 (*Therefore I hate pride and arrogance, corruption and perverse speech*), is an arrogant conceit, a tunnel vision that proclaims that I alone can accomplish any feat I put my mind to. It is a deep satisfaction that comes from the well of self-absorption and is born of anxiety and the need for accomplishment and perfection.

Confidence, on the other hand, is believing that I am who God says I am, therefore, I am sure of my success (*"Though a mighty army surrounds me, my heart will not be afraid. Even if I am attacked, I will remain confident." – Psalm 27:3 NLT*). The sustenance for confidence is God Himself – our sustainer, strength, and guide. And it comes with the caveat that in order to be truly successful, we must surrender to God's will and follow His direction.

How can we walk away from the pride of self and walk into the confidence of being a child of God? Our biggest weapon is honesty. When we examine our own lives honestly in front of God, we will begin to see that we never, ever have done anything completely by ourselves! If you got great grades, you likely have a teacher, parent, or even taxpayers to thank for providing you with a great education! If you won that championship, chances are there was a coach guiding you and teammates cheering you on! If your high school resume afforded you a scholarship to the finest school, likely there was a counselor, student, pastor, or friend supporting you along the way!

And honest reflection will take each of these instances a bit further and reveal that it is God Himself who blesses us with people, intelligence, talent, skill, and resources!

The fact of the matter is that without God, even the best of our intentions would be useless. Turning our backs on our pride allows us to turn and see the glory of the one who deserves all the credit: our God! Our infinite, unchanging, all-powerful, all-knowing, perfect in power and wisdom, faithful, merciful, gracious, loving, and glorious Father. He is our source and our strength. In that we can stand proud!

• •

 **Carrie Christopher** is a writer, speaker, and an encourager – all for the glory of Christ. She walks her faith journey joyfully with her faithful husband Jonathan. Jonathan and Carrie have the honor of raising, discipling and homeschooling two beautiful children, Micah and Ava. Second to Jesus, her family is her greatest treasure. Carrie serves on the board of Directors for Women World Leaders and fulfills a leadership role of Ministry and Development. She aims to awaken women around the world to their glorious callings. She passionately serves Kerus Global as an Ambassador Coordinator, linking hands and hearts to serve the orphan and the oppressed. Carrie loves praying, His presence, worshiping, writing, reading, enjoying the wonders of outdoors, and horseback riding.

Lastly, Carrie is passionate about praying with and for people struck down by disease. Carrie and her husband launched prayingforlyme.com to position prayer around the vicious cycles and ravaging ailments of Lyme Disease, including fighting for those with Neurological Tics and Tourettes.

Listen to Carrie on The Women World Leader Podcast Trio
www.womenworldleaders.com

From Fear to Faith
Carrie Christopher

Chosen. I am chosen. Chosen by God before time to grapple generational disease deploying its efforts to weigh down multiple generations and casting down souls with arrows of declared destruction. The appointment that God has called me to is a position of unrelenting trust and courageous steps of faith. You see, generational disease has sought to denounce my life, the very light of Christ coexisting in me, coming against me and multiple generations. When disease came against our family, the devil emphasized despair-filled, debilitating living. He whispered lies of our demise. He deemed our lives as inoperable, dampened depths of dreams lost. But he is the very father of lies, the deceiver and accuser of the brethren. These devious destroyers came in with carriers of ferocious, fanatic fear. That is the very song that the enemy spews over my life and the lives of my loved ones who are also debilitated by this disease. Our Jesus, though! The very economy of God lets nothing go to waste – not suffering, and surely not the devised destructions of disease. He is a redeeming multiplier, investing in the dark parts of our stories, to come in with the courageous rescue of His power.

My story starts in chains and ends in victory. What the enemy has meant for evil shall be used for good.

Disease pounced on my family as soon as my son was born. It came as a positioned plague of poison unrelentingly pursuing my family. The disease first began to manifest in me, then my son, then my daughter. All our symptoms combined landed us in a sea of distress, constantly ending up in hospitals and urgent care facilities. For years on end, symptoms and illnesses such as toxemia, chronic migraines, hypoglycemia, constant bacterial infections, interstitial cystitis, dizziness, brain fog, onsets of panic and anxiety, ocular migraines, overproduction of scar tissue, traveling inflammation, fatigue, allergies, sinus infections, and female infections plagued me. For my son, it was intense allergies, transient tic disorder, chronic sinus infections, and insomnia. For my daughter, infections, headaches, bladder and bowel inflammatory issues. Perhaps some of the most prevailing pain was the affliction of my four-year-old son when his transient tics disorder began. The doctors were never able to give us conclusive evidence of where and how this disease works or how it began. He underwent a sedated brain scan and many hospital visits, with no help at all. Our hearts were stricken by such strife and war of the hopelessness that this disability deemed upon his life. We suffered years of aching deeply within our hearts. We committed ourselves to laborious prayer – prayer for healing, prayer for a cure, prayer for the true root cause of this disease. Our hearts were surrendered and yet we were utterly crushed. At times, the prevailing ache of our souls felt like we would not survive the pain. It's one thing for my health to suffer, but when it came to my children, there was so much of my soul that questioned and lamented to God, asking, "Why them.... No, not them, God."

That is when the Lord broke through – with a miracle. Although the doctors had left us without answers, the Lord came to reveal His counsel and splendor. The Lord began to speak to me about

Lyme Disease; on multiple occasions He spoke that He would heal Micah! Over the months that followed, God's voice became louder and louder, loosening the bonds of affliction in our life. On one intimate occasion, the Spirit gave me a vision. In the vision He showed me that the neurological tics were caused by undiagnosed Lyme disease. Then He powerfully and pointedly showed me, through the vision, that Lyme disease had spread in utero from my mom to me to Micah and, most likely, to Ava. He showed me that this disease is a painful plague that spreads to multiple generations. The Lord gave me many promises to heal our family! In the months that followed, God orchestrated everything perfectly by providing a Lyme doctor who was experienced in diagnosing this disease.

I remember when the Lord called me first to be tested with an advanced laboratory test costing almost $4,000 just for the labs of one patient. My husband had to trust that God had really given me a supernatural vision and had spoken those words to me. Praise be to God, we went forward with courage and through a wrestling of faith! I remember the enemy whispering lies while we were waiting for the results to come back, spewing that I was wasting my family's money and other falsehoods. I had to daily put my trust back into the Lord. It was through my weakness that God did what He faithfully does. When I was faithless, He was faithful. When I gave up, God spoke up. When I tried to control, God came to carry. When I was angry, God understood my anguish. When I was hurting, God hushed my soul with comfort. When my test came back positive, we went forward with courage to have both children tested. Micah's results were a straight positive, and Ava's was a borderline diagnosis, which meant that a true diagnosis would be determined by her presenting symptoms in the future.

Another layer of the riddled pain deeply wedged in my soul was seeing my mom get sick when I was about 13 years old. Her ailments attacked her ferociously and devoured our family. I had prayed over her many times, asking Jesus to heal her, yet it wasn't the appointed time. As part of this layered vision, it had been my deep prayer for her to be tested. This came with a spiritual fight, only God made a way for this. In June 2020, my mom was tested and diagnosed as positive for Lyme Disease. Some of her ailments included vertigo, blood clots, debilitating arthritis, spinal stenosis, fibromyalgia, anxiety, and depression. The entire vision that the Lord had compassionately revealed came to pass; it awoke to wisdom, glory and dominion of the Lord. The Lord solved the case of medical mysteries that plagued my family for generations, and He did so with a revelation through the heart and the hands of the Holy Spirit.

Underneath the surface of our health crisis, there is a bigger God story. Clearly, the pain and suffering that afflicted my family was intended by the enemy to steal, kill and destroy us. But the Lord, being a God that does not waste, chose to heal the deep layers of my soul throughout this time of physical suffering. Through the fear that had taken a foothold during our many years of unknown health suffering, heaping ashes upon every inch of our souls, the Lord showed me a ferocious, taunting fear that was already woven into my life years before the illness. This health crisis unveiled a story of captivity, woven with threads of pain birthed from fear and combined with the daunting oppression of the weight that I carried. God was using this storm to speak to me of what my soul was lacking, to unshackle me from my own sin and layers of unbelief, fear, anxiety and depression. He looked down on me in compassion and desired to free me from shackles of fear and captivate me with His unceasing love. Jesus came for me.

He didn't leave me to the wild wolves of wanton destruction, or the falsehood of fear-laced lies. Throughout the past eight years, the Lord has been coming against this Spirit of fear and asking me to trust him with my children, with my family and with our disease. It has been like walking a tightrope with Jesus, allowing Him to lead and teach me. If I focus on the possibilities of this incurable disease, I will be paralyzed. Instead, I have to trust His leading continuously, as we travel to heights of impossibilities unknown.

You may be wondering if we are currently healed. We are NOT, but we are expectantly awaiting His promises to my family that He will heal us. Some days we faithfully hold on to this promise and other days, the pain of the suffering muffles His voice and distracts me within. I write this story out of the courageous calling that God has placed on my life to serve him with zeal, before my family's miracle comes to fruition. We aren't serving him to obtain or necessarily chase after a miracle, but rather to follow HIM despite the perfection-based proof of the miracle.

My health may fail. My children's health may suffer. Agonizingly, our family may be riddled with pain, living daily on a battlefield of suffering from chronic Lyme-induced afflictions. The pain plaguing our lives sometimes feels like an inexpressible witness of the enemy's access to our family.

However, the Lord has spoken this triumphant proclamation over our story: to allow my flesh to die in sacrificial love unto the Lord, to allow any of the painful plagues that He has allowed, is to birth purpose instead of death.

> Revelation 12:11 (ESV) – *"And they have conquered him by the blood of the Lamb and by the word of their testimony, for they loved not their lives even unto death."*

It is better to serve the Lord one day in His courts than to be wandering in a sea of purposeless suffering.

You see friend, the surrender that disease produces teaches me that this isn't just about me. But rather about YOU, about others, about God's church and the vital growth of His church. It's understanding that my pain has purpose. If my disease, if my prevailed aching in the secret places of our suffering, allows me to understand your story and fight with you in the gaps of disease, then it serves a pointed purpose of glory for Christ's church. If God is allowing our lament in order to lavish His love on His church and feel the depths of pain together, then it is worth it. A love to see you, dear reader, restored, starts to saturate my life, a yearning to see many obtain salvation, to know the depravity of our sins and the dark ploys of destructive diseases, and to understand this with eyes from inside this suffering-induced coma. Because I am in the coma with you, I feel and know of your pain, which can birth a launching pad of compassion. God sees you, diseased and afflicted one. God loves you. His overarching banner of love is pursuing you, prayerfully generating an ultimate surrender to a God who redeems all the broken pieces of our lives, every ache and travail. As you follow Him, your most heart-wrenching pain and despair will be used for good. His love lives in the dark places, in cocoons of waiting. He is with you in the ashes of your waiting, always caring most about your healing for your heart, because ultimately, your heart determines your place in all of eternity. I ask you, is your salvation secure and anchored in the love of Jesus alone? Or are you still grasping at the world to fulfill you?

I believe that as our hearts look into the beloved eyes of the faithful one, Jesus Christ, and as we love Him above our health, above our sin, above our family, and above ourselves, that goodness and mercy shall follow us all the days of our lives and that we shall dwell in the house of the Lord forever.

God is welcoming us all home: the prodigal, the afflicted storm-tossed one, the diseased. This home is a haven of healing. You see, after He purifies our hearts and links the body together in a radiant display of His everlasting, omnipotent love, I believe He will heal you, my friend. I believe that revival is coming in this very generation and that we will witness a revival in the supernatural healing like that in the first church of Antioch, as we groan and wait and link arms in love. The treasure isn't the healing, however, it's Christ Himself made manifest amongst us. Christ is above healing and is the risen treasure, greater even than prospective physical healing. Treasure the Risen One, who has come to take away the sins of all the earth, who left His throne to defend you and bring you into the complete restorative arms of the Father. His presence is all we need; His love is in us, fighting for us, and giving us HOPE for the healing haven of Christ.

Our loving Father is still good even when life hurts, carrying our every sorrow-filled ache in the seasons of trials. His portion is always enough. Strength pours from the Holy Spirit's presence, reaching every dark cavity of pain and loss. What dies will come alive again. He rose in new life to penetrate every disappointment with new life. This life isn't the end, it is the beginning. Despite my trials, I speak to my soul, hope again, and prosper in His plans. Let every ounce of worth and comfort come from a blanket of soothing trust. He alone is the soul satisfier, my sanctifying power, my water when I am parched and wandering in a weary land. Rest in the Risen One.

Let us not be hopeless or deceived – the subject of disease is under His feet. His feet carry flames of fire, desiring to ravage disease and the persecution of the Christian church, suffering from the droughts of disease. As I have walked this journey, the Lord has whispered with boldness deep in my heart, that HE WOULD HEAL MY FAMILY. It wasn't about just the paralyzing effects of disease within my children or myself, or the spiritual layers He desired to heal deep within my soul, it was about healing a multitude of generational diseases.

I would challenge us all to ponder what it would it taste like to experience a generous giver of healing to the nations, an incense bowl of petitioned prayers poured out as we faithfully ready our hearts to receive the grace, glory and generosity of our Lord. Are you ready, friend, to experience a day and age of the Lord where His love truly abides in the church of believers, where He sorts the chaff from the grain and restores what the locust has eaten as our bodies were ravaged with disease? Can we stand united, imploring our God, who is rich in mercy, to come and make a way for miracles? Not so that we can feel perfect, accomplished or feed our appetites of pride, but so that we can be truly enveloped by His lingering, light-striking affirming love for us. Will you live expecting a revival in His church allowing us to experience the supernatural effects of healing through His lavish love and goodness? Where we can be the church, where our slavery to sin and Satan cease to control us? And where the Spirit's power escorts us into our heavenly places, seated at the right hand of Christ?

Ephesians 2:6 (NIV) – *And God raised us up with Christ and seated us with him in the heavenly realms in Christ Jesus…*

Would you ponder with me a realm where we can fly free, friend, into a sea of expectation, a song of praised revival, a generation of glory? Would you join me in praying for the abolishment of debilitating disease – within Christ's church, the prepared bride of God? Would you hold your neighbor, your sister, your brother's hands inviting them into the haven of the Healer? Would you fight for the diseased, the physically oppressed, imploring the Lord to come quickly to our aid, fighting for us on the besieged battleground?

As I prayed for the Lord to show me which scripture of healing to leave as an inspiration for us all, He gave me the story of a woman named Tabitha. Soak in the story of this saint and wait with hungry expectation. This is for those who never stopped trusting and faithfully pursuing God in midst of your disease, just like that of precious Tabitha. I believe that not only has the Lord Jesus seen and reveled in your faithful service to HIM, but He's seen a faith arise so deeply embedded in your soul that your heart shall never depart from the presence of the Lord. For where the Spirit of the Lord is, there is freedom. Jesus has this Word for you to feast upon.

Acts 9:36–43 (ESV)

Dorcas Restored to Life
36 Now there was in Joppa a disciple named Tabitha, which, translated, means Dorcas. She was full of good works and acts of charity. 37 In those days she became ill and died, and when they had washed her, they laid her in an upper room. 38 Since Lydda was near Joppa, the

disciples, hearing that Peter was there, sent two men to him, urging him, "Please come to us without delay." 39 So Peter rose and went with them. And when he arrived, they took him to the upper room. All the widows stood beside him weeping and showing tunics and other garments that Dorcas made while she was with them. 40 But Peter put them all outside, and knelt down and prayed; and turning to the body he said, "Tabitha, arise." And she opened her eyes, and when she saw Peter she sat up. 41 And he gave her his hand and raised her up. Then, calling the saints and widows, he presented her alive. 42 And it became known throughout all Joppa, and many believed in the Lord. 43 And he stayed in Joppa for many days with one Simon, a tanner.

. . . .

Courage to overcome DISEASE

Kimberly Ann Hobbs

Many of us infected with diseases have a choice of how we view that disease. No disease is easy to withstand, and some are definitely worse than others, but with God's grace we can persevere in steadfast joy.

Throughout the Bible we see examples of individuals inflicted with terrible diseases. We can ask ourselves, why? Why did they suffer and why do we have to suffer? Why do the ones we love have to suffer? It is interesting that the Biblical characters seemed to have purpose for their afflictions and God deemed it valuable enough to share their stories in His Word. These Biblical characters can be an example to us.

Although Job was blameless, upright and feared God, God used his traumas to draw Job closer to Himself. You can read about this in the book of Job, chapters one and two.

Moses' sister Miriam was inflicted with a judgment because of her unrepentant sins against God. The Bible tells us that Moses had to intercede for her healing (Numbers 12:1-15).

When Naaman, commander of the Syrian army, got a terrible infectious disease, he turned to the God of the universe to heal him. He humbled himself, and in faith, turned to God – and God healed him (2 Kings 5:15)!

Then there was the woman who bled for 12 years. Because of her faith, God healed her. Her example has become famous in the Word of God.

There are many examples in the Bible of individuals who were afflicted with terrible diseases allowing their ailments to turn their attention to God. It takes courage to know that no matter what you may be walking through, whatever plagues your body or soul, having faith and trusting in God's plan can position you for joy.

If you knew you could be used by the God of the galaxies to show His miraculous power through your battles of sickness, would you be willing to be a vessel used by Him through it all? Even if it took your life to do it? It takes courage to say yes. It takes powerful courage to trust an illness into God's care and leave it in His hands. Only He can give you the strength to endure and the will to continue on. Pray and surrender any disease to God. Ask Him for the courage needed to seek and find His will in your life through your disease.

• •

 **Lauren Elizabeth Dean** has the heart of a missionary and compassion for the disadvantaged and most vulnerable. She is passionate about promoting the well-being and best interests of children. In 2019, she served in Kenya through various capacities of children's ministry, and mentored children at the United Nations 30th Anniversary of the Convention on the Rights of the Child. She is also founding board member and Vice-President of a non-profit in Palm Beach County that serves children in Africa.

Lauren has a BSBA in Finance and a BA in Corporate Communication with a minor in Spanish, and she has used her skills and knowledge as a business professional at Fortune 500 companies. She likes to travel and experience different cultures; has studied abroad in Rome, Italy and has traveled to over 15 countries and counting. She enjoys sharing a great meal with family and friends, spending time with her dogs, pursuing a healthy lifestyle—and is always up for an adventure!

Lauren cherishes connecting with women all across the world, she is on staff in the ministry Women World Leaders serving as Global Business and Missions Director.

laurenelizabethdean.com

God is Working.
He's Always Working.

Lauren Elizabeth Dean

Trust in the Lord with all your heart and lean not on your own understanding; in all your ways submit to him, and he will make your paths straight. (Proverbs 3:5-6 NIV)

My grandfather was a great man of faith. Orphaned as a child, he was taken in by a loving couple, but even more importantly, he was adopted into God's family. My favorite childhood memories were spending the summers with my grandparents and going to their church. There was something different about them and their lives. Although my family attended mass every Sunday, we didn't pray or read the Bible, and I saw God as distant and impersonal. It took me 28 years to understand that the faith my grandfather had was waiting for me, if I was courageous enough to accept it.

When I was young, God instilled in me a deep desire to go to Africa to care for orphans and to one day adopt children. Once I started dating my high school sweetheart, that desire no longer fit into my plans. I became set on our future together—graduating college, marrying, and having children. I left Florida to attend school in Pennsylvania, and even though I had a passion for children, I pursued a finance degree because I wanted to make a lot of money. My life was all about building Lauren's kingdom, not God's Kingdom. I graduated, got a great job, and six months later my high school sweetheart broke up with me. I abandoned the call God put on my heart to go to Africa, built my life around my boyfriend, and was left with nothing. Instead of making a turn and following God's call to Africa, I turned to alcohol and men.

A month later, I met a man from Israel who was Jewish. I threw myself with reckless abandon into that relationship, forcing it to work no matter the cost. Less than a year later we decided to get married. There were many red flags that I chose to ignore, but I loved him—and I wanted to be a wife and mother.

A year and a half into our marriage, I hadn't become pregnant. I scheduled a doctor's appointment with an OBGYN and my long journey with infertility began. I was diagnosed with polycystic ovary syndrome and started taking medication and following a prescribed medical protocol to improve my chances of conceiving. The first month went by and I wasn't pregnant. The second month, and I still wasn't pregnant. The third month the doctor took my hands and began to pray. I was completely caught off guard and tears began to stream down my face. It was so powerful to me. But when I left her office and drove back into the world, I completely forgot about it.

Trying to get pregnant had been an obsession, but that month I had so much peace. Thanksgiving rolled around, and I realized my period was over a week late. The next morning I took a pregnancy test and, to my surprise, I was pregnant! It didn't occur to me then that this was an answer to my doctor's prayer. I began to cry tears of joy as I ran to wake my husband and tell him. Little did I know the struggle and suffering that lay ahead.

A day before leaving for Florida to spend Christmas with my family, I started bleeding. I had an ultrasound the morning we left and was diagnosed with a subchorionic hematoma (blood between the embryo and uterus). I was approved to travel and told to schedule another ultrasound when I returned.

On Christmas Eve, while shopping with my family, I began experiencing unbearable pain. I was wincing through waves of cramps. As we drove home, I was slammed with a wave of the most excruciating pain I've ever had in my life. But I insisted on attending church that evening. Pad after pad quickly filled with blood. And although I should have been in the emergency room, I was in denial about what was happening. So there I was—in my Christmas pajamas, family huddled around the tree, opening presents. I ran to the bathroom over and over again, curled up on the tile floor and braced myself for another round of writhing pain. Until I felt something pass out of me. That's when my eyes confirmed what my heart already knew.

Miscarriage.

When I returned to Pittsburgh, the miscarriage was confirmed. I was staring at an empty womb. I tormented myself with all the reasons I might be to blame. The pain and sorrow were unbearable. Nothing could comfort or console me. My spiral into a deep, dark depression began. Not a single day passed that I didn't cry. I detached myself from everyone and everything—hoping the numbness would will the pain away. A few months passed, but my depression persisted, so I decided we should move to Florida to be closer to my family.

A year after the miscarriage, I started back on the fertility drug. My faith was in the drug, not God—not even God who could work through medicine, but the medicine itself. Eight grueling months later, I was still not pregnant. Each month when I got my period I would come home and cry myself to sleep. Those nights were the beginning of the unraveling of myself. The coming undone. The brokenness. I didn't have a personal relationship with God, but I remember vividly for the first time ever crying out loud to God in desperation. Distraught, and at the end of myself. Questioning God. Pleading with God. Begging God. Trying to make deals with Him. I actually uttered the words, "If You give me children, I'll never miss church again." These were the desperate cries of a girl who did not know God.

My 27th birthday was approaching, and I had been battling infertility for four years. All around me, newly married couples were conceiving; some friends started having their second child. In the midst of all of this, my grandfather was battling heart disease and was constantly in the hospital. One of my biggest desires was to have my grandfather hold my baby one day. Heartbreakingly, he passed away, and I watched his incredible faith as he kept his eyes fixed on Jesus to the very end, even telling the chaplain at the hospital, "Either way, I win." *For to me, to live is Christ and to die is gain (Philippians 1:21, NIV).* At my grandfather's funeral, the pastor said something so vivid—"We don't grieve as those who have no hope." I couldn't relate to what he said at all. I was the epitome of grieving with no hope. I remember thinking, what hope is he talking about? I had no hope. It devastated me that my grandfather would never get to hold my children. It was impossible now.

A month later, my husband and I were going on a trip to Israel to visit his family. On our prior trip we visited Jerusalem and I went to the tomb of Jesus. This time we visited the Sea of Galilee. I was in awe that I was walking in the same place Jesus had walked. I took a picture sitting on a rock with a map entitled "The Gospel Trail," but I didn't yet know what the Gospel meant. But God was working. He's always working. As I look back on my life, I see God pursuing me in every miracle and every mundane moment.

We returned from Israel right when we would have been celebrating our baby's first birthday. The significance of this date made my mind wander and my imagination run wild, fixating on all that could've been. I daydreamed about every detail of the life my child would never have and I would never witness. What would my child have been like as an adult? Would she have had my eyes, or my husband's sense of humor? Would she have been a lawyer? A doctor? A teacher? What would it have been like to see my grandpa hold my child? I was fixated.

I started coming out of my depression and I began writing a "bucket list" of things I wanted to do: "Go to Iceland, go skiing out West, learn Hebrew, mission trip to Africa, read the Bible from the beginning to end." God was working. He's always working. I bought a Bible and started reading it every morning. I began with Genesis. This is when I read for the first time, *Now Sarai was childless because she was not able to conceive (Genesis 11:30, NIV)*. Then Rebekah was childless (Genesis 25:21, NIV). Then Rachel was childless (Genesis 29:31, NIV). Something stirred inside me. This was not new to God. I was not alone. God and women had been dealing with this since the beginning. And it gave me hope.

I refocused and renewed my efforts on getting pregnant, putting my body through every option my doctors and I could come up with. At one point, I began having extreme pain, so I was tested for an infection and discovered instead that I had an STD. I was in shock. Since I knew I had been faithful in my marriage, the only explanation was that my husband had not been. I immediately stopped trying for a baby until we had worked through this hurdle in our marriage. But a few months later, my husband filed for divorce and my life as I knew it came crumbling down. The same red flags I ignored in the beginning of our relationship followed us into marriage and ended it. The STD was curable, but it likely caused damage to one of my fallopian tubes—increasing my prognosis for infertility. I was two years shy of my 30th birthday, soon to be divorced, and facing infertility. How would I ever find someone to start a family with? I was buried in so much shame. I was exhausted in every way—physically, mentally, and emotionally. So much so that I even came down with shingles. It was a wake-up call that I needed help.

I started working through the trauma with a counselor and began to realize that I had been in a very unhealthy relationship. God started putting women in my life—a sorority sister who was finding her way back to God and a hairdresser who shared her testimony and invited me to church. I was starting to recover my confidence and regain my former self. I took that confidence too far, however, and returned to my former ways of drunkenness and pre-marital sex – actions that left me empty and never satisfied. Around this time, I was in a store and saw a statue of a little girl with angel wings that stopped me in my tracks. God graciously reassured me that my little girl was fine and was being held by my grandfather in Heaven. This entire time I had been fixating on my grandfather never getting to hold my children, I was missing the fact that one of my biggest desires had already been fulfilled. God had done it, just not in the way I was expecting. He made what I thought was impossible possible. He continued to speak to my heart, "You are sad because you want to be a mother, and I have all of these children who have been waiting for you." I could no longer ignore the calling to go to Africa. So I sold my house and car, quit my job, and courageously followed God's call to Kenya.

On Christmas Eve, exactly three years after my miscarriage, I was in Kenya surrounded by children, right where God wanted me, and I could see God's redemption. The name Lauren was too difficult for the local children to pronounce, so I was affectionately called by my middle name Elizabeth, which means "an oath to God."

One day a Kenyan man from a local church came to serve the children. As we were waiting for the rest of the congregation, we chatted over a cup of tea. He asked me, "Are you born again?" I was silent. I had no idea how to respond. I had heard that term once or twice before, but I had no idea what it meant. I said, "Umm..." And he said, "It means that Jesus is your Lord and Savior." I thought, *I'm Catholic; we believe in Jesus.* So I said, "Yes, I am." And he responded, "Oh, you had to think about it for a while."

I couldn't get the term "born again" out of my mind. I had all of these questions stirring in my mind: What does born again really mean? How can other people know with certainty they are going to Heaven? Why am I unsure?

Jesus replied, "Very truly I tell you, no one can see the kingdom of God unless they are born again." (John 3:3, NIV)

When I came home from Kenya, I had no job, no children, no husband—just me and God. In search of answers to the Kenyan man's question, I read the Bible for hours a day, as verse after verse about salvation jumped out at me. My living, breathing prayer to the Lord every moment became, "I don't want anything if You're not in it. The only thing I want is You and whatever You have for me." I would take long walks talking and listening to God. As I was praying, God gave me a vision. And on February 15, 2019, everything became real to me. I was a believer. My eyes were finally opened. In an instant, I saw my whole life up to that point flash before my eyes. I saw a personal God who loved me so much. I saw the weight of my sin like I had never before, in need of a Savior. I was convicted of my drunkenness and sexual immorality. Where I used to see meaningless rules, now I saw a God who wanted the best for me. I saw a God who mercifully restored me when I took a courageous step of faith to go to Africa. I repented, I turned away from my sin and toward God, and I believed the Gospel, the Good News that Jesus died on the cross for my sins, was buried, and was resurrected, restoring my relationship with God and eternal life. He made the impossible possible, something I could never do on my own. I was in awe of God's grace. The mission trip to Africa had saved me.

For all have sinned and fall short of the glory of God. (Romans 3:23, NIV)

But God demonstrates his own love for us in this: While we were still sinners, Christ died for us. (Romans 5:8, NIV)

...that he was buried, that he was raised on the third day according to the Scriptures, (1 Corinthians 15:4, NIV)

For the wages of sin is death, but the gift of God is eternal life in Christ Jesus our Lord. (Romans 6:23, NIV)

Jesus answered, 'I am the way and the truth and the life. No one comes to the Father except through me.' (John 14:6, NIV)

But following Jesus does not mean life is without tragedy. Two months later, I received a text that one of the babies I cared for in Kenya had died. I thought, *Here we go again.* Another loss. A baby I had cared for and held in my arms, now taken away. But for the first time I learned what it meant to grieve with hope. The words spoken by the pastor at my grandpa's funeral came to life to me. ***Brothers and sisters, we do not want you to be uninformed about those who sleep in death, so that you do not grieve like the rest of mankind, who have no hope. For we believe that Jesus died and rose again, and so we believe that God will bring with Jesus those who have fallen asleep in him (1 Thessalonians 4:13-14, NIV).*** Those words rang loud and true to me. This loss was just as tragic for me as the loss of my angel baby and my grandfather—just as heartbreaking, just as gut-wrenching, but it was different this time.

God brought me back to Kenya for eight months. I had to stand strong and courageously when yet another baby passed away. I cried out to God—Why? Why? Why? How many babies, Lord? How much pain and suffering and loss? I went to the baby's funeral and I'll never forget returning to the house, as one of the little girls met me with a wide grin. She asked me if I cried and I said, "A little." "Kidogo," she said—which is Swahili for little. I told her that the baby was in Heaven with Jesus, and that if we believe in Jesus and follow Him, one day we will see her in Heaven too. She looked puzzled. Conversations continued. But after a few minutes her eyes lit up and she said, "Gloria is in Heaven too! And Mary is in Heaven. And Rebekah." My soul smiled the biggest smile ever. We talked about how they are with each other playing right now. I praised God for the strength and comfort He provided. The ability for me to trust Him, unlike in my miscarriage. My heart was filled with so much joy with this opportunity to share the Gospel with this little girl. To speak life. And I could see Jesus redeeming, giving me these opportunities to be a mother in moments. *You turned my wailing into dancing; you removed my sackcloth and clothed me with joy, that my heart may sing your praises and not be silent. Lord my God, I will praise you forever (Psalm 30:11-12, NIV).*

A few days later I visited a fellow church member's home who was grieving the loss of her baby. She shared her story of giving birth and the baby's struggle with sickness. How she and her husband were praying for the baby's recovery, but they saw the baby was suffering and changed their prayer, asking for God's will. The baby passed away. Here was a mom who had the faith to say 'Thy Will be done' and release her baby's life into the Father's hands. I thought about how courageous she was as I gazed out the window overlooking a neighboring slum, watching two children play on the tin roofs, or as I often gazed out of my empty five-bedroom house watching kids play, looking at what I so deeply desired.

My mind wandered back to when I was in Israel kneeling at the tomb of Jesus, the same exact place where Mary Magdalene had been weeping at the empty tomb (John 20). Jesus met her there and called her name. She took her eyes away from the empty tomb and fixed them on Jesus. In the moments when I'm weeping at my empty womb, He calls my name and I fix my eyes on Him. Do I believe that what I need most isn't a child, but Jesus? In the midst of loss and grief and suffering, do I believe in the Gospel? Do I believe that redemption will come? Will I receive God's comfort, and then go out and comfort others in their troubles with the comfort I received? Will I get up from weeping at my empty womb and tell others I have seen the Lord? Will I worship God with an empty womb?

> *Praise be to the God and Father of our Lord Jesus Christ, the Father of compassion and the God of all comfort, who comforts us in all our troubles, so that we can comfort those in any trouble with the comfort we ourselves receive from God. (2 Corinthians 1:3, NIV)*

My story is just one of the many stories on the infertility journey, all with different outcomes and purposes, but the same God is sovereign over them all. The pain is real, and suffering is guaranteed this side of Heaven. But God's love is greater, and the joy found in the Lord is invincible. It is a joy that can coexist with pain, as we cling to the hope that He has given believers. *He will wipe every tear from their eyes. There will be no more death or mourning or crying or pain, for the old order of things has passed away" (Revelation 21:4, NIV)*. But we don't have to wait until Heaven for redemption. He has the power to transform our lives on earth. I used to put my hope in everything the world had to offer, and I had no peace. I thought if I could just have children, I'd finally be happy, but God taught me there is no real happiness apart from Him. I learned that marriage and children are gifts from God to be stewarded, not idols to be worshipped. And as each of those idols was stripped away, it led me to Him. I've desperately crawled through infertility on my own, without God, and now I'm taking courageous steps of faith through infertility with God as He leads me. As I pursue God's design for my life, He has surrounded me with a church family, sisters in Christ in Kenya, daughters of the King from Women World Leaders, and a strong woman of faith who shares my heart for Africa. He showed me what it means to be a godly woman, a godly wife, and a godly mother. And I continue to see Him transform me. *Therefore, if anyone is in Christ, the new creation has come: The old has gone, the new is here! (2 Corinthians 5:17, NIV)*

My dream has always been simple... three little letters, M-o-m. Even to this day, my dream feels so alive to me, and so far away at the same time. I don't know if my dream will ever come to pass. But I do know that if it doesn't, God has a different plan for me. I didn't always accept this truth so easily or believe it wholeheartedly. It took me 28 years. It may look like I'm the farthest away that I've ever been from that dream, but I'm the closest I've ever been to Jesus. And child or no child, I will worship Him.

The same God who settled Sarah in her home as the mother of Isaac, who settled Elizabeth in her home as the mother of John the Baptist, is the same God who settled my great-grandmother as the happy mother of my orphaned grandfather. And I imagine my sweet Jesus at the Last Supper with his disciples the night before He is crucified, singing, *He settles the childless woman in her home as a happy mother of children. Praise the Lord (Psalm 113:9, NIV).*

That is the same God of today. That is the same God that will always be. That is my God. And He can do it again, if it is His Will. In whatever way He wants, in whatever timing He wants, for whatever purpose He wants. A good God, whose ways and thoughts are higher than my own, and I can continue to take one courageous step of faith at a time knowing that with God all things are possible.

Be on your guard; stand firm in the faith; be courageous; be strong. Do everything in love. (1 Corinthians 16:13-14, NIV)

To be continued...

Courage to overcome IDOLATRY

Kimberly Ann Hobbs

Scripture strongly advises us against following any idols other than God. The Bible says we should be living in a righteous manner, above any and all other pursuits of the flesh and the mind.

"Put to death therefore, whatever belongs to your earthly nature: sexual immorality, impurity, lust, evil desires and greed, which is idolatry" (Colossians 3:5 NIV).

These things mentioned in the Word of God can creep into our lives suddenly, catching us off guard, and before long, we can be caught up in a rigorous way of living with idols inside our life. It takes courage to overcome such possessions and take a stand against serving false gods. Be aware that at any time we can fall prey to being drawn away from the Lord if we aren't actively pursuing worship of the true King of glory.

1 John 5:21 teaches us, "Dear children, keep yourselves from idols." To do this we must study God and His Word. God is faithful and so is His Word. His Word endures forever. He will not let you be tempted beyond what you can bear. He will make a way for you to escape. This means we are to look to Him with courage to overcome any idols we are clinging to. Your idol can be anything that replaces God.

If God is not in the primary spot of your life, you may have idols where He should be. Ask Him for the courage it takes to break chains, breaking free from any idol that you cling to. As you courageously walk toward the cross of Christ, the things that once were so important become a shadow and eventually vanish in the light of God's glory and grace.

"Those who cling to worthless idols turn away from God's love for them" (Jonah 2:8 NIV).

· ·

 **Carol Ann Whipkey** is a follower of Christ with much of her time spent writing and encouraging others with uplifting guidance through her written words.

Carol has enjoyed work as a freelance model and participated in pageants as a contestant. She enjoyed her career as a beauty consultant and working in an accounting position for UPS for many years.

She is an artist and was trained by world renown wood carver; Joe Leonard whose work is in the New York Museum of Art. As a hobby, Carol spends much of her time now carving horses and birds for many who commission her incredible talent.

Carol lives in her own park like setting on 52 acres in Thompson Ohio with her husband Mel. She is a mother of 4, grandmother of 6 and great grandmother of 2.

Only Trust Him
Carol Ann Whipkey

My story is a story of courage and faith. My desire in sharing it with you is that it will bring hope to you if you need hope. If my story of standing in faith when the enemy of doubts pounded at my door can help just one person, my tears through the trials were worth it all.

It takes courage to release a life we often grasp so tightly and self-ishly hold on to before surrendering it to Christ. He knows our needs better than we do and asks us to trust Him more than we trust ourselves. My story is a wake-up call from God. He opened my eyes to show me that He is in control and that He is the only way to a life of joy and freedom which is available when I trust Him.

As a young woman in my late teens, I had a great job. I did some modeling and pageant work and had a taste of money, a new car and an apartment of my own. Many would say I was successful in my time. I felt I had it all under control back then – "my control" – and I thought I had achieved the life!

I soon met a man, married him and had a beautiful baby girl, and then two years later, another baby boy. My life was feeling good! My husband loved racehorses, and I loved horses too. He soon bought the kids and me a couple of riding horses. They were just so beautiful to look at. Wow! My life felt complete. Everything I wanted, I received. As I rode horses and had fun with them, I got my exercise and lost the pregnancy weight that I didn't want. Unfortunately, I had gained some weight from having two children, but now that it was gone, I was regaining my girlish modeling figure and getting the attention and glitz and glamour I once had before children. I was on my way to the very top of having it all. My life, my dreams, and my goals – everything I wanted.

But then... like a bad dream, I got pregnant. "Oh no, why is this happening?" I cried. "I have plans!" Little did I know God had bigger plans for my life, a purpose I would never have imagined had God not gotten my attention.

Finding out I was pregnant sent me searching every avenue to end the pregnancy. Since having another child was not in my plans, abortion was my solution. But my dreams of grandeur crumbled before my eyes when I found out that no person or facility would do this procedure. I cried for days. "Why? Show me why. How can I be pregnant now, at a time when everything was going right in my life?" I did not want the weight that I had lost to come back, and I wanted my freedom to enjoy life.

> *"For I know the plans I have for you, declares the Lord, plans to prosper you and not harm you; plans to give you hope and a future" (Jeremiah 29:11 NIV).*

As I cried for days, I held my hands up to God and continued to ask the question "Why?" Was this my turning point of surrender, I wondered? I surely needed courage to face a pregnancy that I did not want! My selfishness was appearing strongly after trying to abort a child given to me by God.

"For you created my inmost being; you knit me together in my mother's womb" (Psalm 139:13 NIV).

My baby boy was so cute and sweet, I fell in love the moment he arrived. He came into this world, arriving on my birthday to boot. Coincidence? NO! What a gift he was, a very special gift given by God on my birthday.

Fast forwarding to a few years later, I was listening to a radio program in my home and heard a word I had never heard before. You must be SAVED. "Born again." I had never heard the word before or what it meant. As God had it, around that time my brother and his wife decided to start a Bible study for the three of us inside their home, which was located in an antique store in the country. We all wanted to learn about God. A man showed up at the door the same night as our Bible study asking to buy an antique for his wife. He was a pastor and he noticed we had a Bible study going on. We invited him to our study that night and he presented us all with the plan of salvation, which none of us had ever heard before. When I went home that night, I went to my knees before the Lord and I repented of all my sin. I asked Jesus to forgive my sins and make my life new, and He did. The Bible says in Isaiah 43:19, "Behold, I am doing a new thing..." and He was.

2 Corinthians 5:17 (NKJV) says, "Therefore if anyone is in Christ, he is a new creation; old things have passed away; behold, all things have become new."

God was now in my life and I found a church, got baptized, and the Holy Spirit began to work inside me. I was now seeing my life had meaning and that God had plans over my life and my baby boy's life whom I almost killed.

Early one morning, my four-year-old boy was asleep after I got my other children off to school and my husband off to work, and I was going to go back to bed and rest. As I lay there, I was thinking about the exciting day that my husband had planned. After work he would be going to the racetrack to purchase a horse that he had been saving a lifetime for. In crawled my sweet boy on the floor, looking strange and laughing. When looked at him, I immediately knew something was wrong. He had just gotten over chickenpox and his eyes could not stay focused on me. They kept rolling back in his head.

I ran to the phone and called the doctor and was advised to immediately bring him to the emergency room. They suspected encephalitis – a pox that went inward had affected his brain. They put me in a room where my courageous steps of faith began. I prayed in that room. There was another couple in the room with me whose son had the same illness. He was in surgery to relieve the pressure on his brain caused by the infection. I sat and prayed with the couple and later found out their son did not make it. As I stayed in that hospital, I learned of several other children besides my child who were suffering from encephalitis. My courage needed to rise as I held on to faith in a ward of beds with sick children everywhere.

Up against a wall, my tiny, helpless baby lay red with fever in a bed way too big for him; with his hair all wet and just a diaper on his little body, he lay in a semi-coma, motionless. I cried and I cried. I was so scared.

"Do not fear for I am with you, do not be dismayed, for I am your God; I will strengthen you and help you; I will uphold you with my righteous right hand" (Isaiah 41:10 NIV).

The doctors put a chair next to his bed for me with a light that seemed to shine on my son almost like he was the only one in the room. That solitude quickly disappeared when I heard buzzers going off all around me. Doctors and nurses ran through the room screaming "code blue, code blue" for a little girl a couple of beds away. I sat horrified at what I was seeing. The nurse came to remove me and seat me in the waiting room with the other parents. Their children had the same illness my little boy had. Many parents had been there for weeks and weeks and not one of their children had a good prognosis.

I asked God again, "Why? Why is this happening?" Could it be that it was because I wanted to end my pregnancy for the glitz and glamour lifestyle I desperately wanted? Was it because my husband was going that day to buy a dream, a racehorse he wanted so badly? I mustered up the courage to ask God to show me the way. Many things raced through my mind, but it wasn't those things at all. God is not a punishing God. He is a forgiving God. As I sat there, God brought me a song we sang often in church. "Only trust Him, Only trust Him now" was a phrase from the song. I realized that was the only thing I could do. I had to trust God with faith like I did when I accepted Him as my Lord and Savior.

When I got back to the bed where my little man lay, motionless and so small in a huge bed, I prayed. I cried. I prayed again. That's when God spoke to my heart, in that moment of courageous faith.

He told me to open His Word and read it. Opening at random, I read Psalms, where my finger landed. Chapter 102, verse 28 read …

"The children of thy servants shall continue and their SEED shall be established before thee." To me, God said, "I will not harm the children of your seed" and He reminded me that I am God's child and my little boy is my seed. Nothing else mattered at that time. I trusted the Word of God and what He spoke to me as He told me He would not harm my child.

As I was praying and thanking the Lord, a nurse came in to tell me the doctor needed to talk with me. I walked into his office and sat at his desk as he began to tell me, "Mrs. B, your son has encephalitis and is in a coma." He explained how the brain swells and has pressure with this illness. I was half-listening to what he was explaining but I kept trusting God's Word to me: "I will not harm the children of thy seed." Then the doctor said to me that they felt that at best my son only had a 50% survival chance. I responded by laughing as he looked at me strangely and said, "I know this is a lot to take in and it's OK to cry." Still laughing, I replied, "Doctor, I heard what you said. But more importantly, I heard from the Lord that my son was going to be just fine." He tried to explain again as if he did not hear me, but I assured him that I heard him the first time, and with courageous faith I answered again, "My baby will be fine because God assured me he will be." The doctor got up and shook my hand, replying, "I wish I had as much faith as you."

I went back to my son's room. He was AWAKE. Nurses were talking to him. As my husband was next to me, one nurse escorted us to another room to spend the rest of that night…In the morning our pastor from church came and brought some little cars for my son. As we approached my son, he immediately looked at us and began to play with the cars like nothing ever happened. A short time later the nurses came in to take him for tests. They did a spinal tap among the tests and guess what? No more encephalitis! He was 100% OK, and in what seemed like an instant we received the OK from the doctor to take our son home.

I sat in complete amazement watching my son play with his new cars. What God did was more than amazing; He gave us a miracle story. He said, "Now, go to the world and tell your story, a story of true love, not punishment." Because of our sin, Jesus came to save us.

"If we confess our sins, he is faithful and just to forgive us our sins, and to cleanse us from all unrighteousness" (1 John 1:9 KJV).

I did this many years ago – I confessed my sins to Jesus, not understanding it all, but completely trusting with my whole heart. Because I had trusted Him years ago, God gave me the courage to take the steps of faith I needed and face whatever would come my way.

I hope that my story somehow encourages you to trust God. No matter what you are going through, I urge you to let go of that which you are trying so hard to hold on to and to release it to God. Our Father knows our needs better than we do, and I guarantee that you can trust Him more than you can trust anyone else – even yourself!

"Trust In the Lord with all your heart and lean not unto your own understanding; In all your ways acknowledge him and he will direct your path" (Proverbs 3:5-6 NIV).

Courage to overcome HURT

Kimberly Ann Hobbs

Many believers have abandoned their relationship with God or their call to serve God because, at one time or another, they have been hurt and then allowed this hurt to control their lives and, in many instances, crush their lives.

There is a large spectrum of hurts – emotional, physical and circumstantial – which can include things like dealing with people or losing a friend or a relationship. Hurt can stem from a change in our lives, broken hearts, lost hope, aging, death, sickness and so many more events that can encompass your mind.

It takes a courageous step of faith to overcome hurt before it consumes you altogether. There have been many Christians conquered by hurt when they let their flesh get in the way. We can be overcome by this one powerful word and it can happen very quickly. Be on guard to war against fret, envy, anger, wrath, and evil. Hurt can cause us to fall prey to these actions. So what is the solution to a hurting heart? Do you think you could trust your hurting heart to someone who can help you?

God is your perfect solution – He never makes a mistake.

Someone who makes no mistakes and loves you and cares about you is always with you. God provides truth in his Word for you to hear. One of those truths is that God loves his children. When one of them is hurting, He knows it. When His child is feeling pain, He feels it and He cares. God is a God of wisdom and He is also just and will take action to protect his children.

"If any of you lack wisdom, let him ask God, who gives generously to all without reproach, and it will be given him." (James 1:5 ESV)

The first step to take is trust God. If you know Him, you will be open to trust Him.

"Keep trusting in the Lord and do what is right in his eyes. Fix your heart on the promises of God and you will be secure, feasting on his faithfulness." (Psalm 37:3 TPT)

Give God your hurts and all that comes with them. God will cover your wounds with His healing power that He so generously bestows on His children.

• •

Ms. Adiana Pierre, is a native of Brooklyn, NY, by way of Miami, Florida. Their parents raised Adiana and her three siblings. She came to know Christ at an early age.

Within the Miami community, Adiana is a gifted and bold voice and is an upcoming author as she tackles women's issues. In her role as a Financial Consultant, Adiana helps families win with money. She is a community liaison with a wealth of business savvy.

She graduated from Miami Dade Community College and received her Master's degree in Criminal Justice from Capella University. She is the mother to Payton and Carter Pierre.

Adiana has her finger on the pulse of today's culture of business and entrepreneurship. During the financial crunch of this national pandemic she asserts, "Now is the time! So many people are in fear and focusing on their failures. I'm walking by faith and not by sight."

Faith Walk
Adiana Pierre

I had enough. They say when you really want to change you have to feel the pain so severely before you will make a move. I used to think that I had a low tolerance for pain until I realized the events in my life were at a threshold of excruciating emotional, mental, and spiritual abuse. The saddest part was, I was hurting myself. When you don't know who you are or whose you are, you allow the worst things to happen. In my case, it was a toxic relationship.

"Toxic relationship" is a phrase that means major relationship turmoil. When a woman hears this phrase, she doesn't normally think about her own actions, but typically blames the man. However, I had to ask myself what part my own personal toxicity played in my relationship.

I am a woman, therefore I am the gateway to sexual and erotic pleasures men want to enjoy. My body was designed by God as a "gate" to enter one way, by one husband. I hold the key to my gate, so why was I giving the key to toxic men? Why was I living beneath the standard God set for me? Why was I constantly wrestling in my flesh to do the very things I did not want to do?

> *Romans 7:15 (NLT)*
> *I don't really understand myself, for I want to do what is*
> *right, but I don't do it. Instead, I do what I hate.*

These questions and many more will be answered as I give you a peek into my courageous steps of faith away from a toxic relationship, but more importantly, from the toxicity in myself. You have heard it said before, "It takes two to tango." It also takes two to be toxic. I have had to look in the mirror of my soul and get nauseated about the stuff I allowed, and even celebrated. I didn't know my worth.

I defiled my temple, my own house. Can you imagine going from room to room in your home with a sledgehammer, knocking holes in everything you could find? Can you imagine never taking the toxic trash out and allowing it to pile up to the roof? If this disgusts you, imagine the toxicity level in our bodies when we share our temple with Mr. Wrong.

> *1 Corinthians 6:19 (KJV)*
> *What? know ye not that your body is the temple of the Holy*
> *Ghost which is in you, which ye have of God, and ye are not*
> *your own?*

Paul was asking rhetorical questions. "What!? You mean to tell me you don't know that your body is the temple of the Holy Spirit? Don't you realize that you are not your own?" If I am honest, the answers to those questions for me used to be "No" and "No."

People, not just men, used me. I was an equal gender opportunist when it came to being used. The women my ex-boyfriend had babies by used me to watch their kids since I was the "nice girl." I was the "good baby-mama," with seven kids swinging from my arms. Two in diapers, three in pull-ups, and two more getting potty-trained. Yep, I was the "good wifey." The only problem was I was not anybody's wife. I desperately wanted to be, and I was putting on a virtuoso performance to be Mrs. _____. I thought if I made him happy, he would love me unconditionally. But a boyfriend, no matter what he says, isn't going to love, serve, protect, and marry a woman just because he's living and sleeping with her. Ladies, don't act like you haven't been there before. I thought pleasing him to prove I was "good enough" was my meal ticket. So I cooked, cleaned, ironed, bailed him out, loaned him money, and even put myself on a strict exercise and diet program because he called me "fat." Am I the only one? Yeah, I didn't think I was. What did it get you? Another sleepless, pillow-soaked night of remorse, regret, and resentment?

My story of courage couldn't come quickly enough, but I almost did not make it. There was a time when life seemed less for living and more for dying. I get frustrated sometimes when I think about where I was. I hope the words in this chapter will take away your own self-loathing and give you the courage to walk away from the toxic woman in the mirror.

Joshua 1:9 (NIV)
This is my command—be strong and courageous! Do not be afraid or discouraged. For the Lord your God is with you wherever you go.

Courage is not required when things are going well in life. Courage is not needed when the bills are paid and your children are behaving well. However, courage is necessary when your money is funny and your change is strange. Courage is essential when you have two crying babies that need diaper changes in the backseat of your four-door sedan in need of a muffler and a new transmission. Courage is needed when you are afraid of life, love, and the woman staring back at you in the mirror.

Courage can only be activated in the presence of fear. Courage needs fear in order to breathe. It's not unusual to be fearful about important decisions and important responsibilities. But God does not *suggest* us to be courageous; He outright demands it.

When God told me to move, I didn't have a clue where He was calling me to, I just knew He was calling me through – through the fire.

I had caught my ex-boyfriend cheating before my planned exodus. I rushed to the clinic to be tested. I never trusted him. Think about what I said. I never trusted the man that I was giving my most precious gift. I was already in the U-Haul when the nurse called, and though I wanted her to tell me my results over the phone, she paused and said, "Adiana, just come in!" *Click.* What? I turned around and went straight to the doctor. I was scared, and rightfully so.

As I walked through the doors of the health clinic, I was frightened out of my mind. I had to be courageous, so I walked to the back and sat down. The doctor told me I had contracted chlamydia, again.

You see, this wasn't my first rodeo. Nor was it my second. It was indeed the third time I had contracted this same bacterial STD, leaving me with the same disappointment, coming from the very same person. Even though I was not new to this, I still had the audacity to be angry with him. They say, "Fool me once shame on you, fool me twice, shame on me." What happens when it's round three? You play stupid sexual immoral games; you win stupid sexually transmitted diseases. I played myself three times too many.

I am in no way downplaying the devastation of contracting an STD. I was able to take meds and get rid of it, luckily. I say luck, because I was playing Russian roulette with my woman parts. I was outside the will of God and could not put any blame on God. I played a part in all of this, but at that moment, I saw red. We have to stop "blaming God" and men for the damage we do to ourselves.

> *Proverbs 19:3 (NLT)*
> *People ruin their lives by their own foolishness and then are angry at the LORD.*

I had so much anger toward my ex I couldn't even cry. After I loaded up the U-Haul to leave, it began to get cloudy and started to rain. The rain was a reminder of the tears I couldn't cry, and the clouds reminded me of the gloom that had me doomed. I kept on stepping toward my destination. The drive was surreal. Before my children fell asleep, they asked, "Where are we going, Mommy?" I told them to just sit back and enjoy the ride. I was bright-eyed and hopeful.

I could not believe I had gained the confidence to leave. This was a woman who was tired of stepping in the wrong direction. This woman was learning her value and renewing her virtue. This was a woman who had been praying for a breakthrough, and it had finally come.

When I arrived in the driveway of my new home 45 miles away, the sun was shining bright and the sky was clear. This was a fresh, new start.

I want to leave you with five things that help me walk with courage – that brought me to a point of breathing again even when fear was gripping my feet in chains. Ladies, I haven't arrived. But I have put my attention on what is in front of me and no longer worry about what was behind me. Jesus has become my ultimate goal.

Philippians 3:12-14 (MSG)
I'm not saying that I have this all together, that I have it made. But I am well on my way, reaching out for Christ, who has so wondrously reached out for me. Friends, don't get me wrong: By no means do I count myself an expert in all of this, but I've got my eye on the goal, where God is beckoning us onward—to Jesus. I'm off and running, and I'm not turning back.

The FIRST STEP of a courageous faith walk is to recognize what is going on around you and in you. Get thee behind me, Satan!

Matthew 16:23 (NIV)
Jesus turned and said to Peter, 'Get behind me, Satan! You are a stumbling block to me; you do not have in mind the concerns of God, but merely human concerns.'

Sometimes Satan tries to surround you by working through the people closest to you. You have to know the world from the Word. World talk is carnal and pleases your flesh. It's when a close girl-friend says something like, "Girl, you know if I was you, I wouldn't do that." This sounds good, but where is it coming from? When you have big dreams and big plans from God, you will be surprised who shows up to the party in all black. They will treat a banquet celebration like a funeral. Jesus looked at Peter, one of his closest friends, and said, "Get behind me, Satan!" Wow. Peter was still Peter, but his words were from Hell.

> *Matthew 22:14 (KJV)*
> *For many are invited, but few are chosen.*

Many people have been invited into my life, but those who are chosen came from God. If your friends don't lead you back to the Word, they are "invitation only" friends – in attendance, but not present and accounted for by God. God chooses those who challenge you and hold you accountable. These are the friends who will tell you the truth even when you don't want to hear it. They truly love you and want the best for you. Put Satan behind you and keep God's chosen friends beside you.

Besides working through those around you, Satan will attempt to work in you – in your mind, will, and emotions. Your mind needs to be regulated by God's Word – not by movies, food, gossip, shopping, money, work, sex, wine, or pornography. What you think says everything about you.

> *Proverbs 23:7 (NKJV)*
> *For as he thinketh in his heart, so is he...*

Your will is the seat of your soul. Whatever governs your will is your master. If your appetite, selfishness, or personal agenda governs your will, God is not your master. The will has to be submitted to Christ on a daily basis. You must find out His will and crucify yours.

> *Psalm 143:10 (ESV)*
> *Teach me to do Your will, for you are my God! Let your good Spirit lead me on level ground.*

Honestly, I don't have the desire to do God's will. It is God working through me that gives me the will and power to do what pleases Him. This is a different level of submission. Doing what you want to do is for girls. Real women submit their will to God. Women of God are known by their love, kindness, and submission. Say amen or ouch; I understand.

The SECOND STEP of a courageous faith walk is to get a vision for the future.

> *Proverbs 29:18 (KJV)*
> *"Where there is no vision, the people perish: but he that keepeth the law, happy is he."*

Ladies, if you do not see beyond sight, then you will never see where you're going. Write down what you want and look at it every day. In my bedroom, I have a mirror with my personal goals written in erasable marker. Every day I visualize myself reaching my goals. I erase each goal after I achieve it and replace it with a new goal. This empowers me and energizes me to keep pushing myself. I encourage myself in the Lord as I reach new heights daily! Do not underestimate the power of an erasable marker. Write it down!

Habakkuk 2:2 (NKJV)

And the LORD answered me: 'Write the vision And make it plain on tablets, That he may run who reads it.'

The THIRD STEP of a courageous faith walk is to forgive.

Forgiveness is therapy for your soul. We've all been hurt, but God gives us forgiveness as a remedy for our pain. It may be hard to swallow, but forgiveness soothes the agony of defeat.

Balm, in the Bible, is healing ointment that comes from Gilead, the mountainous region east of the Jordan River. Have you ever taken some medicine that didn't taste good, but healed you? For me, it's Nyquil. Yuck! I don't like the taste of it, but it does what I need it to do to get me back up and running! Forgiveness tastes sour sometimes, but the healing is priceless. You need that "forgiveness" balm in Gilead.

> *Jeremiah 46:11 (ESV)*
> *Go up to Gilead and take balm,*
> *O virgin Daughter of Egypt!*
> *In vain you have used many medicines;*
> *there is no healing for you.*

Sometimes therapy can help us take the step of forgiveness. I had to force myself to seek Christian counseling because I used to think I was "flawless." For some reason, we women feel like something is wrong with us if we seek help. We have been told to "be strong" and "be the boss" or "never let them see you sweat." We put on a performance, but it does nothing but break our own hearts. Sometimes being strong means recognizing that other sisters can hold you up.

> *Proverbs 15:22 (NASB)*
> *Without consultation, plans are frustrated, But with many*
> *counselors they succeed.*

> *Luke 23:24 (NIV)*
> *Jesus said, 'Father, forgive them, for they do not know what*
> *they are doing.' And they divided up his clothes by casting lots.*

Jesus is our example of forgiveness! If Jesus can forgive me for all my sins while hanging on a bloody cross with nails in his hands and feet, a "crown" of thorns on his head, and goons shooting craps to see who would get his clothes, then who am I to say I can't forgive? With tears in my eyes, and by God's power, I can courageously forgive. Thank you, Jesus!

The FOURTH STEP in a courageous faith walk is to get comfortable with your new identity.

For the majority of my life, I had seen things from my own perspective. But with God's help, I began to see things from His point of view. I am in the same skin, but I have different ways to win. I was winning at the life I thought I wanted, but my prize was always pain. I was a successful loser. I was "successfully" losing at love, relationships, parenting, and my career.

I wanted my identity to be Mrs., but to God, my identity is who I am in Him. A relationship with God is for forever. With Him, I am a new woman, because the old me has passed away. Thank you, God!

2 Corinthians 5:17 (KJV)

Therefore if any man be in Christ, he is a new creature: old things are passed away; behold, all things are become new.

THE FIFTH and final step in a courageous walk of faith is to be a witness for the Lord.

God makes us new so that we can tell others about what He has done in our lives. Your mess can become a message.

Sisters, there are women who need to hear your story. Don't let shame and guilt keep you trapped. Sisters in Christ, Romans 8:1

says, *Therefore, there is now [no condemnation] for those who are in Christ Jesus.* I hope my testimony has helped you lean into your own pain and recognize there is hope. I know how you feel – trust and believe I am still all woman. I know what sleepless nights feel like. I know what unfulfilled promises feel like. I know what trying harder only to be let down feels like. Notice I said "feels like." Feelings come and go, but joy comes in the morning. Where is your joy? My joy is in the salvation of the Lord.

Psalm 51:2 (NLT)
Restore to me the joy of your salvation, and make me willing to obey you.

Nehemiah 8:10 (NLT)
The joy of the Lord is my strength.

There is no other way. Jesus died for [me] so I could be free from so many of the things you read in this chapter. This is only the beginning. Take these five strategies of walking in courageous faith and you will see a life of change that will help you breathe again. Be encouraged, my sisters. God be with you.

Psalm 30:3-5 (NIV)
You, Lord, brought me up from the realm of the dead;
you spared me from going down to the pit.
For his anger lasts only a moment,
but his favor lasts a lifetime;
weeping may stay for the night,
but rejoicing comes in the morning.

Courage to overcome FEAR

Kimberly Ann Hobbs

There are two types of fear mentioned in the Bible. The first type is beneficial and is to be encouraged, but the second type of fear is a detriment and is to be overcome.

The first fear spoken of in the Bible is the fear of the Lord, which brings about many blessings and benefits, and is also the beginning of wisdom.

"The fear of the Lord is the beginning of wisdom and the knowledge of the Holy One is understanding" (Proverbs 9:10 NIV).

The other Biblical fear, the "spirit of fear," can come upon us at any given moment and is something we must overcome.

It takes courage to overcome the spirit of fear. We need to trust in and love God completely to be able to rise above this type of fear. God reminds us that as He cares for the birds of the air, so much more will He provide for his children.

So don't be afraid, you are worth more than many sparrows (Matthew 10:31 NIV).

Is fear holding you back from doing what God has called you to do? Be strong and courageous. Why? Because God tells us not to be afraid of being alone or of being too weak, and He tells us not to be afraid of not having a voice to be heard. He also commands us not to be afraid of lacking physical necessities. There are admonishments throughout God's word covering the different aspects of fear. We should not be stifled from our "calling in Christ" because of fear.

Once we have learned to put our trust in God and courageously walk forward by faith into the unknown, we will no longer be afraid of the things that will come against us. God takes our hand as we take our first step of faith forward.

"Be strong and of good courage, do not fear nor be afraid of them; for the Lord your God, He is the One who goes with you. He will not leave you nor forsake you" (Deuteronomy 31:6 NKJV).

. . . .

Joselie Marcellus is a dedicated mother and wife whose chosen profession is nursing.

She has had a life-long journey with God due to her mother's faithful commitment to Him. Growing up in the church has led Joselie to be surrounded by Christ-followers who were also invested in her development and her relationship with God. The church members became an extended family and created strong ties to her community. She has grown to be a loving and caring woman. Her exceptional decision making and nurturing capabilities have made her an excellent candidate for her nursing career. Today, Joselie acts as a mentor in her church, enriching the lives of women, using her story as testimony.

Understanding Courage

Joselie Marcellus

But he said to me, *My grace is sufficient for you, for my power is made perfect in weakness* (2 Corinthians 12:9 NIV).

Courage: mental or moral strength to venture, persevere, and withstand danger, fear, or difficulty (Merriam-Webster).

I have always admired and been impressed by courageous people. When facing calamity, they have shown resiliency in every aspect of their journey. I have heard and read stories in which people acted courageously and heroically. We have several stories narrated in the Bible where people have demonstrated courage, such as Daniel in the lion's den or Esther when presenting her case before the king. From many of the stories of courage in the Bible, there is one common denominator behind their courage: faith. No decisions were made, no actions taken, no battles were fought without the presence of the Holy Spirit.

Understanding our body

Our body is equipped with the sympathetic nervous system. When we are faced with stressors (finances, danger, distress, sickness, relationships, uncertainties) our sympathetic system triggers emotional and physiological reactions. The body's natural fight-flight-or-freeze response is stimulated; this autonomic response is a major component of how we deal with stress and danger in our environment.

God's work is mysterious, He takes pride in everything that He does and wants to be glorified for everything He does. He purposefully created mankind with a limited innate autonomic response to be dependent upon His power and grace. Many of the most bold and courageous people in the Bible, like Moses, Ruth, Daniel, Peter and Paul, experienced distress, discouragement and depression, but they found their refuge and strength in God.

I believe that everyone on earth, at any moment in life, has to show courage to some extent. The occurrence might be anticipated or unanticipated, an effortless action or a challenging one. For some, it might be easy to get out of bed in the morning and perform our daily morning routine, but even those seemingly "simple" tasks require courage for others who battle with depression.

Understanding faith

To me, participating in this book is an adventure, so to speak. It requires a leap of faith to be courageous every step of the way. Are the conditions favorable? Am I qualified or worthy? Can I measure up to the expectations? I don't know. After considering this, I put aside the incessant questions and started praying, asking God for His presence and guidance. I placed my faith in Him, knowing that *I can do all things through Christ which strengthens me* (Philippians 4:13 KJV). I went forward acknowledging that I have no power to do any spiritual work without His presence, *not by might nor by power, but by my spirit; says the Lord Almighty* (Zechariah 4:6 NIV)

Faith is the essence of a Christian life; it all starts by faith alone in Christ alone; *for by grace you have been saved through faith; and that not of yourselves: it is the gift of God* (Ephesians 2.8 NIV).

The lack of faith in God leads to a transgression of God's commandments. *And without faith it is impossible to please God, because everyone who comes to him must believe that he exists and that he rewards those who earnestly seek him* (Hebrews 11:6 NIV). At some point in my Christian life, I deliberately chose the path of disobedience. I abandoned the Christian values inculcated into me from the early stages of my life. Being raised in a Christian household and believing in God didn't make me take the Word of God seriously. My concept of a relationship with God was erroneous. For a moment in my life, I didn't have peace in God. For one unanswered prayer, so deeply desired, I believed that God had let me down and that He didn't care. I became at war with Him and blamed Him for His silence. My thoughts were that He could have recompensed me for being the good person I had been, which meant to mechanically live as I was taught without understanding that His goodness and favor in my life are unmerited.

I did not realize that having a relationship with God does not imply the absence of heartaches and adversity, but amidst the tribulations was the fortification of my faith and the building of my spiritual maturity. Being away from God's presence is a spiritual suffocation; it's going through life without His peace, chasing after earthly things.

Finally I accepted that God is not a genie in a bottle to answer my demands (needs and wants). I committed myself to letting my faith be tested, growing stronger and living according to His promises. *Now faith is the substance of things hoped for, the evidence of things not seen* (Hebrews 11:1 KJV). *For I know the thoughts that I think towards you, saith the Lord, thoughts of peace, and not of evil, to give you an expected end* (Jeremiah 29:11 KJV).

It became a priority to me to develop a relationship with God based upon His standards, not upon my understanding. It is fundamental for me to have a relationship with God based upon obedience and submission to His Word. *Trust in the Lord with all your heart and lean not on your own understanding; in all your ways submit to him and he will make your path straight* (Proverbs 3:5-6 NIV). I reconciled with Him and took steps to restore our relationship. *So then faith comes by hearing, and hearing by the word of God* (Romans 10:17 KJV).

And this became my life verse: for He said to me, *My grace is sufficient for you, for my power is made perfect in weakness* (2 Corinthians 12:9 NIV).

From a Personal Experience

I have been a registered nurse for many years, working in different specialties and areas to promote health while providing comfort and care to patients by using a compassionate and holistic approach. One evening, I left my home for work, unbeknownst to me that my work night would be destroyed by an unfortunate event. I would endure a situation that would leave me shaken to the core, questioning my profession, work and values.

I work as a unit care coordinator. As I was assisting one of the staff members with a challenging patient, I was unexpectedly physically assaulted and beaten. The initial emotional and physical shock was devastating. I couldn't believe what had just taken place; my brain felt short-circuited. My emotions rapidly went from fear to disbelief to rage and anger. While my body expression remained calm and in control, it did not match my feelings and emotions – I felt confused, lost, degraded, betrayed, invaded, and robbed. Surely this was just the beginning of how this event was going to affect me. Being a nurse, I am well aware of the risks; I have heard many stories, but to experience this kind of violence took me to another level of distress.

I knew that experiencing such a sudden and fearsome event would forever influence my ways of living and working. I was confronted by a situation where I felt helpless. I was angry at myself and at others. I often asked why this had to occur to me. I was consumed and stagnant, consistently reliving the ordeal, which caused me a great amount of anxiety. My days were filled with tears and my nights with nightmares. Anxiety is physical and emotional suffering. I remember this particular week when I felt the effects of depression and discouragement tightening their grip around my body, mind and soul. More dreadful news showed up at my door and took me deeper down into depression. I turned to God, prayed and implored him for strength. I have faith in His healing power and I cast all my burdens upon him. "Come to me, all of who labor and are heavy laden, and I will give you rest" (Matthew 11:28 ESV). I started worshiping God through songs and music throughout my days. Subsequently, my perspective on my situation shifted, and I started to see how, through it all, God had never left my side. I started to give Him praise and thanksgiving for sparing my life on that night. My heart became lighter, my mind clearer and my days brighter.

The blessing to have the unconditional love of a family, the emotional support from friends and the spiritual support of partners in faith is one of the utter proofs of God's love for me.

While the dread, created by this incident, of going back to my work environment was a challenge I had to walk courageously through, I also had to cope with the new reality of Covid-19 in the healthcare industry. I have seen many people, via social media, asking for the year 2020 to be erased and restarted. The Covid-19 pandemic has impacted and continues to impact people across the world on different levels: economic, educational, physical, and psychosocial, to name a few. The world's foundation is shaken by the disease; the world as we knew it will never be the same. In Psalm 11 David asked and gave the answer to the question, *When the foundations are being destroyed, what can the righteous do* (Psalm 11:3 NIV)? *In the Lord I take refuge* (Psalm 11:1 NIV). This is the time for all of us children of God to strengthen our faith, stand in the gap, draw closer to God, and pray for the spiritual, physical and emotional healing of the land. We cannot be a spectator in the army of God, but must be true participants, no matter what our position is.

As a healthcare worker, my position is to work on a Covid-19 unit. I've seen firsthand how the disease affects the lives and well-being of the population. My coworkers and I have to face a new reality – running many codes and rapid responses, and transferring patients to the intensive care unit every shift. Taking multiple trips to the morgue every week has become the norm. Like everyone else who has to leave their home for work in spite of knowing they may potentially contract this frightful disease, I am concerned. This disease has accentuated the stress in a workplace that is already emotionally, mentally and physically demanding.

Every day I pray to God for the courage to perform my work without fear, because I know how the fear of contracting the disease can compromise my job performance. I believe, more than ever, that I am making a difference through my work while I am giving emotional support to staff, patients and family members. I go to my workplace assured of God's help and presence. *Fear not, for I am with you; be not dismayed, for I am your God; I will strengthen you, I will help you, I will uphold you with my righteous right hand* (Isaiah 41:10 ESV). As a Christian, it is imperative that I also pray for my work team, the patients, and their families.

Today I understand that faith is contingent on my relationship with God. I have learned how easy it can be to let the unexpected distract us from God's purpose in our lives when we don't have faith. Difficult times can make us lose sight of His words and promises. We cannot pray while having doubts about God's will to fulfill His promises. Faith is also the courage to accept God's plans for our lives, because His ways are not our ways, His timing is not our timing, and He holds our future in His hands. To put our faith in Him is to have perfect peace to get through life's challenges. God does not tell us about how big our faith needs to grow, but He tells us how to begin and encourages us to continuously work toward growing our faith in Him. *He replied, If you have faith as small as a mustard seed, you can say to this mulberry tree, 'Be uprooted and planted in the sea,' and it will obey you* (Luke 17:6 NIV). You and I just need to take the first step toward faith. Courage may be like a seed watered by circumstances of life, but faith is the seed watered by the words of God. *Now faith is the substance of things hoped for, the evidence of things not seen* (Hebrews11:1 KJV).

Courage to overcome
DEPRESSION
Kimberly Ann Hobbs

Depression is a problem many human beings often face. Proverbs 12:25 (NKJV) says, "Anxiety in the heart of man causes depression, but a good word makes it glad." Depression is a mood disorder that causes a persistent feeling of sadness and loss of interest. It affects how you feel, think and behave and can lead to a variety of emotional and physical problems.

Many who suffer depression as a result of lack of hope find themselves facing trouble. We walk through life with a bleak outlook on circumstances as our mind becomes saturated with the weight of discouragement. Before we know it, we are drowning in the depths of depression. God in his Word tells us clearly that we don't need to be weighted down. Why?

"Come to me, all who are weary and burdened, and I will give you rest. Take my yoke upon you, and learn from me, for I am gentle and humble in heart and you will find rest for your souls. For my yoke is easy and my burden is light" (Matthew 11:28-30 NIV).

When you are experiencing a depressed heart – look to Christ. God says, He is making known the glorious wealth to you of this mystery, which is Christ in you, the hope of glory. (Colossians 1:27).

Your joy comes from salvation which can only be obtained through asking forgiveness for your sins, believing Jesus died for them, and confessing with your mouth, which allows you to share in the eternal joy of living life forever with God.

If you are feeling depressed, identify the causes, and if that is difficult, ask God to reveal those causes to you. He will do this. It helps to know what you are fighting against so you must take this to God in prayer. Then read the scriptures. Psalms is a beautiful place to read. All throughout the chapters you will hear of ways to combat depressive thoughts. Read Psalm 91—the whole chapter.

God tells us in 1 Peter 5:7 NIV, "Cast all your anxiety on him, because he cares for you."

Psalm 34:17-18 reminds us that "When the righteous cry for help, the Lord hears and delivers them out of all their troubles. The Lord is near to the broken hearted and saves the crushed in spirit."

Christians can take comfort in knowing that they do not suffer alone. There are many who will walk beside you who are strong and faithful leaders of God. Set your sights on God and draw strength from Him. Surround yourselves with believers who will speak life into your life. Women World Leaders is a group that can encourage you, strengthen you and empower you in our Lord. Reach out to someone who will truly point you to the God of glory to restore your soul.

. . . .

Dr. Jennie Cerullo and Dr. Marcia Ball

For over twenty years Dr. Jennie Cerullo and Dr. Marcia Ball have provided strategic consulting and training for governments and large Christian ministries throughout the world who are interested in promoting character development, life skills and the prevention of HIV/AIDS. They met as consultants through CRU and utilized their expertise in public health and education as they assisted with the development of *Life at the CrossRoads*, a worldwide intervention to stop the spread of HIV/AIDS. Both left their university positions in 2000 to launch Kerus Global Education, enlarging their ministry footprint to include many of the world's largest Christian organizations, Samaritan's Purse, World Vision, TWR, Willow Creek Global Missions and others, with their *It Takes Courage! (ITC!)* Program. *ITC!* is a multi-tiered approach to HIV prevention including curricula, leadership training, youth rallies and an oral drama program called Grandma's Village. Collectively, their works have been translated into 23 languages and available in over 56 nations around the world. Marcia and Jennie's passion for Africa's orphans and the grannies who care for them, led them to Soshanguve, South Africa where they teamed with local entities to establish the Kerus Go Amogela Orphan Care Center. Recognized as a best practices model in South Africa, the program serves as a beacon of God's love that mobilizes leaders from local churches and schools to care for the orphans and widows around them. Jennie and Marcia's unique blend of art, science, and compassion has made them sought-after speakers, trainers, and technical experts for organizations around the world.

Dr. Jennie Cerullo is an engaging and exciting international speaker and trainer whose sense of humor and joy in life is as contagious as her passion for hurting and vulnerable children. From Vietnamese refugee camps in Hong Kong, to working with Mother Teresa in Calcutta, to the halls of academia in California, she has fervently poured herself into countless lives and communities with life-changing messages of hope. Jennie holds academic degrees in education, human resource leadership, and cross-cultural education and has taught in the graduate education program at Azusa Pacific University. She is a Birkman Method senior consultant and loves helping leaders to be courageous and effective influencers. Jennie loves to write music, sing and play the guitar, and take long walks on the beach where she can spend uninterrupted time with her heavenly Father. She also enjoys quality time with friends and family over a delicious meal, sharing from the heart, and laughing for hours!

Dr. Marcia Ball is a gifted communicator and writer with a passion to uplift and protect women and children living in communities challenged by poverty. As a tenured Associate Professor in the Department of Health Sciences at James Madison University in Harrisonburg, Virginia, Marcia taught a variety of undergraduate and graduate health education courses. The service-learning health education courses where she took students to Honduras and Haiti were her favorite. She has written and directed numerous state and federal grant projects related to the prevention of teen pregnancy, alcoholism, and sexually transmitted diseases. She is a senior-level Birkman Method consultant and enjoys helping individuals and teams to reach their full potential and thrive with confidence. Marcia feels the closest to God sitting quietly in nature with a great cup of coffee in-hand. Her free time is spent exploring portrait and wildlife photography, inventing delectable gourmet meals for family and friends, gardening, and playing a robust game of pickleball.

It Takes Courage!

Drs. Jennie Cerullo and Marcia Ball

"It takes courage!" We've shouted that phrase countless times during conferences with amazing teachers, pastors, and government leaders in over 50 nations around the world. Many days we've quietly said it to ourselves as we care for fearful orphans and weary grannies in South Africa. It has become the rallying cry for more than five million people around the globe who are a part of the ever-expanding Kerus network.

Kerus is a Greek word that means to do something with all your heart and passion. When we chose that name for our nonprofit organization in 2000, we knew God was taking us out of our university classrooms to walk hand-in-hand with a hurting, desperate world. Kerus ministry tools would be educational; the strategy centered on the love and hope of Jesus. Our journey would require courage and great sacrifice. Only a God-given passion would make it possible.

We were both professors from different areas of the country. I, Jennie Cerullo, was at Azusa Pacific University, School of Graduate Education, in California; and I, Marcia Ball, taught in the Department of Health Sciences at James Madison University, in Virginia. We were brought together as consultants through a ministry called CRU, formerly Campus Crusade for Christ. As educators with expertise in public health and cross-cultural communication, we served as strategy consultants and writers of the HIV/AIDS prevention curriculum and training program, *Life at the CrossRoads.*

By the mid-1990s, the HIV/AIDS pandemic was at its peak. In Africa and other developing nations, pastors were weary from burying so many members of their congregations. In our travels, we held babies dying of AIDS, witnessed youth projects selling cardboard coffins, stood among rows and rows of fresh graves ready for the Saturday burials, and looked into many eyes full of fear, grief, and desperation, having lost loved ones. A culture of fear permeated everything; stories of those with AIDS cast out of homes or put in outhouses to live like dogs crushed our hearts. Hopelessness led to suicides; the pain was unimaginable and at times it felt like we didn't have enough tears. Heartbroken and filled with compassion, we were compelled to help change this story.

Our work has taken us around the globe to over 50 nations, conducting world-wide conferences to train educators, health and human services workers, and members of the faith community to work harmoniously and effectively to prevent the spread of HIV/AIDS. We partnered with CRU, working to elevate the impact of the CrossRoads ministry, implementing effective strategies and training nationals to be conference instructors, and showing the JESUS Film.

Kerus worked alongside CrossRoads for ten amazing years, reaching over five million leaders. Eventually, other influential ministries such as Samaritan's Purse, Trans World Radio (TWR), World Vision, and Willow Creek Global Partners were seeking assistance with curricula and training for their global out-reaches too. In response to the many requests, we created our *It Takes Courage! Educational Program,* which includes our *It Takes Courage!* curriculum, *Grandma's Village* radio program, *Courageous Leaders!* training, and our soon-to-be released *Courage to Care! Sex Trafficking Prevention* training and curriculum. Our *It Takes Courage!* program is a character education approach to reshaping young lives and saving them from the tragic life choices that would rob them of their future. Its power is in challenging them to exercise the courage needed to live differently, to make wise choices, to harness the power of Godly principles, and ultimately, to know the God who created those principles and loves them dearly. Kerus has trained organizations to take these tools all over the world.

For over 20 years we have served on the front lines of the church's response to the HIV/AIDS pandemic, elevating the ministry impact of large organizations and local churches as they stepped out in courageous faith to use their resources to stop the spread of HIV/AIDS and sex trafficking. It has been so humbling and thrilling to be part of this movement of courage and to witness millions of professionals and children all over the globe meet Jesus through the *It Takes Courage!* program.

Over 12 years ago, we felt a deep tug in our hearts to start a grass-roots project in the township of Soshanguve, South Africa. Our hearts were breaking for the millions of orphans and their grannies struggling to provide for them in their tiny shacks. What started as a small dream of caring for a few orphans has grown to Kerus leading an amazing community outreach program. We have the privilege of caring for 130 orphaned children at our Kerus Go Amogela Orphan Care Center, providing food, help with home-work, medical assistance, spiritual enrichment, a safe place to play, and most importantly – LOVE. Kerus has two Safe Houses where children at risk for sex trafficking can be placed for care and safety. Our grannies receive practical support and the older children are learning computers at our Academic Enrichment Center. We work with 20 incredible African leaders that run the programs. Our precious children always yell, "We Are Family!" And, indeed we are family! As two single women who always thought we'd find handsome godly men, marry and have children of our own, God gave us the blessing of 130 children instead! Ok, so we are still searching for those handsome men, but we have so many precious kids!

The tragedy of AIDS brought the two of us together in friendship and ministry, but we never realized we would become a non-traditional family too. Four years ago, we took perhaps the most courageous step of all…we took responsibility for a beautiful 13-year-old orphan, Gontse, who walked into our lives and hearts at our orphan care center when she was a tiny five-year-old girl. Many years ago, on an Easter Sunday at church, Gontse's grandmother Jane (very sick with diabetes) was worried about Gontse's future safety. She asked if we would take her Gontse should she pass away. There was no healthy alternative for Gontse's living situation. At the time we promised we'd care for her. Eight years later, that tragic day came and Gontse's precious grandmother passed. We applied for guardianship and took Gontse in as our own. We are learning to navigate parenthood as two single women, still open to marrying "Mr. Right," with an African child, as we all live on two continents. What an incredible blessing Gontse has been in our lives! She is now seventeen and we love and treasure each day that the Lord has given us together.

Looking back, our journey has been full of excitement, intense joy, deep sadness, scary times, unpredictable situations – all perfectly "right" when you pull back the curtain. It is obvious that God prepared us each individually to say yes to the work of Kerus! Both of us took huge courageous steps of faith to leave our comfortable and predictable lives as professors on university campuses – a big move from certainty to faith. But it didn't just happen. For each of us, it was the result of having excellent role models in our lives, lessons learned through opportunities and experiences, and a deep understanding of how we are all loved by Jesus.

Jennie's Journey

Some of my sweetest childhood memories are from my parents' days as traveling evangelists. I stood in awe, watching my animated father preach with the passion that brought crowds to their feet, shouting praises to God. I watched hundreds of men, women, and children pour into the large tent, filled with anticipation of what God would do each night. At the close of each service, my father would invite those suffering with illness and hurt to come forward. As a young child I had the privilege of sitting on the organ bench beside my talented and tenderhearted mom as she played inspirational music. From that bench on the platform, my eyes danced in awe as I witnessed individuals leap out of wheelchairs, tear braces off and toss crutches in the air. It was thrilling! But one night, in particular, changed my life. I can still see the beautiful blonde-haired girl about my age being wheeled up the ramp by her parents. I remember tears trickling down my face as I prayed for a miracle. My faith-filled father dropped to his knees, speaking of faith and trust, and slowly started to pick her up out of the chair. I heard bones cracking as her legs straightened, and soon she was able to stand. JESUS had performed a miracle – actually two! That night one little girl walked out with new legs. The other walked out with a calling to bring health, healing, and hope to a hurting world.

Many years later I found myself on a plane headed to Hong Kong with one of my best friends, Marilyn Hale, filled with the anticipation and excitement of teaching English and sharing our faith. For a year we lived that dream, savoring every moment. Then we were asked to join World Relief as education coordinators in a Vietnamese refugee camp in Hong Kong. Our world was about to turn upside down. For the next three years, we worked at their receiving camp as boatloads of refugees poured in, sick and terrified, in desperate need of our help to start over. I remember Kin and Kong, ages two and four, survivors of a heartbreaking voyage that took the lives of all but four on their tiny boat, including their parents. Kin and Kong had screamed in horror as their parents disappeared into the dark ocean, claimed by an overpowering wave. In the sad and uncertain days after their arrival, Kin would scream when anyone would come near him. I remember walking up to him, only to have him start screaming and kicking me. Unable to settle this precious little boy's fear, I finally grabbed him and held him for several minutes, wrapping Kin tightly in my arms and whispering, "I love you. It's ok. I love you." After what seemed like an hour, he melted into my chest, and the trust began to grow. The boys became like our kids. A year later, I watched with bittersweet tears of gratitude to God as a wonderful French couple who had volunteered at the camp adopted them.

Marilyn and I finished our time in Asia working in Calcutta, India, volunteering at the Home for Dying Children run by Mother Teresa. Hong Kong had sucked the life out of me in many ways. I wasn't sure I could handle this assignment, but it seemed the place we were supposed to be. After the surprise of meeting Mother

Teresa personally and hearing her words of love and encouragement to us, we felt eager and ready to help. Our first day, we walked into the Home for Dying Children and were met by rows and rows of cribs holding dying emaciated babies and toddlers. I remember touching the arm of a precious baby girl thinking it was small enough to be like holding someone's finger. Unwanted dying babies and children were picked up each morning along the Ganges River where they were left in the night. We helped care for them and love them, giving them a place of dignity to die. Day after day the heartache continued until I thought my heart couldn't take much more. But we continued to serve, and the calling I had felt as a child continued to grow.

Returning home to California exhausted and heavy-hearted, I "recovered" by returning to the classroom, earning a Ph.D. in Cross-Cultural Education, and then equipping others as a professor at Azusa Pacific University. My position allowed me to continue traveling, and one trip took me to a completely different part of the world. Russia had always fascinated me with its stark contrasts of intriguing cultural diversity yet dark and brutal treatment of humanity within its borders. A small group of colleagues and friends that worked with me in Hong Kong and I had been recruited to help smuggle Bible Study materials to a Russian-Finnish church group on the outskirts of Moscow. Dangerous but exciting! When we arrived in Moscow, the air was crisp and cold, but the stifling spiritual heaviness could have been cut with a knife. After receiving a detailed orientation to the task ahead and a stern warning that we would be on our own, the gravity of our task began to settle in. The next day, we cautiously executed a series of covert exchanges and convoluted connections, taking care to follow every instruction to the letter. At the end of our arduous adventure we met a group of loving and incredibly courageous Finnish believers, hungry for the materials we were delivering. That night we listened to countless stories about loved ones lost over the years due to their faith, many sent off to Siberia to work camps. I was deeply humbled by their sacrifices for their faith. I returned home with an even greater fire in my heart.

As the years went by, I settled into my life in California. I had reached a comfortable point in my career and was happily living on beautiful Balboa Island and making a difference in the lives of my students at Azusa University. However, my heart could not let go of the calling from years past. I continued to ask God, "How do I get back to my first love...working overseas and touching the least of these with the love of JESUS?"

One day I ran into an old boyfriend who was accepting a position with the International School Project, a part of CRU, and was assigned to Russia as a project organizer. As he talked, he described a very different Russia than the dark and frightening one I had encountered years earlier when Russia was a closed country to foreigners. Slowly his words found their way into my aching and searching heart. In a very short time, I found myself teamed up with CRU and traveling throughout Russia, teaching thousands of teachers, principals, and school administrators Christian morals and ethics. I loved the new door God had opened for me to serve abroad.

Several years later, CRU was beginning a new ministry called CrossRoads. I was asked to help establish the CrossRoads project, serving as the educational coordinator and helping a team of writers create the "Life at the CrossRoads" curriculum and training. Marcia joined us to consult in the area of HIV/AIDS and, providentially, we became a team. It became clear that the previous years of the endless twists and turns, the joys and heartbreaks, frustrations, and challenges were divine preparation for this next chapter. And God was giving me my heart's desire in ways I could never have imagined.

Marcia's Journey

I grew up in a faith community that highly valued world missions. As a child, I saw movies from faraway places like Papua New Guinea, Africa, and the Amazon. I heard stories of miracles and tragedies of men and women murdered for their faith. I distinctly remember myself as a toothless kindergarten student sitting cross-legged on my gray mat during morning assembly and listening to Barbara Cotton, a missionary working with disabled children in the country of Haiti. My heart broke for those children and I was in awe of this lady's love and commitment. I also remember writing a 7th-grade paper about wanting to be like my Aunt Sara, who was a missionary in Hong Kong.

My life path wasn't missions, it was academia. I ended up at James Madison University as a professor and loved every minute of it. I had the privilege of co-facilitating May Session courses in Honduras with my dear friend and colleague Dr. Patricia Brevard. For many years we would head out with a group of 10-15 students, rent 4x4s and trek out to remote areas to do health projects.

Patcie was fluent in Spanish, while I, on the other hand, ran around with flashcards in hand. One evening while standing with my host and a group of university students, we saw HUGE spiders in the cracks of the ceiling. I said, Yo estoy "miearda" instead of "mieada". Everyone burst out laughing. I essentially told him I am sh#%#%, instead of scared! I could prepare the team, drive through rivers, take care of emergencies, or handle the changes in logistics with ease, but my Spanish language skills were sorely lacking!

It was late May when I boarded my night flight to Guatemala City. I knew I needed language school; I had prayed about it and was at peace to go alone, but I was nervous. I walked through the airport doors after clearing customs about 11pm…and saw no one standing with a sign for me. I called the school – no answer. Five times I called – no answer. I was standing all alone in the airport of one of the world's most dangerous countries, after 11 pm, trying not to panic.

A very tall and handsome man walked up and said, "You're in trouble, aren't you." Hesitantly I said, "Yes." He had been behind me at customs as we fed our bags through the machine. I explained my situation, feeling very foolish that in my naïveté I had no backup plan. Flashing his badge and a beautiful smile he said, "I am Rauel, part of the USA Drug Enforcement Agency. I am here to lead a workshop and I'm staying at the Westin. If you'd like I can take you there; we can sort something out tomorrow." The choice: A handsome man heading to the Westin or a stranger in a taxi hopefully taking me to another hotel? Inwardly freaking out, I climbed into the car with handsome Rauel and we were off. This is when my mother would interject in the story and say that when I get to heaven my guardian angel will punch me out…

The next day Rauel took me to the home of the Guatemalan Chief of Police. They were intensely speaking in Spanish and looking over at me. Rauel turned to me and said, "She thinks you should go home today. There is a flight this afternoon back to the USA." I was stunned! It was too dangerous to try to drive to the language school. I looked at him, looked at her, and said, "What time is the flight?"

I had not wanted to spend the summer in language school but I felt like the Lord was leading me to go there. I needed language skills. I obeyed. Did I hear from the Lord about going to Guatemala? Was it just my plan all along? It was wise to leave, but now what?

A friend of mine, John Harris, called a week later. John was an AIDS activist and he loved Jesus. I told him all about the Guatemala adventure and he said, "Great! I'm glad you are free. Campus Crusade for Christ is going to call and ask you to be part of the team to write an HIV/AIDS prevention curriculum that they can use around the world. They want you to serve as the technical AIDS expert." Had I been in language school I never would have been available. I never would've helped to write the curriculum, traveled the world-leading conferences with other amazing professionals, or met my future ministry colleague and dear friend, Jennie.

I was becoming the kind of professor that I promised I would never be – too busy for my students. I loved being a professor and I loved the AIDS work that was now consuming my time. I knew I had a life choice to make.

It wasn't until I found myself chatting about the situation with my mom and I heard myself say, "I worked hard to be Dr. Ball, I like being Dr. Ball, I've never been anything but Dr. Ball" that the light bulb went on. She just looked at me; her gentle gaze, raised eyebrows and long silence spoke volumes. I quickly got out of the conversation and decided to go for a walk. I didn't even get to the top of the driveway when it dawned on me and I started to chuckle. Laughing, I said, "Lord, I guess if I were you, I would be getting pretty annoyed with me by now. I keep asking and asking what to do, but my life this year has been full of such joy. I'm needed, people are dying due to AIDS and they don't know who you are. I don't know what else you could do to show me that this is to be my life path." I was quickly realizing the barrier for me was "Dr. Ball" and the respect it brought – my ego was the chain to confusion.

I prayed, "Lord, forgive me for this whole 'Dr. Ball' thing. I'm going to give you two weeks. Two weeks from now I'm going to my boss and resign. If I'm being weird here, and you still want me at JMU, you have two weeks to communicate that to me." Two weeks later I handed in my letter of resignation.

When I started to share my choice to leave the university, so many people filled my ear with "But you worked so hard", "Lifetime security – don't throw it away!" But I knew the Holy Spirit made it crystal clear…I didn't know what the path would bring, but I knew I was supposed to be on that path.

My heart had started the Kerus journey on that kindergarten mat. Guatemala taught me that I could walk with the assurance of His protection. I was ready to be what I was created to be. And God had prepared me my entire life.

We can't tell you the number of times we have prayed, cried, and questioned why God allowed AIDS to happen. We've said early goodbyes to dear friends, and we've stared into countless eyes that were deep pools of pain. But we've also laughed a lot, had amazing adventures, and enjoyed moments of deep and meaningful relationships. We've seen and experienced change, in others and ourselves. As only God can do, amid a horrible disease like HIV/AIDS and its accompanying issues of rape, sex trafficking, and abuse, God's love shines. He is always present with broken people and in messy situations; He is always working for our good. Through Jesus, there is a reservoir of peace, forgiveness, joy, strength, and a personal relationship with God.

We are always prepared for what he calls us to do; it often takes courageous steps of faith, but He provides everything we need. Our prayer for you and ourselves is, "Dear Jesus, make us courageous, loving, passionate and yes, dangerous women that will storm through the darkness of injustice and abuse and change this world through your power and love. Amen!"

Courage to Overcome Temptation

Julie Jenkins

The need to stand strong against temptation is something we can all relate to. Even though the temptations that each of us face may look different, we can combat them by using the same three-pronged weapon: AWARENESS, WISDOM and FAITH IN GOD.

We see the scenario of temptation played out over and over in the Bible. Let's look at a couple of examples:

In Genesis 3, Satan tempted Eve to eat of the fruit of the tree of the knowledge of good and evil – and when she gave in, it was forever recorded as the first sin, the Fall of Man. As we read the scripture, we can see Satan's plan unfold like he is following a playbook. Satan approached Eve on her home turf, where she was comfortable and surrounded by beauty that had been gifted her. She was UNAWARE of the attack about to come against her. And though she knew that she was not to eat from the tree, she did not have full WISDOM to understand the parameters – this is clear because she told the devil that she was not to even touch the tree, an instruction that was never given by God. And finally, Eve didn't have FAITH IN GOD and in His perfect plan – she fell to temptation as she listened to the devil's words forecasting that by eating, she would see good and evil.

In Luke 4 we learn by a positive example that we can overcome the devil's powerful temptations by following God's game plan. While in the desert, Jesus was tempted for 40 days during which He fasted, clearly AWARE of the evil lurking around the corner, and called on the power of God to help Him resist that evil. When tempted, Jesus relied on the WISDOM of the Bible to come against the devil's temptation – stating truth against lies. And Jesus kept His FAITH IN GOD – standing on the fact that God is who He says He is and need not ever be questioned or tested.

We must always be AWARE that as long as we walk in human form, the devil will not give up. Remember to look twice at every situation, recognizing that temptation is always around the corner.

We must continually go to God for WISDOM regarding His will. This wisdom comes from prayer, from listening to the heartbeat of the Holy Spirit, and by arming ourselves with scripture daily.

Finally, we must stand on FAITH IN GOD, believing that He is who He says He is! Remember God's goodness and His fulfilled promises. And if you can't think of any – keep reading! This book is full of God's promises!

"Stay alert! Watch out for your great enemy, the devil. He prowls around like a roaring lion, looking for someone to devour." 1 Peter 5:8 (NLT)

• •

Originally from Wisconsin, **Leecy Barnett** has lived in Boynton Beach, Florida for almost 30 years. Education has always been important in her life, so she has a BA in History from Duke University, an MA in Church History from Trinity Evangelical Divinity School and an MA in Library Science from the University of South Florida.

Although she never married or had children, being a part of God's forever family for 48 years has been a wonderful adventure for Leecy. Her first career was in Christian ministry to college students from America and later primarily to students and scholars from China. After she moved to Florida, Leecy began a second career as a librarian. However, she never stopped her involvement in ministry, teaching the Bible and writing for her church. Her second book, *Ten Life Lessons Worth Learning Over and Over Again,* has just been published. In light of her struggles as her mother's caregiver, Leecy has recently co-founded the *Common Ground Friends Caregivers Support Group.*

Knowing Who I Am in Christ Gave Me Courage

Leecy Barnett

On the *Family Life Today* broadcast, the host used to ask every guest he interviewed, "What is the most courageous thing you have ever done?" As I listened to him ask this question, I thought to myself, *How would I answer?* My response always was: The most courageous thing I have ever done was to call the Palm Beach County Sheriff's office to Baker Act my mother. To understand why I see calling the sheriff as my most courageous step of faith, I need to explain not only my own history but my mother's as well.

You might call my mom a "miracle baby." My grandmother had been pregnant with her during the Influenza Pandemic of 1918 when she contracted the disease. Both mother and child survived the ordeal and my mother was born healthy. However, my grandmother began to suffer from debilitating migraine headaches which she told everyone began "right after Helen was born." Mom's childish interpretation of this was that she was the cause of her mother's pain. Mom felt that her mother did not love her and that her mom would have been better off if she had never been born. This inferiority complex undoubtedly made mom's lifelong struggle with depression more difficult.

As far as I know, Mom's first crippling bout with depression came when she was a small-town music teacher. The fog of sadness which totally enveloped her destroyed her ability to function, so she quit her job and moved back home with her parents. This was in 1942, when the United States was beginning the fight of our lives known as World War II. The move back home turned out to be providential as about a year later, when she was feeling back to her old self, Mom met a pilot in training at the local Army Air Corps base. Only in this national emergency would a Georgia peach like my mom meet and fall for a Yankee from Wisconsin like my dad. Evidently Dad knew right away that Mom was the one, but she was less sure about getting married because there was a good chance that a bomber pilot like my dad would not return once he went into combat. By the time my dad proposed, my mom was once again battling depression due to the death of a favorite uncle and the serious illness of her beloved aunt. Mom said she did not know if she would actually go through with the wedding until she began walking down the aisle. Six weeks later my dad shipped out to England and flew 64 successful bombing missions over Germany before he returned home 10 months later.

Growing up I was always close to my parents, especially my mom. I strived to please my parents through doing well in school. My sister was the rebel in our family, and I played the role of the good girl so my parents would be proud of me. I first became aware of my mom's fight with depression when we were on a family trip from Wisconsin through the western states with a final destination of Disneyland. Being cooped up in a station wagon for three weeks with four kids is enough to drive any mom crazy. For Mom, anxiety was usually the trigger for depression. The harrowing trip we had through the treacherous Tioga pass (which at that time was a narrow road up the side of a mountain with no guardrails) did her in. Staying at the Yosemite Lodge that hung off over a cliff did not help either. Mom was depressed through San Francisco, down the beautiful California coast and even the 'happiest place on earth' did not make her happy.

When I was 15, mom had a complete nervous breakdown. She was in the mental sanatorium for several weeks. I remember the shame I felt when we visited her there. I told my friends that my mom was in the hospital, but I did not tell them what her disease was. In fact, it wasn't until many years later that I told anyone that my mom was mentally ill.

Growing up I had always believed in God. My mom had been one of my earliest Sunday school teachers and often read to me from the *Children's Bible Story Book*. Mom's faith was very real to her, whereas I was attending church out of habit. In high school, I thought it would be a good thing to read the Bible for myself, so I started in at the beginning in Genesis, but only made it nine chapters, through the story of Noah. It was boring and totally irrelevant to my life as a teenager in the early 1970s.

When it came time to go to college, I chose to go to Duke because it was academically challenging and its location in North Carolina promised much better weather than I experienced in my native Wisconsin. Since Duke had been founded as a Methodist school, there is a massive chapel in the center of campus. I tried out for the chapel choir but because I didn't sight read music, I did not make the cut. So I stopped attending chapel since when they prayed the Lord's prayer, the Methodists used the words 'forgive us our trespasses' and I, having been brought up a Baptist, said 'forgive us our debts.' (It is amazing what trivial excuses we come up with to keep us from worshipping God!) I vowed to find a church in town, which I never did. So out of laziness, I let my habit of church attendance drop. Honestly, I didn't miss it much because Christianity was just a religion to me, and worship was only a duty.

On Easter of my freshman year, my parents came to visit, and we attended chapel together. The worship only served to point out how far I was from God and how empty my life had become. The very next day, I ran into a friend on the inter-campus bus who was on her way to a Bible Study group. This was the first time I had ever heard of people studying the Bible outside church, so out of curiosity, I decided to join her. The girls at the study talked to me about having a personal relationship with Jesus. They told me that the Bible promises, "But as many as received Him, to them He gave the right to become children of God, even to those who believe in His name..." (John 1:12 NKJV). This offer captivated my imagination, but I was not quite ready to accept it. A few weeks later, I visited a local church that the girls in the study attended. I sensed the presence of God in a way I never had before. As we knelt down for prayer, I opened my heart to Jesus, received his love, and was born again as a child of God.

I was eager to learn about my new life as a member of God's family so I decided to give reading the Bible a second try, this time starting with the Gospel of John. I felt like an owner on one of those home renovation shows, who, on the day of the reveal, steps into their house and says, "This can't be the same house!" Only my revelation came as I now read the Bible with the illuminating presence of the Holy Spirit and said to myself, "This can't be the same book!" This was the beginning of a lifelong quest to base my identity not on what my parents or anyone else say about me, but solely on what God says about me in His word: I am His beloved child, fully forgiven in Christ and sealed by the Holy Spirit for the day of redemption.

Knowing that I am who God says I am enabled me to take a courageous step of faith during the most difficult season in my life.

Fast forward 32 years later. I had moved to Florida more than a decade before to be near my aging parents and became the primary caregiver for my mom after my dad died. Somewhere along the line, my mother's illness had been diagnosed as bipolar disorder. Up to this point her main struggle had been with the periods of depression. Her manic phases had been relatively harmless periods of embarrassing grandiose behavior. For example, one time she called up Jerry Zucker, producer and director of blockbuster movies including *Airplane* and *Ghost* (I had attended high school with him) to pitch him the nonsensical screen play she had written. But I was soon to learn experientially that the first major manic episode for those with bipolar disorder often occurs later in life.

Early in 2004, I was inspired to write what I had learned over the years about my identity in Christ in as daily personal affirmation:

- I am a child of God. I have been adopted into God's family. I am completely accepted in His Beloved Son. Long ago He settled on me as the focus of His love and no matter what happens, He will keep on loving me. God sees me through the lens of Christ as holy and blameless above reproach.

- I belong to God. I have been bought with a price, the very precious blood of Jesus, therefore my life is no longer my own. I glorify God with my body, honor Him with my tongue, I worship Him with my mind and trust Him with my heart. No matter who signs my paycheck, I work for God. Whatever I do I give it my all. I thank God for the good things He has given me and rely on His promise to meet my needs today.

- I am a new creation in Christ. I enthusiastically join God in the work He is doing. I am Christ's ambassador encouraging people to be reconciled to God. God's Spirit lives in me and works through me as I embrace His call to service.

- This is my birthright, my inheritance in Christ. Although I am far from perfect, I do not dwell on my past (and neither does God). Instead I press on, always striving to know God better and become more like Him. I may face hard times, but I won't quit; I may get discouraged, but I won't give up. This world is not my final destination. I'm on my way to the heavenly city. My reward is to see God smile and say well done.

- Today, God's mercy is new, so by His grace, I will live this day for Him.

I said this out loud to myself every morning for a couple of months, not realizing how I would need to rely on these truths in the very near future to take a courageous step of faith.

In February, we celebrated my mom's 85th birthday. With my two brothers and sister in attendance, Mom was feeling on top of the world. But less than six weeks later, I noticed that she was then acting over the top. I said to Mom, "I think you are a bit manic." Mom dismissed my concerns, saying she was just feeling great for a change. But over the next couple of weeks, my concerns proved to be justified. On Good Friday, Mom called her pastor at 6:30 am and told him she needed to see him immediately. He graciously came by as soon as he possibly could, likely as disturbed as I was about

Mom's state of mind. When the pastor arrived, Mom told him that she was going to die that day and be resurrected on Easter just like Jesus had been. When I heard this, I became distressed because I knew delusions like this were a sign of a psychotic break and I was anxious she might take action to make the first part of her delusion a reality (thank God she didn't). But I knew I needed help handling the situation, so I called my sister to come assist me with Mom.

My sister dropped everything and arrived early the next week. Since there was someone to stay with Mom during the day I was able to keep working, but the situation continued to deteriorate. We discovered that part of the problem was that my mother's psychiatrist had moved away a couple of years before. She had visited a couple of other psychiatrists but did not find one she liked. So her primary care physician told her not to worry, he could take over prescribing her psychiatric medication. This was a big mistake. Looking back, I think I should have been aware of this and insisted that my mom be under the care of someone fully qualified to deal with her condition. I am not sure it would have made a difference, as mom trusted this doctor implicitly. It turned out that he had been prescribing an antidepressant that should not have been given to someone with a bipolar diagnosis. My sister and I tried to get my mom to stop taking this medication, but she became belligerent, accusing us of being ungrateful children who were trying to deny her the happiness she deserved. She even told her housekeeper and my brother-in-law that we were demon possessed. My sister stayed for several weeks, putting up with Mom's tantrums and public rants against her, but she had a family at home that needed her as well, so she had to leave. By this time, Mom was completely living in her own world with delusions that her neighbors were spies or terrorists. She even wrote a letter to President Bush to warn him of the situation in her development. I was trying to keep working so I asked my aunt and uncle to come stay with Mom during the day after my sister left. But they could not handle the situation and they thought Mom's behavior was putting her in danger of self-harm. They called me at work, begging me to come home. When I did, I realized the gravity of the situation. I prayed and took a courageous step of faith to call the sheriff to come take Mom to the south county mental health facility. Mom was livid, but I knew it was the right thing to do.

According to Wikipedia, "The Florida Mental Health Act of 1971 commonly known as the "Baker Act," allows the involuntary institutionalization and examination of an individual…Examinations may last up to 72 hours." No provision is made for medicating an individual against their will, so naturally my mom refused medication and was released at the end of three days—no better off than when she went in.

I had no idea what else I could do. Fortunately, with God all things are possible, so now He stepped in to handle the situation. Mom decided she would drive up to visit my aunt and uncle who lived about 20 miles north of us. Because she thought a terrorist was following her in a semi-truck, Mom got off the highway and got completely lost, ran out of gas and was stranded and totally disoriented on the side of the road. By the grace of God, a passerby called the sheriff, concerned about this little old lady. This time the sheriff took her to the north county mental health facility. The manager of that facility knew my mother needed more help than the 72 hours that the Baker Act allowed. She said if I filled out the forms to begin the process to declare my mother mentally incompetent and sign a release to have her medicated against her will, she would probably get better long before we would have to go to court. Thus, Mom was able to get the treatment she needed but didn't want.

Every day she called me from the mental hospital, the agitation in her voice clear, her irritation rising along with her volume, convinced it was her right as my mother to be obeyed immediately, threatening to call her lawyer, pleading, like a prisoner facing the firing squad, "Get me out of here!" The vile, nasty things she said to me stung even though I knew it was her disease talking. At this point, I was no longer the beloved child of my mother, but I knew I was a beloved child of God. During this time, I was given a nightshirt that had scripture verses on it including "I have loved you with an everlasting love" (Jeremiah 31:3), "Nothing can separate us from the love of God" (Romans 8:39) and "You are precious and honored in my sight and I love you" (Isaiah 43:4). I wore this every night during this time and God's words comforted me as I slept.

Thankfully, the treatment at the north county facility worked and after a few weeks, Mom was back in her right mind and we were able to get expert care from a geriatric psychiatrist. For the last five years of her life Mom still had depressed moods but she never had a manic episode again.

All this happened 16 years ago, but I have rarely talked about it because of the stigma mental illness still has. If you are sick with any other illness, your church family and friends will rally around and often bring you meals. But Kay Warren calls mental illness the "non-casserole disease." I hope the story of my courageous step of faith will encourage those who battle mental illness and their families to heal spiritually, realizing they are not alone, and to share their struggles as well. Remember, if you believe in Christ you are a child of God, who says to you, "Fear not; you will no longer live in shame. Don't be afraid; there is no more disgrace for you..." (Isaiah 54:4, NLT).

· ·

Courage to overcome SHAME

Kimberly Ann Hobbs

Are you plagued with shame's message of "I am bad "or "Did I do something wrong?" Shame identifies that we are unacceptable, dirty and disgraced. Unfortunately sin leaves guilt and shame in its wake, even after forgiveness has been sought and granted.

Sadly, shame is found in victims of abuse, which is grieving to our hearts. We can feel shame because we are sinned against. Shameful or sinful acts against a person can leave them vulnerable to shame. Verbal abuse, physical abuse, neglect, sexual abuse, and trauma can all result in leaving a person with a feeling of shame.

We can look at the Biblical example of Tamar, who was raped by her brother, Anon. "And she laid her hand on her head and went away, crying aloud as she went" (2 Samuel 13:19 ESV).

Shame can arise from a past sin, even though it's no longer a part of you. When this shame is experienced, you must remember your sin is nailed to the cross and it no longer has power over you. It is one thing to believe your sin has been removed from you, but another to KNOW that there is a divine love that can never be removed from you, no matter what you've done. Jesus says, "Take heart, son; your sins are forgiven" (Matthew 9:2 NIV).

Shame hinders us in many ways. It can hinder you and prevent you from finding your purpose. It can hinder you from creativity. Shame brings on insecurities which can hold you back from fulfilling things that God has equipped you to do for Him. Shame hinders relationships from thriving because there are tendencies to distance yourself to protect yourself from the other person in your relationship due to past fears. In many ways you may feel ongoing hurt in areas you have no control over anymore affecting the other person.

Shame disappears in a relationship with Jesus. Faith in Christ heals us from shame, bringing us true freedom. Jesus' mission on earth was to set the captives free—free from the prison of shame. Remember to reflect on the truth that God is not ashamed of us. Jesus died for our sin and shame. It takes tremendous courage to walk away from any form of shame and refocus on the praise from Almighty God.

Don't allow your own self-evaluation or that of others to set your mind off course. Look to God's Word for your help. 1 Corinthians 4:1-13 may help you to name the shame. Identify your shame and nail it to the cross once and for all. You can then move on to freedom in Christ alone. With Him you will find true inner joy.

. . . .

Diane Cheveldayoff has owned a successful business as an independent meeting planner since 1996. She worked in Hotel Sales and Marketing for 18 years prior.

Diane was born and raised in Alabama and moved to Florida in 1985. God blessed her with a wonderful strong Christian man in 1991, who continues to be her rock, keeping God first in all he does. They were blessed with 3 daughters, beautiful inside and out.

Their number one love in life is traveling with family and like-minded friends. Their best family past time is biking together. They also love hiking, nature, water and most anything outside. The family motto is "As long as we are together that's all that matters. We don't have to do anything fancy or even do anything at all as long as we are all together, that's what's important."

She and her husband enjoy music, ministry and mentoring pre-marriage and newly married couples. Hearing the Holy Spirit and seeking His will is of the upmost importance in their lives. His ministry HALO Highway: Healing Arts Life's Oxygen. HaloHighway.com

For Such a Time as This

Diane Cheveldayoff

A career woman already climbing the career ladder at age 29 meets a missionary man, age 23. Yes, there was an immediate attraction, yet I was not in the frame of mind to allow a man into my life, much less one who wanted children, was in ministry going off to developing countries, and had NO money. That was just not in my plan, my goals, nor did it fit into my lifestyle. While I kept the friend barrier up and looked at the world from a materialistic viewpoint, something kept drawing me to him. As God kept tugging on me, He also kept opening my eyes and changing my heart. It wasn't a simple process, nor one I felt necessary in my life. After all, I was independent and accustomed to doing everything on my own. God was pulling me away from my own self-focus, a "tug-of-war" that I never would have imagined would take courage and faith to overcome. Roots of career-minded success had been deeply embedded in my mind and had been lived out in the years of my life until this point. I had no idea that this struggle, claiming my career as most important, was only the beginning of another struggle with quite the opposite mindset. Both needed to be uprooted by the POWER of God working within me as I began taking the steps of faith needed through this career-focused journey. I know this is where God stepped in and reshaped all I thought I wanted. "Commit to the Lord whatever you do, and He will establish your plans." (Proverbs 16:3 NIV).

Let's scroll back a bit farther for more background. Although I grew up in church, I now know I had no personal relationship with Jesus. After I spent many years putting everything else in front of God, He still continued to pursue me. In every new city I moved to, He prompted me to find a church, yet I never put Him as a priority. Another move and the end of another relationship forced me to look deeper into my life and where I was going. Fortunately, something deep inside told me to go to church, and I turned to the yellow pages. As I turned the page, my first glimpse and impression were: Why do you want me to go to that BIG church downtown? I guess I gravitated back to my roots of a small church, so a big church was just not in my comfort zone, but I went reluctantly. No Bible and no Sunday-best clothes, but I went. Little did I know how that day, those couple of hours, would change my life.

It was that day I heard the story of Jonah like never before. Although there were many distractions, something seemed very different, I sensed a real joy and transparency. Something I just couldn't put my finger on at the time but was soon to be revealed. When arriving home, I went directly to the bookshelf where my Bible sat, dusty and unused for years. I proceeded to open it and found the church bulletin from two cities prior, approximately four years earlier, and guess where it was? Yes, you got it, the book of Jonah! As I sat on that floor alone and wept, I knew this was where God wanted me. Of course, all those years and my focus on worldly things was still part of who I had become. The next Sunday I went back as a different person. In true Southern Baptist style, when the invitation was offered, I came forward. Afterward, in counsel, I'm sure when asked, "Why would God allow you into heaven" I answered, "Because I'm a good person." Nothing about Jesus, a relationship with Him or all He had done for me. I don't think I ever really recognized the void I had all my life, but I knew something had to change. Past life carried me from one man with a vice to another...an alcoholic, a cheater, an abuser and all types in between; all while God was trying to get my attention. I wasn't completely clear on exactly why and how this was all to unfold but reality hit me, and after all, I had just ended a very unhealthy relationship and knew there had to be a better way. God slowly revealed His way, but it all started that day, knowing I had been like Jonah – going the opposite direction from what God intended. This was the beginning of a new life for me, a change in lifestyle, perspective and pursuit.

The girl assigned to counsel me that Sunday was not an accident. She became a friend, and guess who was also her friend? Yes, a beautiful missionary man of 23, singing in the choir that Sunday morning when this 29-year-old career woman came forward. This girl was a great godly influence and I know was put in my path by no mistake. She poured into me by spending time talking about Biblical principles I had not applied in my life. She helped form a new outlook through those early years, developing my walk of faith. As God opened my eyes and changed my desires, He also gave me the man who could show me what was most important – how to look up to God for answers and not out to the world. The following three months of his pursuit and me fighting my feelings were much like a yo-yo. Come here, go away, come here, go away... Fortunately, despite the waves created by my emotions, as clearly as God told me to give him a chance, God also kept him from giving up on me. Over the next year and a half, God walked us through many steps of obedience and developed the best friend and mate we soon became. After being married for three years, we decided to have children. Now, you have to remember, I was deep into my career and he, being over six years younger, had just begun his. Therefore, the question most couples have to face is: Who is going to raise our child? In today's world, most families depend on two incomes and children can present some difficult decisions. Since my income could sustain us, it became evident to us that I should continue to work so one of us could raise our child. This career woman, now mom, saw vividly how God was changing my heart. Following through on this decision took courage every single day. Me, waving goodbye as I drove off to work each morning with my heart aching. Him, giving up the flying career he loved to be Mr. Dad, feeding a baby, changing diapers and wondering, "What am I doing here?" I continued to climb the corporate ladder, knowing neither of us was 100% happy, yet recognizing that it was our best solution for such a time.

To help financially, and I think to keep his sanity, he started doing odd jobs of most anything where he could take our firstborn daughter. Imagine a man with his tools and a pack-and-play in tow. Quite the scene, I'm sure! We had settled into our new norm when, unexpectedly, only seventeen months later, daughter number two came along. The challenges increased and changed daily. As any woman who is working full-time, commuting an hour or more each way, and then feeling the void of not being home raising her kids OR, as a man giving up what he loved to stay home and try to find purpose in his new role, it's easy to become bitter and resentful. We both went through the motions, the ups and downs, always making the best of the situation.

Life was busy, yet change was inevitable. My job security became threatened as new management entered the picture and my value was questioned. A total disruption engulfed us in all that was considered vital at this time. We navigated through new waters as I was presented with the thought of starting my own consultant business. Something I had never even thought of was now, with two kids at home, not only necessary, but appealing. I knew in my spirit that my position would likely soon be eliminated. I wasn't blind to their motives but what was meant for evil, God turned for good (Romans 8:28). Questions raged in my mind. *How can I still provide the income we need? How can I balance work at home with all the distractions?* Doubt and fear flooded my mind as I tried to work through all the new uncertainties and emotions, yet I knew this was my only option. The risk was great, but the reward could be a life-changer for us. Having the freedom to be home and make my schedule was very attractive, but I knew nothing about creating and organizing my own business. The continued struggle of being career-focused vs. mom was still buried deep inside.

It wasn't easy! There were learning curves and financial challenges, but God continued to provide. Those courageous steps of faith are quite amazing as I look back and recognize God leading us the entire way. I can now see how He worked together through previous job experiences, connections and my entire past for such a time. My husband was and always has been so supportive of every decision and was a vital part of getting the business started. That was in 1996, and it took years of digging deep for the courage to keep going and trudging through what was laid in front of me.

When we had our third daughter, my desire to be a mom grew even deeper. I always felt guilty when working and not spending time with the girls. I was heavy in prayer, but my prayers changed and became very specific. As I prayed for income, I was also praying for more time as mom – and I saw it happen before my eyes. Like a scale tipped to one side, I saw my time shift to more time with the kids, yet business grew. I guess I didn't feel that not working at all was an option and in hindsight, maybe I should have been even more bold and specific in my prayer request to be a mom and not work at all.

Meanwhile, my husband started pursuing his career again, shifting away from his passion for flying and turning into a passion for music and ministry. A door soon opened, leading him to Orlando for an acting role portraying Christ. After commuting to this job for three long years, we knew it was time to move north. I knew that I was still to be the main financial support for our family, and yet felt God's calling for my husband. Again, we were in agreement regarding this major life decision which would affect our whole family. Although we both felt God opening this door, moving had its challenges which required courage. We had to uproot our three girls from wonderful friendships with positive godly influences, leave our own friends, church family, and the work of God that we loved doing through our church. The kids were devastated to leave the church they loved. Once the move happened, the fact that I worked out of our home made it difficult for me to develop friendships in our new community. Adding all this to the already planted questions and resentment pushed deep inside made destructive questions continually resurface. Why should I continue to carry the heavy financial role? Wasn't this the role of the man? Despite these questions, I knew it was a decision we had made together for the betterment of our family, but that was then, and this is now, right? When Lord, when?

My husband continued to progress in ministry but let's face it, ministry is not a way to get rich. Not that I expected the "rich" part, but I longed to maintain our lifestyle without my income being a key factor. Although he progressed, so did the expenses of three girls, school and the lifestyle we had created. As my business grew, I continued to be the primary income for our family, yet that desire to relinquish the financial role was still shoved to the sidelines and just not an option. The thought of not having a choice made it worse. I began asking, "Where is MY ministry?" The question surfaced more often, and I'm sure my support in his ministry was lacking due to daily gnawing questions and allowing my mind to capitalize on the wrong priorities. However, life keeps rolling past and we don't always take the time to really dig deep. We don't sit and evaluate how we can make the changes needed, but instead we keep plugging along in life as we know it, too busy to see it for what it is, but not too busy to keep us from blame and bitterness which allows resentment to take root. It is still so vivid in my mind remembering exactly where I was when crying out to God asking, "Where is my ministry?" He clearly told me, "If you didn't do what you do then he couldn't do what he does. This **IS** your ministry!!" Whoa, it seemed so clear – so succinct, yet not the answer I wanted to hear. It was like a blow to the head, with such a shock knowing how much sense this really made, that I couldn't argue. Now I'm not saying my attitude suddenly changed, and I'm sure I don't always accept the situation as graciously as I should. However, that little conversation between me and God has been what I've hung onto for years, knowing this is where God wanted me for such a time as this. When we look at the paths we've taken and where they have led us, it's important to recognize why we took those paths and to see God's hand in it. One of my favorite sayings is: When you can't see His hand trust His heart! Trusting in God's heart is necessary in business, family, our journey, our kids' journeys and whatever life throws your way. God does not delight in our suffering but in our development. He'll give us the foundation to build upon and will teach us all along the way. It's not always easy, we don't always get it right, and it can be very uncomfortable as we grow through it. My husband and I find reassurance in recognizing that we are both in God's Word and that the Holy Spirit is speaking to us. Praying, we both are listening to the Holy Spirit, but also asking that He unite our hearts together in His will. We pray, "Please God, either change his heart or change my heart!" This certainly makes it a lot easier to handle the internal battle.

What I've learned is that although we have specific desires in our heart, we must always trust that God puts us on the path most perfectly suited for each of us and for those we have been called to serve. It takes courage to walk the unknown roads, getting out of our comfort zone or taking risks. It takes courage to find a way to follow your heart, or to stand strong for what needs to be done while letting someone you love to follow their heart. God's call is not always easy, and not always what we yearn for, but we must trust His way and His provision. It takes courage to hold hard lines to Biblical truths even when friends don't agree, when it's not socially accepted, or in business, where it is not the norm. We must change our perspective and recognize how He uses us right where we are. He wants us to be useful planting seeds regardless of our job. You may be right where you are supposed to be and that could be your ministry for such a time as this! On the other hand, sometimes we are called to change paths, as I was when I met the 23-year-old man that God had provided for me. It is natural to want to stay in the comfort zone, the known. It takes courageous steps of faith to keep walking even when we feel alone in our questioning. We can be strong and courageous knowing that Jesus is beside us walking the hard or lonely road with us and at times, even carrying us through it all. When we really seek Him and allow Him to shape our desires and Him give us the desires of our heart, we can truly see His faithfulness (Psalm 37:4).

As that 29-year-old career woman, my plan, my goal was financial security. And I almost missed all that God had for me because that was my idol. Even today I recognize that finances are my greatest sense of security, which results in my greatest fear, a lack of. To leave that fear behind means continually taking courageous steps of faith toward God, sometimes into new territory, sometimes following a new path that He shows me. Following the path that God had for me so many years ago led me a to fulfillment of my heart that I never knew I longed for – the opportunity to be a mom of three amazing girls. Though that new territory initially created fear, the fear created the need for more faith. 2 Timothy 1:7 – We need to learn through our experiences and not ask God to improve our circumstances but use our circumstances to improve us. His answer may not be what we thought we needed or was right, but His desires, His timing and His plan will unfold before our eyes. So be strong and take courage walking *your* road, just as Esther (4:14) was placed at that moment…**for such a time as this!**

Courage to Overcome Deception

Julie Jenkins

Deception is one of Satan's favorite tools. That's why he is known as the father of lies. The more we know who Satan is and the tactics he uses, the better prepared we can be to stand against his attacks. We can learn a lot about Satan by focusing on what he isn't, and we can do that simply by putting our eyes on God and gazing on His attributes.

Our God is PEACE. *May the Lord of peace himself give you peace at all times and in every way* (2 Thessalonians 3:16 NIV). Because God is peace, following His will, even though it may not make sense by the world's standards, will always produce a peace in your spirit that cannot be denied. Although Satan may try to deceive you into thinking his way is better, his way will never provide that deep-seated peace.

Our God is LOVE. *God is love. Whoever lives in love lives in God, and God in them* (1 John 4:16 NIV). Following God's way will always hinge on love – love for God and love for others. Satan will try to deceive us with two of his big coverups for love: lust and conceit. But true love is pure, not self-seeking, and is unfailing.

Our God is HOPE. *May the God of hope fill you with all joy and peace as you trust in Him, so that you may overflow with hope by the power of the Holy Spirit* (Romans 15:13 NIV). True hope produces joy and peace, and an assurance that good will prevail no matter what. The devil doesn't give hope, but he deceives us with fear instead. Although hope and fear on the surface seem like two sides of the same coin, the origins of each are completely different. Hope comes from God. Fear comes from the devil. We must turn our backs on fear and walk in the hope of the Lord.

Satan will try to deceive us that he has the attributes of God that our souls crave. He will try to convince us that he has the power to make our lives complete, full, fun and exciting. He will try to trick us into thinking that what he has for us is better than what we have in Jesus Christ. So how do we know if we are falling under the veil of Satan's deceit? The simplest way is to ask God! James 1:5 tells us that when we ask God for His wisdom, He will give it to us generously and without finding fault. God wants us to come to Him and He wants to show us His truth. God will never deceive us – only the devil can do that!

. . . .

Lisa Morrison is the God-given mother of her South African daughter Mathapelo (Thapi) Tebele. Thapi is the long-filled desire of Lisa's heart to have a child. She is the greatest gift God has ever given to her, and when God brought them together in 2015, both their lives changed drastically in ways they never could have imagined. God called them to a Hebrews 11 journey of faith. By faith, Lisa and Thapi set out ... (You will read their summarized journey of faith in their chapters.)

Lisa is an ordained minister in the Church of the Nazarene. She has been a lead pastor and staff pastor in a number of churches, taught at the college level both in America and South Africa, served in district leadership positions for her denomination, and has a passion for preaching and teaching God's Word.

Her loves outside of ministry are international travel where she enjoys experiencing different cultures, reading biblical fiction stories and being in God's creation encountering His beauty in nature.

Out on a Limb
Lisa Morrison

"How are you two mother and daughter?" she questioned as she stared at us sitting side by side in a Kansas City church – a white woman with fine, straight hair and a black young lady with thick, curly hair. Continuing to inspect us she added, "Your love for each other is strong."

I met Thapi in 2015 when she came bouncing up to me my third day at Nazarene Theological College in Johannesburg, South Africa, where I was a guest lecturer for the semester and she a student. She was wearing a red and white letter jacket and a big smile that lit up her whole face. In that brief moment of time, neither one of us could have ever imagined what God had in store for us nor how far out on a limb of faith He would call us.

With less than three weeks to the end of the semester, God woke me up at dawn one morning and said, "Thapi is the daughter you have always wanted." He then shot a burst of love in my heart for her. I was in awe of God's unbelievable gift to me. I wondered how this mother-daughter relationship was supposed to work. Thapi was 21. Did she really need a mother to take care of her? She lived in South Africa. I lived in North America. How is one to be a mother of someone who lives over 8000 miles away on a different continent?

With nervous anticipation, I told Thapi the night before I was returning home what God had communicated to me about her being the daughter I always wanted. Her face registered understandable surprise and it was evident that she didn't know what to say. After what seemed like endless moments, that big smile lit up her face as she said she felt the same way about me.

The next morning our schedules unexpectedly got changed and we didn't even have a chance to say good bye. Little did we know that within a matter of a few short hours, God was about to reveal his plan for when we would see each other again to establish our mother-daughter relationship and how much it would require us to take courageous steps of faith.

On my plane ride home, God spoke to me about inviting Thapi to come and do an internship with me at my church where I pastored outside of Boston during her upcoming Christmas break. I loved the idea of her coming in just six weeks, but it was a financial impossibility for me at the time. I paid all my expenses to volunteer in South Africa, and upon arriving home, I found out a mistake had been made with my salary and I owed the church half of my December income. Also, due to my busy schedule, it had slipped my mind to pay my quarterly self-employment taxes the entire year. As I wrestled with this, I sensed the Lord asking me about whether I would take a courageous step of faith and say yes to his will.

My out-on-a-limb 'yes' set God in motion to turn my insufficient funds into his sufficient ones. A friend called and said, "The Lord laid it on my heart to send you $1000. It is for you, not for your church, and I have no idea what it is for." I replied, "Let me tell you about God's gift to me and her coming to America. The

$1000 is to cover her plane ticket." Another person handed me $300 cash. Others contributed smaller financial amounts, as well as grocery store gift cards. In the end, God made what was insufficient sufficient.

Our month together as mother and daughter in tandem with being pastor and pastor-in-training was truly anointed of God. Learning to be a mother was fulfilling, yet terrifying at the same time. Who knew how much love could flow out of a mother's heart, or that trying to feed one's child could be so difficult at times, or how uneasy her black child would feel entering an all-white grocery store? Who knew that co-preaching, co-teaching and co-counseling with your pastor-in-training daughter could be such an immeasurably blessed experience?

When it came time to say goodbye, it was emotionally charged. My heart was full from all we had experienced, yet was breaking from not knowing when we would be together again. Watching her turn the corner after walking through security brought a deafening silence that echoed through the chambers of my heart.

In my quiet time with the Lord, I was trying to process what His bringing us together meant. I was seeking understanding when He asked me if I would be willing to lay my life down for Thapi. He wanted to know if I would say yes to stepping down from leadership and standing behind her to support His calling in her life. Saying yes would require a complete change of direction for my life, one which I didn't see coming, and I felt like the wind had been knocked out of me. I couldn't breathe. Saying no wasn't an option. I had experienced too many self-made painful messes because of my no's to God in the past. A slow, soft yes came, not knowing what it would mean going forward.

It wasn't long before God revealed the next phase of His plan. This phase was not going to require a step of courageous faith, but a running leap that would take us farther out on a limb than either of us had ever been.

God's desire was for Thapi to come to the Nazarene College in Boston to receive her Bachelor's degree in Religion. This was overwhelming for both of us. Neither of us saw this coming, and again, it took my breath away. I sensed God asking me if I would be willing to take on the responsibility of Thapi and her education, and while I was working on my struggles in North America to say yes to God's will, Thapi was working on her struggles to say yes to God's will in South Africa.

I wanted us to be together but I had no idea how I could afford to send my daughter to college. This was a greater financial impossibility than her coming at Christmas. I hadn't saved any money for a child to go to school since I hadn't had a child. I pastored a church of twenty-five people that offered me a part-time salary and I supplemented it with adjunct teaching at the college where I had graduated and where Thapi was being called to attend. Her annual school bill was going to be more than my yearly income.

As I tried to make a possibility out of an impossibility, it was clear I had an insoluble financial deficit on my hands. Sure, God had provided for her to come for a month, but that was a couple thousand dollars. Now we were talking thousands upon thousands of dollars for a college education.

Riddled with anxiety, wondering how this could even be a remote possibility, I found myself reading Joshua 6:2 where Joshua is facing his own impossibility – the impenetrable walls of Jericho. The

Lord says to him, "See, I have delivered Jericho into your hands." God did not say, "I *will* deliver" but "I *have* delivered." The victory already belonged to Joshua and the children of Israel. They just needed to take possession of it.

The secret of their victory lay in their shout of faith. Their shout dared to claim a promised victory solely on the authority of God's word even though no physical signs of victory existed. God would deliver His promise in response to their faith. Confirming I was to walk by faith, I read God's promise in Matthew 9:29, According to your faith will it be done.

I was to solve my insurmountable financial wall problem with a shout of faith, believing God *had* already delivered Thapi's schooling into my hands even though I did not have the money showing victory existed. This was going to be an act of God based on my shout of faith. He would provide for Thapi's school bill according to my faith, not according to what was in my bank account.

A year after her Christmas visit in 2015, we took our courageous leaps of faith for her to come to college, knowing this was God's will. We both were dealing with inner turmoil when she arrived. She left all she loved behind in South Africa to come to a foreign land to attend college, not because she wanted to, but out of obedience to God's call. For me, God had let me know earlier in the year that I was to leave my pastorate and move close to the college so we could live together.

I was overwhelmed with my new responsibility of caring for a daughter, paying college tuition, no longer having a ministry position, and on top of this, I couldn't find a place for us to live near the college. With so many changes occurring all at once for both of us, we began to argue, and with our personalities being as opposite as our skin colors, we became like clashing cymbals. In less than a month's time, we were both ready to put Thapi on a plane back to South Africa.

At long last, after a six-month search, a month into Thapi's first semester, God provided housing for us. It was right on the corner of the campus. It was ideal, but it came with a catch. It was only available for five months. We talked it over and knew this was God's will, so we stepped farther out on a limb, trusting that in five months He would provide a new place for us to live.

When we moved, we were still arguing nonstop. I sensed we were dishonoring God since He was the one who had called us to this journey together. It was time for us to honor Him in the way we communicated with each other. We spoke about this and acknowledged that changes needed to be made. I'd love to say all of our arguments ended after our conversation, but that would be unrealistic. We did put in the effort, though, to honor God in the way we communicated and to show a greater love for each other.

Our courageous steps of faith led to more courageous steps, taking us farther out on a limb. I couldn't imagine how I was going to pay a college bill plus living expenses for two on what had been a meager income before I resigned my pastorate, and now it seemed God wanted to stretch my faith even further. He impressed upon my heart that I was to be a stay-at-home mother. The new mother in me was excited and could understand being a foundational support for Thapi since she was encountering major changes, but 'responsible me' fell apart. Not an ounce of logic reasoned this was a successful financial plan. It spelled disaster, and I spent quite a bit of time stressing over this illogical plan. God's response was found in his promise in Philippians 4:19, I will supply all of your needs according to the riches of my glory in Christ Jesus.

He kept His promise as we took one step after another of courageous faith. Little did we know when we said yes to the five-month apartment that it would be our longest stay in one location during Thapi's first year. When our five months were up, we moved ten times in the next three months. We felt like the Israelites wandering in the wilderness, following the cloud by day and fire by night. We never knew where we might 'pitch tent' when the sun set. Through all of the uncertainties, God kept guiding us. Not a night passed without a place to rest our heads, even if it was in a living room on a twin air mattress that lost all its air by morning. After our three-month wilderness wandering, God provided our Promised Land home where we stayed until Thapi finished school.

Just as God provided places for us to stay, he also provided financial manna and quail for our journey. We continually were asked to share our story at different churches. We would get paid each week for preaching, and sometimes a love offering would be taken for us or individuals would hand us cash or send a check. Often, when I went to the mailbox, I would find a check with a note saying, "Your story inspired me and I want to support you on your journey." At the start of her third semester, right before it was time to pay her tuition, a check arrived that more than covered her expenses for the semester.

When it was time for graduation in 2019, God had delivered my financial impossibility of Thapi's schooling and our living expenses into my hands by a shout of faith, just as He had delivered the city of Jericho into the Israelites' hands as they shouted out in faith. It wasn't because of anything I had done. It was all because of what God had done. He was the one who made the impossible POSSIBLE.

After graduation, we thought Thapi would go home to South Africa. Little did we know God had another phase to this journey, and of course, it was going to require more courageous steps of faith challenging us to go even farther out on a limb.

God revealed He wanted Thapi to continue her education at our denomination's seminary in Kansas City to obtain her Master's degree. My thinking was that she would go on her own since she had experienced living in the States and would be twenty-five when it was time for her to attend. I had no desire to move to Kansas City, being a New England girl my entire life, but per usual, my thoughts weren't God's thoughts. He let me know I, too, was to move to Kansas City in order to continue our God-ordained journey together.

This new phase came with more financial impossibility. Yes, God had delivered Thapi's college education into my hands as I shouted out in faith, and I was trusting He would do the same with her seminary education, but I didn't have the money to pay the expense of moving halfway across the country and to furnish our two-bedroom, two-floor apartment, as we were moving from a one-room apartment. In the midst of trying not to stress about this new financial insufficiency, a check arrived in the mail for $8000! The note attached read, "This is to help you move." I wondered, *Who receives an $8000 check in the mail with a note addressing your exact need?!?* Honestly, it might as well have been signed ~ GOD!

Way out on a limb, I arrived sight unseen and jobless in Kansas City in June 2019. I had hoped it would be possible that a ministry position would open since Kansas City is the headquarters of our denomination. Not even a remote possibility became available. To my disappointment, it was all too clear that I wasn't going back in the ministry. I knew I should be trusting God, but I was now facing my greatest fear – securing a secular job. Panic attacks and endless sleepless nights ensued. I was at a complete loss as to what to do.

Three months later, out of desperation, I applied for and was hired for two part-time server positions. Even with both these jobs, I was facing a financial deficit at the end of each month. God assured me of His sufficiency by communicating "you do your part and I'll do mine," which He did by "…supplying all of our needs" (Philippians 4:19).

We settled into a peaceful rhythm in Kansas City until the Coronavirus hit in March 2020, unsettling all of life. My two part-time jobs came to an abrupt halt, causing me to be jobless again. I sensed the Lord directing me not to look for another job at the height of the outbreak or to seek unemployment because we were on a God-ordained journey. It was God's responsibility to supply our needs, not the US government. Farther out on a limb, I took more courageous steps of faith, trusting God would provide for as long as I was without an income.

As I write this, I am heading into my fifth month of not working due to Covid-19. In this time, God has sent over $13,000 to meet our financial needs. Thapi will graduate in less than a year (May 2021) with her Master's in Theological Studies. God has already provided sufficient funds for her tuition for her final year. What I saw as a financial impossibility, God saw as a financial possibility with each step of faith I took. What was my insufficiency became God's sufficiency.

It has not been logical not to work as much as I have while taking on the responsibility of Thapi and her education. Logically, it seems, I should have been working more, but just as God's plan was unique for Joshua and the Israelites conquering the impenetrable city of Jericho, God's plan has been unique for me. The only way to explain my financial insufficiency being sufficient is GOD. No other explanation exists. He delivered Thapi's schooling into my hands just as He promised.

"How are you mother and daughter?" she asked, and then stated, "And your love for each other is strong." It is evident to the eye that we cannot be biologically related because our external differences say so, but I believe God brought us together because internally, we are alike. Even though we didn't choose one another or this journey, God did because of our faith. We are women who have been willing to follow God's call to lay our lives down for His purpose, and each phase of His plan has called us to go farther and farther out on a limb. Taking our courageous steps of faith these past five years through some rough terrain has fastened us to one another, producing a strong bond of love. We have been blessed to travel this God-ordained journey. Through it all, the praise goes solely to our God who made the impossible POSSIBLE by one courageous step of faith after another. To God be the glory!

. . . .

Courage to Overcome
FOOLISHNESS
Kimberly Ann Hobbs

As we walk through this life, we are all too often faced with foolish behavior – whether it be in the actions of others around us, in the lives of those we know, or even in our own behavior. In the Bible, God admonishes us for our own foolish behavior and warns us of getting "caught up" in others' foolish acts. God tells us that avoiding such actions as foolish behavior would be wise.

"Whoever trusts in his own mind is a fool, but he who walks in wisdom will be delivered" (Proverbs 28:26 ESV).

The Bible has much to say about fools. The word fool usually means a "senseless fellow" with weakness of intellect and lack of judgment. The Bible defines this word as "someone who disregards God's Word" and teaches us about many characteristics of a person who behaves as a fool, often contrasting him with one who is wise. How often do we hear the phrase "what a fool"? Unfortunately, this statement is usually made in a derogatory comment toward a specific person.

The opposite of being a fool is being wise, and the Bible has much to say on wisdom as well. The Bible says, "For the message of the cross is foolishness to those who are perishing, but to us who are being saved it is the power of God" (1 Corinthians 1:18 NIV). For the foolishness of God is wiser than man's wisdom and the weakness of God is stronger than man's strength.

Foolishness is completely being out of phase with God's wisdom. In order to step out of the actions of foolish behavior, we must ask God for His wisdom. It is His wisdom that is working in US that allows us to make proper choices and move forward by faith into our calling. We need to pray for God's wisdom. It's something I, as a believer, personally ask God for each day. I am confirmed in my heart that when I ask God for His wisdom, He provides it.

If any of us lacks wisdom let him ask God and he will give generously to anyone who asks (James 1:5).

By believing God's word as truth, we can believe God answers that verse by "asking through prayer" and relying on the Holy Spirit's indwelling power to grant wisdom and reject foolishness. With godly wisdom, even our thoughts can please the Lord, and we are enabled to make decisions that glorify God as He enriches our lives. Ask God for wisdom in your choices day by day and move forward with that wisdom benefitting yourself and all those around you.

. . . .

Mathapelo (Thapi) Tebele is an Ambassador of Christ and she is completely sold out to Him. She was born and raised in South Africa and has an older sister and brother. She now lives in America with her God-given mother **Lisa Morrison.**

Thapi is currently earning her Masters in Theological Studies at Nazarene Theological Seminary, where God has called her to go.

Her greatest desire is to serve the Lord by being a witness to His people in "Jerusalem, Judea, Samaria, and to the ends of the world." And her fulfilment is found in doing God's will and carrying out His purpose.

Home Is Where You Are
Mathapelo (Thapi) Tabele

"I will go wherever you send me…" These are the words a 10-year-old me would utter every time I had a conversation or prayed to God.

Life Growing Up

I grew up in a Christian home where I lived with my extended family, which consisted of my grandmother, mother, sister, uncles and cousins, my grandmother being the head of our home. My grandmother was a very strong-willed woman who L-O-V-E-D to serve the Lord wholeheartedly. Because of her character, everyone who lived under her roof had to abide by her rules, and one of her non-negotiable rules was to attend church on Sunday. If we decided not to go to church, she would lock us outside and take the keys with her, and we would have to wait for her to come back to access the house.

Not only did she "force" us to go to church, she brought church to us. Yes, exactly what you are thinking… we were "home-churched!" She designed our home-church service program, which included different duties that we were required to carry out. For example, if it was my turn to preach for the Monday evening service, then my sister would be a worship leader, while my cousin prayed for us. Everyone was expected to be hands-on every single day, and because of the everyday services, we had no choice but to read our Bibles and prepare to preach that evening. That is how much my grandmother was dedicated and obedient to God. She lived by this scripture: "*Train up a child in the way he should go, and when he is old, he will not depart from it*" (Proverbs 22:6 KJV).

I became so consumed with church that I began to be interested in this God that wanted my attention 24/7, and not only did He want my attention, He also expected me to be like Him! The 10-year-old me could not wrap my head around the thought of Him being the Creator of everything or the fact that he didn't have any parents. Who does not have parents? So where did He come from? Who created Him then? These are the questions I would ask my grandmother. She would try to answer most of them but would soon get annoyed and brush me off.

The more I thought about God, the more fascinating I found Him to be. I started directing my questions personally to Him, and even though He did not respond audibly, deep down I knew He heard me. I had so much faith in Him that I cannot even begin to explain how and why I trusted Him so much at a very young age. As I was learning more and more about Him, both at home and at church, I started developing this burning desire to serve Him and, although I could not fully understand who He was, I found myself wanting to be like Him. "*I will go wherever you send me...*" I said these words without entirely comprehending what they meant.

> *"You will be my witness..."* These are the Words I heard from God as I was kneeling down in front of the altar as streams of tears were dripping down from my face to the ground.

The Calling

Eight years later, God took me at my word; remember when I was 10 years old, I had promised Him that I would go wherever He would send me? God responded audibly for the first time in my life. It was Saturday, the 27th of April 2013, and the sun was bright, just like any other day in South Africa. The only difference about that day was that we were visited by the President of our Nazarene Theological College (South Africa) and some of his students. They came to do a "college promotion" (called summer ministry in America), and it was in that service that my life would be completely changed forever.

I remember having a conversation with God as I was kneeling down at the altar telling Him that I would do anything for Him except this one thing, and that was to be a preacher of His Word. God was calling me into ministry at the age of 18, just when I was getting ready to go to college and pursue my dream of becoming a pathologist. I pleaded with Him and tried to negotiate my way out of this request that would turn and revamp my whole life. But He took me back to when I was 10 years old and reminded me of all the questions that I used to ask Him, the conversations I had with Him, and yes, the burning desire to serve Him and be like Him.

It was at that point that I realized that it was Him all along: the questions, the conversations, and the burning desires. It was God Almighty who put all those things in my heart at that tender age. This realization was accompanied by a very warm feeling of assurance and a peace that surpassed my understanding. I could not resist anymore, and I said yes to His call upon my life and again I said "I will go wherever you send me…"

After deciding to take the courageous step of faith and saying yes to Him, I knew I was faced with the task of telling my family, which wasn't easy for various reasons. First, I was considered very young to become a preacher, and a female at that. Second, in South Africa we pay school fees from kindergarten until college, so you can imagine that almost every parent would want their children to make a decent living for themselves, and that would not be the case for a pastor. The only person that understood God's calling upon my life was my grandmother, and that was no surprise to me. Eventually, though, everyone came on board and supported me.

It was by faith that Abraham obeyed when God called him to leave home and go to another land… **Hebrews 11:8**

Going to College

Part of saying yes to God required that I go to college for training and, without any further hesitation, the following January (2014) I went to the Nazarene Theological College in South Africa. I can actually recall my first day entering through the college gates feeling overwhelmed with so much joy and peace and thinking to myself, *This is going to be my new home.* Indeed, my first year went exceptionally well, although I had a strange feeling that God was not done with me yet. I felt as though God was still calling me, which left me confused because in my mind I was where He wanted me to be and I was fulfilling my purpose for Him.

And then it hit me that when I was young, I desired to be a "missionary" in the rural areas around Africa, especially in the impoverished areas. In my mind I concluded that God was the one who put those desires in my heart, so the only explanation was that He wanted me to go and be a missionary in the rural areas, somewhere in Africa. My heart dropped at that thought, but I guess I knew this would come. And hence I started preparing my heart because I thought that after I graduated in 2016, God was going to send me somewhere in Africa.

But God had a different plan, one that would require a courageous step of faith. Nazarene Theological College regularly hosts volunteer lecturers from both South Africa and other countries. In August of 2015, we had a guest lecturer from the United States of America. Miss Lisa Morrison was not the first American lecturer, but what made her outstanding and unique was that she raised funds for her Ethics class to attend an "It Takes Courage" conference which was originally scheduled to be held in East London, South Africa – quite a distance from Johannesburg (where the college was located). Because driving that distance was not an option, she was going to pay for all 12 of our plane tickets. Bear in mind, none of us had ever flown before, so we were excited. Unfortunately, the conference was moved to a different location only an hour and thirty minutes away, so we ended up driving instead of flying.

It was evident that Miss Lisa's goal was to invest in the students, and she was very intentional in doing that. I had witnessed the volunteer lecturers come and love on us, and when they had to leave it would be very painful. Hence, I decided not to be close to Miss Lisa and spare myself the heartbreak. All I did was admire her from a distance. I just hugged her every morning and smiled— that was about it.

Little did I know that the woman I was avoiding so much was soon going to be inextricably linked to me. Three weeks before her departure, she approached me and asked if she could take me out for lunch since she got to spend time with all the students except me. I agreed to go with her, and to my surprise we immediately clicked, and God began working in our hearts. We decided that we would have lunch again the following week. On our way back to the college she asked, "How do you see me?" Shocked at her question, I responded, "I see you as my mentor." She looked rather disappointed at my response, and I could not understand why because most people would be honored to have that kind of response.

On a Sunday night in November, the night before she left, I went to Miss Lisa's apartment to say my final goodbyes... this very moment was the reason why I had been avoiding her the whole semester. I hated goodbyes. When I got to her apartment, we exchanged gifts and it was time for me to head back to my room, but she said she wanted to talk to me. I could sense that what she wanted to tell me was very serious and so I sat down. She began, "One morning I was sitting in front of my door, reading my devotion, when God suddenly told me that you are the daughter that I have always wanted..." I paused, not knowing how to respond to that because I already had a mother, and what kind of a mother could she be since we lived oceans apart from each other and she was leaving the following day?

The day she left was bittersweet for me because we never got to explore what God meant concerning this mother-daughter relationship. Three days later, after she had left, Miss Lisa asked me if we could Skype because there was something very important that she needed to disclose to me. She then asked if I could go to a private space where no one could hear us. Me being me, guessed that she was pregnant, and she had no one else to tell since she is a pastor. When the time came for us to connect via Skype, the first thing she uttered was, "Please promise that you will not tell anyone," Now in my mind I was thinking, *I knew it...she is pregnant.* But what she was about to say would blow my mind away.

"On my flight back home, God began speaking to me about you coming to America to do an internship with me for two weeks..." she said. I froze upon receiving the news, and trust me, it was not a "too excited, I don't know what to say" kind of freezing. It was a hurtful and painful kind of freeze. I was not excited or happy; I just sat there not knowing what to say. Words cannot even begin to describe how I felt. I knew God was up to something, although at that time I could not perceive it. In faith I said yes, and we began my visa process as quickly as possible because it was mid-November 2015, and the plan was to go there for Christmas.

America???

What am I doing? I kept asking myself over and over again when I boarded that flight. I could not believe that I was actually flying for the first time, by myself, to North America, to visit my "mom" that

I hardly even knew. I was a little bit nervous. "God," I said, "this is all for you." Nevertheless, we had an amazing time doing ministry together in my mother's church. It was truly a God-anointed time, and I got to visit my American grandmother, uncles, and cousins for the first time. To be honest, I still could not understand what God was doing, but somehow God had bonded us together as mother and daughter.

When my time was up, I had to go back home to South Africa to finish my last year at Nazarene Theological College. I was sad because I had built relationships with my American family and people from the church, but I was ready to go home. I had no desire to go to America in the first place, and when I got there, I did not like it at all. Not knowing when my mom and I were going to see each other, we said our last goodbyes and that was the end. Well, not quite…

The following year, 2016, God began speaking to me and my mom separately about me going to college at Eastern Nazarene College in Boston. "What?" I kicked and I screamed because I had no desire to go back to America. *"Will you still follow me wherever I send you?"* God asked. I always had a sense that I would end up in a foreign country, but I never thought or dreamt about America. "God, America?" I said. "But we have a Nazarene University in Kenya (Africa); why can't I go there?" Later on we would learn that this was not just about going to school, but about being obedient.

Eventually I gave in. My mom was worried about the financial piece because she had a small church and had never saved money to send a child to college. As if that was not enough, God asked her to close her church down in October of 2016, before I came, so that she could focus on being there for me the following year.

So basically, she had no job at all, and yes, she was worried about how this was going to play out because we all know how expensive college tuition is. On top of that she had to move closer to the college so that I could walk to classes. Fortunately, we found a place that was right at the corner of the college and it was not that expensive to live there. The unfortunate part was the lease was for five months. And after that we moved 10 times in three months before we got settled in a new home. The following year, 2018, the unthinkable happened and I lost my grandmother in South Africa. As painful as it was, God was faithful through it all! I graduated from Eastern Nazarene College and I was happy to finally go back home to South Africa, even though home would never be the same without my grandmother. Once again, God wasn't finished with His plan.

Where is home?

When I was in my last year at Eastern Nazarene College in Boston, ready to leave America and go home after my grandmother's death, God began asking me, "Are you willing to go deeper?" He was nudging me to attend Nazarene Theological Seminary in Kansas City, Missouri. Despite my desire to move my life back to South Africa, I courageously said yes.

My mom had no intentions of moving with me, but God began speaking to her as well. It was as if God was saying, "Your journey together is not yet over." So my mom moved to Kansas City in June, without even having visited and without a job, while I was in South Africa, as it turned out, "visiting" for the summer. We were back to square one, only this time we had a permanent place to live in. Because we never thought that God would end up calling me to go to seminary, my mom and I never thought of saving money for tuition while I was in Boston

God, being the provider that He is, took care of us financially and also took care of my tuition, just like He did in Boston. I followed God's call knowing that my mom was not a "rich" American, and the beauty was that God proved to be all we needed. My mom and I are living this faith journey together as we watch God lead, guide, and provide. The journey is not over yet, and the puzzle is still blurry because we still do not fully understand why God has us on this journey. Sometimes it is hard for us to live miles away from our family, but God reassures us that *Home is wherever He is!* All we need to do is Trust and Obey!

Taking these courageous steps of faith required obedience and dying to self in order to fulfill what God has called us to do. "If any man will come after me, let him deny himself, and take up his cross daily…" (Luke 9:23 KJV). My mom and I come from two different worlds and God brought us together in the most unusual way, the God way! Sometimes what God does makes no sense to us, but that is who He is; He defies logic. I am graduating in May 2021 from seminary and I still do not fully grasp why I had to come to America and study. I might not know what the future holds, but I know Who holds the future. Where He leads, I will follow because *Home is wherever He is!*

. . . .

Courage to Overcome Disobedience

Julie Jenkins

Being a contributing member of a team requires obedience – obedience to follow the vision of a single leader so that the team can work toward the same goal and take steps together toward that goal. In order to be obedient, a team member must have confidence in her coach, a clear objective, and knowledge of what her part is in the process.

As Christians, the Bible is our game book, and the short book of Titus is a pep rally intended to cheer us on.

In his opening Paul reminds us of the Lord's credentials. God is the one who gives the hope of eternal life, who does not lie, who is eternal, and who brought us His Word at the appointed time (Titus 1:1-3). Our God is a flawless leader whom we can respect, love, admire, trust and put our faith in.

The objective of the Christian is stated clearly – that we *encourage others by sound doctrine and refute those who oppose it* (1:9). Sounds simple, doesn't it? As Christians, we don't have to be frustrated trying to understand what we are supposed to do – we only need to, in obedience, follow the vision of our leader who KNOWS what we need to do. *Whoever gives heed to instruction prospers, and blessed is he who trusts the Lord* (Proverbs 16:20 NIV).

Then the game plan is presented – leaders today often call this the "how." Paul tells us in the book of Titus that Christians must stand strong in obedience to the Lord despite what others say (1:10-16); be an example, and therefore a teacher, of faith (2:1-15); and submit to and obey authority and, in humility to all, avoid foolish controversies along the way (3:1-11). I don't know exactly how this speaks to you or where your struggle of obedience is – but what I do know is that when you sit with the Holy Spirit, He will disrupt the peace in your soul in the area in which you are being disobedient.

So here's the thing: God doesn't actually need our obedience to win. He is quite capable of overcoming the battle going on in the world all by Himself. But how gracious He is to allow us to be part of His team! To be part of His assured victory! When we walk obediently in the path that He has called us, we will celebrate the victory from the field, rather than as a spectator on the sidelines. We *can* run our own race, play our own game, call our own shots – but it is only as a contributing and obedient member of God's team that we are able to experience the true thrill of victory.

· ·

Christine Mallek is a wife, mother, grandmother, retired corporate professional, and published author. Her most recent writing is in "Tears to Triumph", an anthology of testimonies intended to bring hope and healing to others. A leader of women's initiative programs throughout her career, Chris also facilitated programs aimed at assisting women to acquire job search skills and led financial workshops for both adults and kids. Chris currently leads the Finance Team of Women World Leaders Inc., a ministry that empowers women to embrace their beautiful purpose God has designed for them.

Chris holds several financial services licenses and is a graduate of Montclair State University with a Bachelor of Arts in Mathematics and Accounting.

Originally from New Jersey, she and her husband of 45 years, Marty, now reside in Hobe Sound, Florida, have two married children, and one grandson. Chris loves all that comes with being a grandmother, and in her spare time enjoys traveling, yoga, keeping fit, deep sea fishing, and the beach.

God's Not Done with Me
Christine Mallek

Some of you reading this may know the beginning of my story from *Tears to Triumph*. When the *Tears to Triumph* book went to print, I had just started treatment for a recurrence of Stage 4 endometrial uterine cancer which had metastasized to my lungs. To briefly summarize and bring us up to date, I was diagnosed with endometrial cancer in 2015. I know this may sound strange, but the silver lining in this is that it brought me so much closer to God and stirred in me a strong desire to really know Him. I grew up Roman Catholic and never spent much time reading the Bible or feeling like I had a relationship with God. For some time, I felt that something was missing in my life. Through this health challenge I was awakened to the healing power of Jesus and so much more. My eyes were opened, and I got a glimpse of the healing power of our Lord. I began praying intensely to Jesus to heal me and trusted that He would. Fighting cancer was a three-pronged approach for me – spiritual, nutritional, and medical. Early in my healing journey, I accepted the Lord as my salvation and have been blessed with nothing short of a miracle. Since my diagnosis, the cancer returned two additional times, Stage 4, and with the Grace of God, I am continuing to defeat it.

Before this recurrence, everything was going well, my tumor markers and scans were consistently good, I was eating well, and I was working with a functional/integrative medicine doctor to help my body be healthy so cancer would never return. My husband Marty and I were caring for our new grandson a couple of days a week and loving it, I was taking group fitness classes to rebuild my strength, and overall, I felt surprisingly good. Life was moving forward, and I thanked God every day for healing me and giving me a second chance at life! I have been so blessed through this entire journey and want to share what has happened since then and how the Lord continues to walk right beside me and bring me through any challenges I face. God is working things out in my life and shaping me to be the person He wants me to be.

> *"I know the Lord is always with me. I will not be shaken, for he is right beside me" (Psalm 16:8 NLT).*

One of the most remarkable experiences we had early in my journey was when the Holy Spirit showed up and spoke to Marty. Three years ago, Marty attended a men's workshop. At the end of the last session, he received the Holy Spirit and was blessed beyond belief. Wow, the Holy Spirit overcame Marty so powerfully that day! He felt an intense rush of heat and the next thing he knew he was speaking in a foreign tongue. Strange words, not English or any language he had ever heard. The words came out as – "In a ma gauche sa tee, a a tee in ma sa." He kept saying these words over and over as others continued to pray with him. At some point, Marty no longer heard anyone, was exhausted, and felt as if his senses had been paused and he was in a zone of peace. Something had happened that he never experienced before. He kept saying to himself, *What did those words mean?* He would soon realize they were powerful words indeed! Marty rarely recalls his dreams, but that night he dreamt he was to take me to the beach on Sunday morning at sunrise. I was to go into the water and when I came out, Marty should rub frankincense oil on my abdomen and repeat the words he was given the prior day. We went to the beach as instructed and did exactly what his dream told us to do. As we performed those steps, the sun came through the clouds and the wind began to blow an amazing formation in the clouds that appeared to us as the face of God. The sun shone through his eyes and mouth as if directly on us. As the sun came up, Marty said to me, "You are in remission – you will be fine." It was a powerful experience and one that changed our lives forever, in a way we will never forget! Without this confirmation, we might have given up and would not have had the courage to keep pushing forward.

Where Am I Now?

I have become a new person since all this began. I have a much closer relationship with the Lord and trust Him with all my heart. I turn to Him for peace, wisdom and comfort and am no longer fearful of test results or what the doctor may tell me. I may still have to walk through this season, but God has healed me!

> *"O Lord my God, I cried out to You for help, and You restored my health" (Psalm 30:2 NLT).*

I completed radiation and chemo treatments over the summer of 2019, and again the Lord carried me through. Both Marty and I received more signs from God that I would be ok, but this was part of my story and I had to keep walking in it. A PET scan in

October showed no live cancer in my body and significant reduction in the size of the nodules in my lungs. Praise the Lord!! The next step in the medical process was to begin an immunotherapy treatment which consisted of a daily pill and IV every three weeks. Immunotherapy is a treatment that uses the body's own immune system to destroy cancerous cells. I knew the side effects from this treatment could be devastating, but I believed I was under God's protective shield. He helped me handle side effects previously and would do so again. I trusted He would protect me and work through my doctors, so I decided this was the right way for me to go. I agreed to begin this treatment.

Starting on the immunotherapy medication was hard and scary! Until we got my dosage right, I experienced some severe mouth and throat sores, intestinal problems ... ugh! All issues I never had prior to this. At one point, it was so bad that Marty thought I was heading toward a stroke. I lost more weight and was really starting to feel down about everything. Sometimes it felt like the bad physical side effects would never go away. I remember sitting in my oncologist's office one day and crying because I felt so defeated. This was so not me! I needed to remember what, or better said Who, had brought me through so far, and continue to have faith that the Lord would not let me fall.

"I can do all things through Christ who strengthens me." *(Philippians 4:13 NKJV).*

A new year begins. Strength is my word for 2020 and I pray to the Lord every day to grant me strength in Him that I know only He can provide. Strength to build my body's own defenses to keep fighting this disease and any side effects, strength to equip and empower me, to take control and fight with Him right by my side, strength of my faith and my spirit, strength to be there for my children and grandson, a renewal of my physical strength and healthy body weight, and strength to make the right (sometimes hard) decisions and move forward in faith.

I learned to lean on God every time I face a difficult situation. For example, having bloodwork done or setting up an IV is really a challenge and always fills me with dread. I know it will take two or three tries, and I always end up with sore and bruised arms that last for weeks. I pray very specifically and right up to the successful start of the procedure – asking the Lord to help me with this. I recall one time the nurse was having a tough time finding my vein and getting the blood to flow. I closed my eyes and earnestly prayed to God right then to help me with this. And He did! A moment later everything was flowing as it should, and all was well. Thank you, Father God!! I told the nurse what brought us success; she looked at me intently, smiled and replied, "Yes, God is good!"

Then the Covid-19 pandemic hit. For the next four or five months, life got even more challenging. My oncologist said my risk level of contracting this coronavirus was 10% higher than a person of my age not facing health challenges. Someone else commented I looked frail. Yikes! Suddenly, I was compared to a declining 75-year-old. That hit me hard and I realized how critical it was to stay healthy, strong, and safe. I did not want to die from the cancer, and certainly not from Covid. But very interestingly, through this time I still have a feeling of peace and a lack of fear. Peace that I am going to be ok, that with the Lord by my side I will not be defeated; and peace that when it is my time to leave this earth, I will see Him face to face, which also leads to excitement for all that awaits me in Heaven for all eternity.

Quarantine and social distancing became a part of life, as did wearing masks and not spending time with or hugging my children or grandson. I know we all experienced these circumstances in different ways. I loved the extra time I now took to be closer to God, to trust and remain focused on Him. I would come outside, sit in a comfortable chair, give thanks that He gave me another beautiful day, and just experience the sights and sounds of His masterpiece all around me. Birds, butterflies, frogs, rain, thunder, clouds, blue sky, trickling water, and walking through my neighborhood which was so quiet except for the sounds of nature. It was all so refreshing and calming. Our God is magnificent!

"You will keep in perfect peace all who trust in you, all whose thoughts are fixed on you" (Isaiah 26:3 NLT)!

A follow-up PET scan in April 2020 was still good – praise God!! Everything was stable and no new cancer cells were detected. I continued for another three months on the immunotherapy treatment. Side effects continued and, in some cases, worsened. I prayed every day for the side effects to completely go away, or at least for me to manage them better. The Lord equipped me with knowledge of what I could do to improve my health and overcome physical issues. I needed to keep following His direction and fighting to do everything I could to keep this cancer at bay.

"I shall not die; but live and declare the works of the Lord"
(Psalm 118:17 KJV).

And while the emotional roller coaster continues, I declare complete healing over my body, in Jesus' name! A follow-up PET scan in July 2020 again showed everything was stable. Not entirely gone, but not worse, and the doctor said, "You're still winning." Marty and I praised the Lord for this outcome and the fact that I was doing good! Then God presented me with a different way of looking at it – *not worse is NOT good enough.*

With the support of my medical team, I am taking a break from the immunotherapy treatment for a few months, but I know that getting rid of remaining cancer cells is critical to my beating this disease. So I will see a radiologist very shortly to determine if advanced, targeted radiology therapy will help me, and I pray for wisdom and discernment to make the right decisions. I know God is leading me along the path He wants me to follow. I trust in Him and believe He has more in store for me here, so I need to keep moving forward, with Jesus right by my side.

I encourage you to listen to your body, this temple God has given each of us. While endometrial cancer affects mainly post-menopausal women, no matter what stage of life you are in … if something does not seem right, see your doctor right away and don't procrastinate like I did. Endometrial cancer is not as well-known or publicized as some other cancers, but it is just as serious, accounting for 6% of all women's cancers. I also learned Stage 4 is not always what it used to be. There are many different treatment options now, and new ones coming all the time, so there is no reason to automatically give up hope. And standing on your faith is key. God is in control!

I am so grateful that God stepped into my life when He did and prevented me from walking straight over the cancer death cliff. He stopped me, got involved and intervened in my life, all because He loves me. I love and thank you, Heavenly Father! Battling cancer and the journey I am on has taught me how to push past the immediate risk of death due to the cancer and move to being spiritually prepared for death when it ultimately comes. And that is all anyone could ever want or hope for. What a gift!

. . . .

Courage to Overcome Defeat

Julie Jenkins

Because of the Lord's great love we are not consumed, for his compassions never fail. They are new every morning; great is your faithfulness. – Lamentations 3:22-23 NIV

When we read these verses written by the prophet Jeremiah, we might be tempted to think that it was easy for him to have a good outlook, because his world was just fine. We may feel, because of the optimism in these words, that he could never understand the trials and the feelings of defeat that you and I face on our worst days: the death of a loved one, the loss of a job, children who turn against us, even a country that seems woefully unstable. How wrong we would be to think that he couldn't understand!

Jeremiah is the author of two books in the Bible: the book of Jeremiah, in which he predicts the destruction of Jerusalem; and this book, Lamentations, where he responds to that destruction of his home. Jeremiah understood the meaning of the word defeat.

I challenge you to read Lamentations – it is a vivid description of heartbreak and mourning. Five chapters of literal crying out to God for mercy:

...All her friends have betrayed her... (1:2)
...All who honored her despise her... (1:8)

...Her fall was astounding; there was none to comfort her... (1:9)
...My eyes fail from weeping, I am in torment within... (2:11)
...He has weighed me down with chains... (3:7)
...I have been deprived of peace... (3:17)

That is what defeat feels like, isn't it? Jeremiah knew. God knows.

But defeat is final. It signifies that something is done – finished. And what the prophet Jeremiah knew even in his misery and despair was that, no matter how bleak the outlook is, we, God's children, are never defeated. In the middle of those five chapters of outpoured anguish, we see hope. Hope that all is not lost.

I say to myself, 'The Lord is my portion; therefore I will wait for him.'
The Lord is good to those whose hope is in him, to the one who seeks him;
it is good to wait quietly for the salvation of the Lord. – (3:24-26)

If you have given your life to Christ, if you have invited Him into your heart as your Lord and Savior, if you willingly submit to Him, you will never be touched by defeat. If you are in need God's presence in your life, will you turn to Him now? Pray with me!

Dear Heavenly Father, I confess that I am a sinner and that you hold the key to my forgiveness. Jesus, I ask you to come into my life as my Savior – the one who will never be defeated! I give you all praise and honor as I walk with you! Guide me and lead me into your righteousness. Father, I surrender all – and it is in surrendering that I know I will never be defeated. Amen!

· ·

Natalie Mellusi is a daughter of the Most High King! She loves serving in her church and community. She has a degree in Child Development and worked as a preschool teacher in her earlier years. Natalie has volunteered and worked at Hannah's Home of South Florida, a non-profit home for pregnant women. Natalie has served with Nick Vujicic from Life Without Limbs over the past five years. She currently is a publicist and national event coordinator for the founder and keynote speaker of Your Life Speaks, Nathan Harmon. Her passion is for youth and she is dedicated to their social, emotional, and behavioral learning through her resources, research, and work.

Natalie resides in South Florida with her husband and is a mother to three boys. Her oldest son recently married and now she has a beautiful daughter-in-law. She enjoys reading devotions, exercising, walking her dog Bandit, and watching sunsets.

~ For nothing will be impossible with God ~
Luke 1:37

Believe

♡ Natalie Mellusi

His Will, His Way, My Faith
Natalie Mellusi

October 5, 2008 is a date that I will never forget. My boys were
11, 7 and 5 years old at the time. A few days before October 5th, I
called our precious babysitter, Savannah, a teenager in our church's
youth group, to see if she could watch the boys for a few hours so
my husband and I could go to see the movie *Fireproof* with several
other couples from church. Savannah excitedly agreed to watch
the boys. Thursday evening, Savannah came over – the boys were
so thrilled to see her. They were jumping up and down and asking what candies she had in her purse for them. She dug through
her purse and held up a bag of M&M's. Although she was very
playful, she did not seem quite herself. I asked her if she was all
right. She told me she was fine, just a little tired. We said goodbye
to the boys and Savannah and headed to the movie, not having
any idea what would happen in just a few days. Sunday evening,
I received a phone call from a church friend who was in sheer
disbelief. She just blurted out, "Savannah died; she took her life!"
I did not believe I had heard her correctly. This could not be true.
She was just in my home a few nights ago, standing in my kitchen
digging through her purse, giving my children M&M's. My mind
was racing. All I could think was, *Lord, this is not true, this cannot be
true! She loves you with all her heart, she serves you, she is an obedient
daughter who has the Holy Spirit dwelling within her!* As my friend

repeated those chilling words, I dropped the phone, screamed, fell to my knees, and sobbed. My husband ran in asking what had happened. I could not catch my breath or even utter those words to him. I was finally able to get the words out. He dropped to his knees, wrapped me in his arms, and we sobbed together, not knowing how to make sense of what just happened. Savannah's death broke the hearts of our church family and all who knew her. Our community experienced grief like no other. **Psalm 34:18 MSG –** *If your heart is broken, you'll find God right there; if you're kicked in the gut, he'll help you catch your breath.*

My church lost this beautiful 17-year-old young woman to suicide in 2008. Unbelievably, in 2016, a close neighbor and friend of more than ten years also committed suicide. She left behind two children, 12 and 14 years old, who were good friends of my own boys, once again intimately rocking our family. This shook our community to the core, and we were left with so many questions that would never have answers. Our town lost several more teenagers between 2015 and 2018 in a string of suicides. It was as if a contagious disease had spread throughout our area. I knew something needed to be done, but I was hesitant to believe I could make a difference or even know where to start. I felt a deep desire to help our broken community through a time of great pain, grief, and hopelessness. A few weeks after my friend's death I was in the shower crying uncontrollably, hitting the shower walls, falling to my knees sobbing. I cried out to God that I didn't have much to offer. I am not a mental health specialist. I am not capable. I do not have the credentials to talk to our community about suicide and all the brain psychology that professionals have. As I laid all this at His feet, I realized I had a great desire to serve Him in a way I had never served before. I told God that my heart and life belonged to Him, and to please use me in any way that He saw fit, and I would obey. Although I surrendered, I did not hear Him answer my pleas. As the weeks went on, the Holy Spirit was preparing my steps, which I was unaware of. I began to feel a strong urge to move forward and step out in faith. **Psalm 61:2 ESV** -*From the end of the earth I call to You when my heart is faint; Lead me to the rock that is higher than I.*

Proverbs 16:9 NIV – In their hearts humans plan their course, but the Lord establishes their steps.

Later that week I received a phone call from a friend asking me if I had heard of an international evangelist and motivational speaker named **Nick Vujicic,** founder of *Life Without Limbs*. I told her that I recalled watching him on YouTube once. "He is the man without arms and legs, right?" "Yes," she said. "He will be speaking at Christ Fellowship this Sunday. You should bring your family to hear him speak." So we went, and I was in awe of this man's courage, confidence, and sense of humor. Also mind-blowing was Nick's holy and humble dependence on the Lord. He was not superficial; he exuded the love of his KING, Jesus Christ! I had never listened to or watched someone praise God for his disabilities and have such peace in his life despite those disabilities. One of Nick's extraordinary quotes is *If you can't get a miracle, become a miracle.* I said to myself, *He is one of Jesus' apostles!* God was the author of Nick's story and I soon came to believe that He is the author of my story. After the service was over, my family and I discussed how Nick used and embraced his disabilities to encourage others, and that through God all things are possible, even when you are faced with life-challenging struggles. Nick is a role model for the hopeless and he lives his life to glorify God.

The following week I received a phone call from the same friend who invited my family to hear Nick speak. She shared with me that some of Nick's team members were looking for an opportunity for Nick to speak in a Palm Beach County high school to address bullying and suicide. She told them she knew of a person who might be interested in helping them. The next words out of her mouth were, "Would you like to get involved?" I was thrown off guard, I hesitated, I was fearful and stumbled on my words. Then I heard a voice within say to me, "I am answering your cry." The next word out of my mouth was YES! **Isaiah 30:21 NIV –** *Whether you turn to the right or to the left, your ears will hear a voice behind you saying, "This the way; walk in it."*

The following week I was meeting with the ministry director of *Life Without Limbs* in my friend's living room. He shared with us that Nick had just finished writing a book called *Stand Strong*. The book was written to help middle and high school students overcome bullying and to never give up (suicide). Nick wanted to start his tour in Florida in my county. LWL team members asked if I would put a few feelers out in the school system. My ears could not believe what I was hearing, but I knew that God was orchestrating this meeting. Again, I said "YES!" I had no clue what I was doing, but I knew that God would lead the way. Look what He had done already.

I was not given much instruction on how, what or who to contact to start the process. The LWL team totally left it up to me. As I reflect now, without a doubt they put their trust in God, and He appointed the person who had cried out in the shower a few years earlier.

I found a school for Nick to speak in – it was the school that both Savannah and the children of my late friend had attended. Again,

God prepared and guided my steps all the way. I attended local support groups for families who had lost a loved one to suicide. As I listened to their agonizing, heart-wrenching stories, I wept with them like Jesus weeps with them, and I embraced them, wanting to offer some sort of hope. I invited them to come hear Nick speak at the high school and set up a green room where Nick would address the family members privately. As a community, we need to support and grieve together. *People don't really care about how much we know, until they know about how much we care!* As I worked diligently to prepare for the school event and fundraiser, I could feel God in front of me, behind me and beside me. Faith involves a choice. You will either choose to go God's way or not, and the choice to go His way requires your willingness to be courageous and afraid at the same time. *Deuteronomy 31:6 – Be strong and courageous. Do not be afraid, for the Lord your God goes with you.*

The big day arrived, January 23, 2016. My stomach was in knots. It was here! I was eager to meet Nick and to watch God work through him, bringing some healing to the hurt and speaking boldly on bullying and never giving up. His car pulled in. Every move seemed like it was in slow motion, as if I were watching one of his YouTube videos. As I was waiting for him to exit the SUV, he jumped in his chair, rolled over to me with a big smile on his face and said, "Natalie, thank you from the bottom of my heart and give me a hug." I hugged this limbless man and knew my life would never be the same. We proceeded into the school and entered the green room, where around 30 people were waiting to meet Nick and hear some words of comfort and hope. Nick hugged every person in the room and expressed that though "I may not know your pain of losing a loved one to suicide, pain is pain, grief is grief. I weep with you and you are not alone." God worked through Nick in that room that day and brought comfort to the mourning. My late friend's children and ex-husband were present, along with the families from the suicide support group I had attended, as well as a few pastors from our area who came to pray with the families. Nick then proceeded to talk to 1,000 students in the auditorium, and the assembly was streamed on the county's education network so other schools could join in. Indeed, lives were touched that day! We prayed lives would be saved here on earth and eternally. **Matthew 5:4 NIV** – *Blessed are those who mourn, for they will be comforted.*

That evening we attended the fundraiser I had organized with my friend. Nick was the guest of honor and keynote speaker. I will never forget how God spoke to me that evening with pure, undeniable love through Nick's words. After he spoke, Nick came over to me, smiling from ear to ear, with the bluest glistening eyes I have ever seen. His eye color was different shades of the sea with shimmering light exuding from within. He got close to my face and said, "I feel like I have known you my entire life. I love you! Do not be afraid! What took place today in the schools and tonight was amazing! God has a calling and a purpose in your life, and you must be obedient. Say yes and move when you hear His voice. I have a feeling you will be used as a vessel with teenagers and LWL ministries will be in your future." My eyes welled with pools of tears, my head nodding yes! In that moment I physically, emotionally, spiritually, and tangibly felt the presence of God. The Father does not share secrets with just anybody. The Father shares hidden things in His heart with His sons and daughters. Draw near to the Father, receive His heart, and then step out in faith. It really was a test as I look back; God saying, "Do you trust me?" **Jeremiah 33:3 NIV** – *Call to me and I will answer you and tell you great and unsearchable things you do not know.*

That evening when I came home, I was so overwhelmed with gratitude and wept over the events, conversations and healing that took place that day. I once read that the opposite of faith is doubt. Faith is believing in what you cannot see. Faith is measured by your feet, not by your feelings. When you move in step with a big God, you really are exercising big faith. If you keep God small, then you are going to take many steps, but you will not be exercising much faith. The multiple steps of faith I took included believing God for who He says He is, moving forward in faith even when I was afraid, having a willing heart, being aware of the calling, and being obedient. There was fear, but perfect love casts out fear (1 John 4:18). Nick uses an acronym for **FEAR – False Evidence Appearing Real,** and for **FAITH – Full Assurance In The Heart.**

I would have never imagined that God would answer my cries in the manner that He did—that He would lead me into ministry work with the world-famous limbless evangelist *Nick Vujicic* from *Life Without Limbs.* God ordained the weeks and years to come in my ministry work for sharing the gospel message, lifting the stigma on suicide and bullying in schools. My "yes" became the beginning of working with Nick and an extraordinary team of people. I was part of launching Nick's anti-bullying and suicide tour in schools on the east coast of Florida. We reached over two million students, opening the door to preach the gospel message of Jesus Christ to millions of students and adults. Savannah's mom was able to have some one-on-one time with Nick and to share her daughter with him. Nick became a dear friend and brother in Christ. He became a mentor, sharing the Word of God with me. When visiting my area, he would have dinner with me and my family. God is so amazing! He was preparing me from the beginning to be in the current role I am in now. I have been working with another motivational speaker, **Nathan Harmon** from *Your*

Life Speaks, since 2018 as his national school event coordinator. I speak to principals, guidance counselors, teachers, students, and parents on the topics of mental health.

As we know, life brings trials and sufferings. Kingdom work brings persecution. When you are answering God's call, be on guard. The enemy does not like kingdom work. The devil will try to use any person, obstacle, lie or circumstance to instill doubt and fear, and to cause discord and division. At times, the enemy used my own family to persecute me. I was gossiped about among friends. My brother disowned me because of my faith. I had many other struggles along the way. I suffered in silence some of the time; however, I communicated my struggles and fears to trusted people to help see me through. The power of prayer, keeping my eyes on Jesus and knowing God is faithful and good saw me through. He kept me strong within his might and power. He sustained me and his grace was always sufficient. **James 1:2-3 NIV** – *Consider it pure joy, my brothers, and sisters, whenever you face trials of many kinds, because you know that the testing of your faith produces perseverance.*

Ladies, choose to live loved wherever you are in your journey and know that what God has in mind for you is so much more than you can ever imagine! I read this quote recently from Christian author Lysa TerKeurst: **There is an abundant need in this world for your exact brand of beautiful!** Your life is the greatest platform you will ever stand on. Be the person God created you to be. Believe it, pray about it, seek God›s will through it, and answer your calling. Step out in faith, be courageous and do not hesitate when the Lord calls you. When the Holy Spirit lays something in your heart, move without hesitation. You have no idea who may be depending on your immediate obedience. Your story is someone else's story. Your story, both what is happening now and what has yet to happen, is meant to be shared. God calls the unqualified. All He wants is our faith in Him, our heart, and our obedience – whether you are in mourning or in a season of pure joy. Go to the extreme; ask Him to reveal Himself to you like you have never seen before. Wait and watch to see how He will choose you for this moment to be a light and vessel. Whether it is for one person or for a million people, the angels in heaven rejoice the same. God is the author of all our stories! I hope my story ignites a flame in you, to bring you hope, a new level of faith, courage and a testimony that God will use you through *HIS WILL, HIS WAY and YOUR FAITH.* **Ephesians 3:20 NIV** – *Now to him who is able to do immeasurably more than all we ask or imagine, according to his power that is at work within us.*

This chapter is dedicated in loving memory of Savannah and Tonya: and to their families and to all the people who have suffered the loss of their loved ones to suicide. May God give you daily strength and carry you when you are weak. May He heal and mend your broken heart. You are missed daily, and your story will not be forgotten!

If you are struggling with any aspect of life, please reach out to someone and share your struggles. Talking about your struggles to someone gives you freedom and can start you on the road of recovery. If you are depressed and have suicidal thoughts, please call The National Suicide Prevention Lifeline at 1-800-273-8255.

. . . .

Courage to Overcome Hesitation

Julie Jenkins

Have you ever gone tubing in the mountains? A mountain stream does not rush consistently for miles but has areas of calm and peace allowing you to, at times, float and enjoy the wonder of God's creation. But before long, your tube begins to pick up speed as the water begins to move toward the quickening rapids, and you have a choice to make. Do you want get out of the water and retreat to the safety of the dry land or do you want to allow the current to take you as you brace for the upcoming rush and prepare to put a foot out to push off a rock or to position your body to plunge through a rapid without falling off the tube? This adventure is not for the faint of heart – and the choice to hesitate or to attack the situation with zeal is serious.

Life is sometimes like a mountain stream. We can be floating along enjoying the presence of God, when suddenly, we are pushed into an adventure or a trial, and we must respond to the circumstances we are plunged into. How we react, with hesitation or with zeal, will determine our course.

Mary was a young woman who was flush with joy for her upcoming marriage when an angel of the Lord appeared to her as the water suddenly rushed around her. She chose to react with zeal: *I am the Lord's servant...May it be to me as you have said* (Luke 1:38). Imagine what a blessing Mary would have missed if she had hesitated!

Lot and his family were thrown into the rushing water when the Lord warned them to flee Sodom and Gomorrah before its destruction. Lot's wife hesitated as she looked back, and she was turned into a pillar of salt. As she watched her home being destroyed, she was also destroyed (Genesis 19). What a story she would have had to tell if she had not hesitated!

The disciples had just gotten used to hanging out with the risen Jesus when they heard the rushing water ahead. Jesus told them it was time for Him to go, but that they should wait in Jerusalem for the gift of the Holy Spirit. They could have hesitated and walked away, but they responded in zeal, bracing themselves for the coming rapids (Acts 1-2). What an adventure they would have missed out on if they had hesitated in their response!

What about you? When the water begins to pick up speed, will you hesitate, or will you zealously follow His call for you? God's voice is perfect – His words of warning and His words of instruction are sure. We may not understand what He is up to as the water starts swirling ahead of us, but trust me, you don't want to miss it!

When you hear His voice, will you hesitate, or will you respond with zeal?

* *

Carrie Denton is a wife, mother of three, and a Gigi of four. She is currently a proud baseball mom, a full-time sales coordinator, with a passion for public speaking and event planning. She in the process of writing her first full book titled, *GOD IS BIGGER THAN CANCER; A story of surrendering to walking in faith through the fear*, the full story of her husband and her families battle through stage 4 colorectal cancer.

She is determined to share her testimony as much as she can through Podcasts, Retreats and social media as well as her book.

Faith + Surrender = Courage

Carrie Denton

On Wednesday, January 20, 2016, four days before my husband David's 35th birthday, he went for a colonoscopy because of issues he was having going to the bathroom. Shortly after the procedure was complete, I joined him in the exam room waiting for the doctor. The doctor came into the room very different than the upbeat doctor we had met before. He was no longer smiling and had become solemn. He put his hand on David's leg and said to us, "I'm very sorry to tell you, but I found a mass. I've taken several biopsies of it and sent them off to the lab. Even without lab results, I feel comfortable telling you it definitely looks like cancer, and it looks like it has been there for a while."

I can't explain the way this kicks the air out of you. Immediately I looked at my husband as tears came down his face. I couldn't breathe, much less cry. I tried to console him and encourage him that we would beat this, but my heart was about to beat out of my chest.

My brain was running a thousand thoughts a second. *Oh my God, he is going to die? Our kids! Our baby is only four years old! Carter needs a dad! I need him! I cannot do this life without him! How do I comfort him, when I feel like I am about to fall apart myself?*

It was literally more than I could process. This was the first time God intervened. A nurse walked in and sweetly said, "Mrs. Denton, can we borrow you for a moment?" As I walked into the hallway, she guided me into an empty exam room. I was about to hyperventilate. She hugged me and said, "It's going to be okay. You need to breathe." Once I was calmer, she held both my hands and looked me directly in the eyes and said, "Do you believe in God?" I replied, "Yes." She continued, "Then let your faith guide you. David needs you to be strong right now. He needs to be the one who gets to be scared today. God is bigger than cancer." I couldn't even reply with words, I just nodded okay and went back to his room. They scheduled him for a full body scan for Friday.

We left there and barely spoke a word all the way home. Over the next two days we agreed we wouldn't tell anyone. We decided we would get through his birthday weekend and wait until Monday for the scan results. However, we talked about cancer all day, every day.

A few days later, out of the blue, he looked at me and said, "Just as long as it isn't Stage 4, you know?" I replied, "Why do you say that?" He answered, "Because there is no Stage 5. It will mean I have no chance to survive."

We knew so little about cancer and stages of cancer or what any of that meant. We just knew that Stage 4 was the end.

I began to Google everything I could find about colorectal cancer. I quickly found out Stage 4 meant that the cancer has traveled to another organ, making it a metastasis cancer. I didn't share anything I was learning with him. The more I was learning, the more scared I was becoming. The frightened little boy inside my brave husband had no desire to Google anything. I believe he was far too scared to learn more and wanted to only think positively.

As we were sitting on the sofa that Sunday afternoon, the day of his 35th birthday, the doctor called to speak with him personally. I could only hear David's responses. "Yes sir. Yes, I understand. Yes, Wednesday at 10am."

I knew that getting a call from the doctor on a Sunday couldn't be positive, but I was still praying for good news. When he hung up he said, "I now have an oncologist. We meet her Wednesday at 10am." Again, I felt my stomach turning and a giant lump in my throat. He continued, "The scans are not good. It is also in my liver." We cried and held one another. He again repeated his hopes. "I just hope it's not Stage 4."

Later that evening I sat him down and said, "Baby, on Wednesday the doctor is going to tell you it's Stage 4." He was angry and hurt by what I had just said. He replied aggressively, "Why would you even say that?" Carefully I explained everything I had learned about cancer stages. He didn't say a word. With his tears beginning to fall, he just stared off into space. I too began to cry as I assured him we wouldn't give up and that we'd fight this to the end. I repeated what that nurse had told me in the exam room. "Our God is way bigger than this cancer." However, if I am being honest, our fear was growing out of control. I realized at this point, we needed to begin to take courageous steps of faith to make it through this journey. *Matthew 7:7 KJV – Ask and it will be done; seek, and you will find; knock, and it will be opened to you.*

That night I couldn't sleep. I was up all night crying and praying, then praying some more. The next day before work, we sat on the end of our bed. I was scared for him and I could see the fear in his eyes. I said to him, "We cannot fix this. There is literally nothing we can do to make this go away. We need to completely surrender our life to God and walk in faith. I mean absolute blind faith, trusting God every step of the way. That means us never losing our faith, no matter what." He wiped the tears from his eyes, nodded okay, kissed me goodbye and left for work. I collapsed on the floor the minute I heard his truck drive away. Who was I fooling with this strong act? I was literally falling apart inside. Although somehow I knew I felt God telling me to trust Him no matter what was going to happen.

The morning we were scheduled to meet his oncologist, I was sitting on the side of the bathtub drawing a bath when David came into our bathroom. He looked different to me as he said, "I am going to do what you said." He stood there looking so strong, with his shoulders pushed back and his head held high, as he said, "I'm going to surrender it all to God. I'm going to walk in faith. I'm going to fight this to the very end, no matter what the outcome is. If I end up losing this battle, I will go home grateful for this life he gave me with you and our kids." Hearing him speak so strongly and courageously not only made me incredibly proud of him, but also devastated me inside. Hearing his fearless words made me realize that trusting God's plan also meant trusting the possibility that God's plan wasn't at all what I was so passionately praying for. That maybe we bury him too early and I become a widow with a four-year-old. That maybe God's plan wasn't MY plan at all. However, David was making it clear that he still wanted me to trust God.

My ever-faithful husband put out his hand for me to hold and said, "I need you to promise me that you'll never stop trusting God's plan. Promise me that no matter what happens, you'll never blame God. Promise you'll always know the plan had the perfect ending, no matter how this ends." I nodded yes even though I felt broken inside. That moment turned out to be one of the most powerful moments in our marriage. My husband, the leader of our family, was asking me to be stronger than I think he even thought I was capable of. I will never forget it.

Psalm 62:8 KJV – Trust in him at all times; Pour out your heart before him; God is a refuge for us.

At David's first oncology appointment, his oncologist seemed way too young to be the person I was trusting to save my husband's life. She was lovely and extremely kind, but also very direct. She confirmed what we already knew; he was in Stage 4 colorectal cancer with metastasized cancer to his liver. The liver lesions were so plentiful they were actually stacked on top of each other, making it hard to determine exactly how many we were dealing with. With that kind of disease in his liver and the large mass in his colon, he was not a candidate for surgery. Instead, they started chemotherapy and radiation to begin the battle.

David's first round of chemo began the first week of February, accompanied by a liver biopsy. His parents came to town to be with us. Before his first chemotherapy treatment started, his oncologist sat with David and me. She bluntly asked, "Do you want a prognosis?" I held my breath waiting for him to say yes, yet scared to death to hear what she would tell him if he did. He looked at me, waiting for me to reply, but I just smiled and nodded as to say, "It's whatever you want."

He strongly and very matter-of-factly said, "No, I don't." So she didn't give us one and that was that.

Often people would ask him throughout his battle, "What's your prognosis?" and he'd say, "I'm kicking cancer's ass." And for some reason people just accepted that as a logical answer. However, his parents weren't as easy to please with no prognosis. They were scared for their son and needed more answers. At one point, David's very worried father and I cornered the doctor and Dad said, "Give it to me straight, Doc. I know he doesn't want to know, but I need to know. His mother and I BOTH need to know his prognosis."

With great hesitation she said, "I will respect his wishes and not give him a prognosis. However, I'll tell you that people in his condition, as sick as he is, usually last between 12-18 months." His dad hung his head and walked back into the room, heartbroken yet somewhat satisfied that he at least had something factual to hang on to. I just stood there, speechless and scared. The doctor very tenderly put her hands on my shoulders and said, "Carrie, please put Carter into counseling as soon as possible. He will need to learn how to say goodbye to him." And with every piece of breath I could muster I said, "I'm sorry. I just don't accept that. Our God is bigger than this cancer." She smiled and said, "Oh Carrie, I do believe in miracles, but I cannot promise you one this time." I smiled back and said, "That's okay, you aren't who I'm asking for my miracle from."

James 4:8 NKJV – Draw near to God and he will draw near to you.

The following weeks got rougher as my tenacious husband made his way through session after session of the strongest cocktails of chemo they could cook up for him. He was becoming weak. He couldn't touch or drink anything cold, couldn't keep food down, and began to lose feeling in his extremities, all as side effects of the chemo. But he never gave up and always told people, "God is working a miracle in me. I can feel it."

Twelve weeks into treatment we were ready to scan, to see how his body was responding to treatment. As we sat in that cold waiting room, we tried laughing and making small talk, but it was only to cover up the fact that the waiting was horrible. The doctor came into the room and got to the point. I'm sure she knew we were waiting to exhale. Then she said it: "The chemo is working. Things are starting to shrink." We were completely overjoyed! We knew we still had a long, tough road ahead, but that was the first small piece of positive news we both needed to hear to keep going.

About a month later, because of the miraculous shrinking of David's tumors he was now a candidate for surgery. We were sent to Indiana University Hospital to meet with the team of surgeons that would discuss taking the tumors out of both his liver and colon.

Finally, we were on the books for surgery for July 5, 2016, to remove the tumors. David's liver was down to only four remaining lesions. It was remarkable to think how far he had already come! As they prepped him for surgery, we told his surgeons that the bowel prep hadn't seemed successful, that very little stool was released. We assured the surgeon that he had followed the instructions closely. We knew the tumor was large and blocking his colon, but if the surgeons didn't seem concerned, then neither were we.

The liver resection portion of the surgery was first and went off without a hitch. Once the colon portion of the surgery began, to the doctor's surprise upon cutting into his colon, loads of backed-up stool began to flood his abdomen. The surgeon began flushing and irrigating his abdomen while his partner removed the last tumor. Hours of irrigating went on until they decided they needed to close him up and sent him to recovery with several drainage tubes draining out loads of brown stinky fluids. By hour 12 post surgery, David's fever was rising and the medical team was scheduling him to be opened back up for a more intensive irrigation. The doctors sat me down and explained, "Despite our best efforts to clean him out, we are sorry but your husband has become septic and is very ill."

Scared and helpless, I waited by his bedside as I watched his temperature rise to 106.1 and noticed his blood pressure was continuing to drop. I recall a sweet young nurse hurrying in and out of our ICU room. She gave a comforting smile while bringing David yet another bag of adrenalin. Eventually, after several blood transfusions and multiple bags of adrenalin, I heard her outside of David's room on the phone with the surgeon in a calm but shaking voice. "I have given Mr. Denton the blood transfusions and the bags of adrenalin you ordered, but his blood pressure is still dropping. What would you like me to do next?"

For the first time I realized that this was really bad. I got on my knees and began praying. I could not even string together a full sentence. My fear and my emotions were at the level of a full-blown panic attack. All I could get out was "Help him, Jesus-help him, Jesus" over and over. I prayed that simple prayer for hours.

They put David into a medically induced coma to help him heal while on the ventilator. As the days went on, we had two failed extubation attempts, but he was still too weak to breathe on his own. While the days turned into weeks in that ICU room, they eventually put in a tracheotomy.

I watched my 6'3" strong 240-pound husband wither away to 174 pounds. Each morning I would wake up on the small couch tucked in the corner of the room. No matter how many mornings I continued to open my eyes in that ICU room, it never stopped feeling like I was living out the worst nightmare of my life. The first thing I noticed each morning was the small red numbers on the side of his bed—digital numbers showing David's weight as it was dropping little by little each day. However, God had a plan, and I mean a BIG plan.

Day 25 in the ICU rolled around, and my fighting husband was still alive! Not only was he alive but he was healing. He was beating sepsis. They began to wake him up from his coma but his body mass had wilted and muscle atrophy had set in. He was too weak to sit up in a chair. He could not walk. He could not hold a pen or a ball. He was literally a shell of the man that walked into that hospital 25 days before.

On Day 29 of being in the hospital, he was progressing and healing. They moved us to a progressive care unit. I say "us" because I had not left the hospital since Day One. Our poor son was being juggled and moved around from family members to friends until Mommy and Daddy BOTH were ready to come home.

We worked on David's physical therapy all day, every day. Every minute he had the energy, we got him up and worked. He learned to sit up, he learned to walk, he learned to write and throw a ball. We did whatever we could do to help him regain his strength. He never gave up. We knew God was right there with us. We could feel God in that room with us and I believe the staff could feel it too.

God pulled David and me through that time. Today David is a healthy almost 40-year-old man who coaches our son in baseball and football. He has had two full years of clear scans, which blows our team of doctors away.

Although that stretch of time seems like a living nightmare, through it we learned to trust God more fully. The courageous steps of faith that we both had to take through this entire journey taught us firsthand that with God all things are possible. I've learned that even when I don't understand God's plan, I can trust it. Faith + Surrender = Courage.

Proverbs 3:5 NKJV – Trust in the Lord with all your heart, and lean not on your own understanding.

. . . .

Courage to Overcome Loneliness

Julie Jenkins

Although we often see the word "isolation" as part of the definition of loneliness, loneliness has less to do with *being* alone than it does with *feeling* alone.

In Psalm 25, David is calling out to God – lifting himself up, begging for God's guidance and forgiveness, and proclaiming his reliance on the Lord. And then he gets to verse 16, where we truly see the heart of David's anguish mount:

Turn to me and be gracious to me, for I am lonely and afflicted. The troubles of my heart have multiplied; free me from my anguish. Look upon my affliction and my distress and take away all my sins. See how my enemies have increased and how fiercely they hate me! Guard my life and rescue me; let me not be put to shame, for I take refuge in you. May integrity and uprightness protect me, because my hope is in you. – Psalm 25:16-21 (NIV)

David begins by putting words to his distress – he is lonely and afflicted. He expands on these descriptions by saying that his troubles have multiplied, and then he begs God to free him, to take away his affliction, his sin, the hate of his enemies. David trusts that God can rescue him from this loneliness and affliction, and he vows to take refuge in God, in whom he puts his trust.

What we see is that David's loneliness was caused by his isolation from God, which came about as he focused on his troubles, afflictions, distress, sin and enemies. The cure came when he looked to God, took refuge in Him in obedience, and allowed his hope to grow.

There is no worse feeling of loneliness than turning away from the love of God. On the other hand, when we practice the presence of God – crying out to Him in joy, despair, gratefulness, or repentance – loneliness and affliction fade as hope and love are ushered in.

If you are feeling lonely, will you reach out to God? We all go through peaks and valleys in our lives, stages of community and isolation. Perhaps God draws us into times of seclusion in order to draw us closer to Him. Did you ever think that maybe God is lonely for you? That He is yearning for your presence? I've heard it said that if there are 1000 steps between you and God, God will take 999 – but you have to take one to close the gap. You are never alone, friend. And with God by your side, you need never be lonely again.

• •

Michele Hughes is a Christ follower, devoted wife to husband Mark since 1997, retired teacher, and co-owner of Go Life Savers, LLC.

Michele enjoys traveling and was blessed to visit the Holy Lands, March 2020, right before everything shut down due to the pandemic.

She grew up in church and accepted Jesus as her personal Lord and Savior in 1983 and followed up with baptism and again with her husband in the Jordan River in 2020. Growing up in church instilled a love for music and is part of her soul.

She prays to be a light in the darkness, loves her family, has a passion for children, and enjoys all things water.

Her prayer is to encourage others to follow Christ and stay in His will.

He called you to this through our gospel that you might share in the glory of your Lord Jesus Christ. 2 Thessalonians 2:14 (NIV)

Never Say Never
Michele Lynn Hughes

> *Joshua 1:9 NIV – Have I not commanded you? Be strong and courageous. Do not be afraid; do not be discouraged, for the Lord your God will be with you wherever you go.*

The plane was taking off and I was ready for a fun, new weekend adventure with my husband. I have an adventurous spirit as long as I know I have a safe and secure place in which to return. Like most people, I've always liked being in control of my situations. I like to think of it as being a planner, and I had my life all planned out…I'd live near my family forever, I'd be a teacher and retire in my hometown, I was **NEVER** getting married, and I was **NEVER** moving away.

> *Proverbs 16:9 NIV – In his heart a man plans his course, but the Lord determines his steps.*

As a child, I grew up in a loving, Christian family of six in a small town in northeastern Ohio. We were a very close family. My parents and I were best friends. I have one older brother and two younger brothers. We attended First Christian Church with pastor Jay Cooper. Peeper, his wife, was the choir director and biggest influence of music in my life. The songs of scripture I learned have settled in my soul and have spoken to me throughout my life's journey.

Psalm 95:1 NIV – Come, let us sing for joy to the Lord; let us shout aloud to the Rock of our salvation.

My mom is an exceptional role model and lover of Jesus. I thank God that he chose her to raise me. We spent many hours in the kitchen around the meat block cooking together. We enjoyed playing cards and board games. We had routine shopping trips in Canton, Ohio and ate lunch together at TGI Friday's. She patiently sat through many hours of various dance, band, and majorette classes and recitals. She helped me navigate through the awkward childhood school years and boy/girl drama. As a professional young adult, my mom was a vital volunteer and support in my teaching career. And best of all were the life talks...we were best friends.

When I went to college three hours from home, I stayed on campus with Gina, my best friend from high school, and started working toward my Elementary Education degree. I also earned another degree in Special Education and later added a degree in Early Childhood. Throughout all of this, my parents visited frequently and we enjoyed the Bob Evans Farm Festival in Rio Grande, Ohio.

During my freshman year, I met a particular fellow who caught my interest. However, I drove home almost every weekend because, I was **NEVER** getting married.

Isaiah 55:8 NIV – "For my thoughts are not your thoughts, neither are your ways my ways," declares the Lord.

Our friendship grew as he frequently asked me to cut his hair and help him with his homework. During those years, I invited his family to a picnic pool party at my house so our families could meet, which worked out great as we were all from Ohio. His mom brought the best potato salad that included a lot of farm fresh eggs.

Eight years later, I got a call from the "fellow" from college. Our friendship picked up where it left off and he told me he knew I was the one he wanted to marry. I knew I was **NEVER** leaving Ohio so I told him if he ever wanted to move, I wasn't the girl for him. As I thought about getting married, I asked my mom how she and I could remain best friends if my husband was supposed to be my best friend. She said she wanted him to be my best friend and she would be my best girlfriend. She always has the right words. That worked for me and I continued on in peace.

Mark proposed at Marblehead Lighthouse in Ohio. I soon married my one-and-only love and became Mrs. Hughes. Since my husband always wanted land, we bought 62 acres and built a ranch home – it's good to have one-level if you're **NEVER** going to move. My husband was working at a YMCA and I was an educator in the local public-school system. My dad helped us plant fruit trees and a walnut tree farm that would provide potential income in retirement. We had a coonhound, raised chickens and guineas, and did a lot of mowing. Our weekends were spent caring for the property and visiting family.

My husband always wanted to live in Florida. He had been submitting resumes and out of nowhere, he received a call from Mississippi. They said his resume came across their desk and they wanted to schedule an interview with him. When I found out, I calmly said, "Oh, that sounds like a great experience. Check it out." After all, I knew we were **NEVER** moving so why show resistance, right?

Mark traveled to Mississippi for the interview and the company was so interested in him that they wanted to fly us both back so they could meet me. Again, I calmly said, "Great. Whenever it works for you, but it has to be on a weekend." I was a classroom teacher at the time.

When we both arrived back in Mississippi the following weekend, we attended church with the man conducting the interview. During the service, they played the Indiana Jones movie clip where he gets to the edge of a cliff and they say, "It's a leap of faith." It would definitely take courageous steps of faith to step out into the unknown. During the dinner social, he introduced us to people who told me I could easily get a teaching job there. Everyone was painting a rosy picture to make the move. I was definitely feeling the "Southern hospitality."

After a great evening, we were taken to the airport. When we were dropped off, they offered "us" the job and wanted an answer within a few days. I knew we wouldn't be able to accept the offer. After all, I was **NEVER** moving. I would have to know I had a teaching job lined up, where we would live, how we could sell our house and land...

Meanwhile God had it all worked out but I didn't know it.

Later we were sitting in the airport to head back to Ohio and I started sobbing. I knew God was telling me to GO. I knew He was letting me know I could take a leap of faith and He would be with me. I told my husband and he said he felt the same way. We both cried and prayed right there in the airport. (*Take it to the Lord in prayer* – Song by Nolan Williams, Jr.)

As we arrived back in Ohio, we knew we needed to tell our families, but we didn't know how or when. We got back into our routines and doubt started rising. I began to feel as if maybe things wouldn't work out. But the next Sunday, God gave us a sign. We were attending church when an actual telephone that was sitting on a table on the stage just rang and rang – God was telling US to answer.

My husband accepted the job offer. They wanted him in 30 days. This threw me into a tailspin. Our house instantly sold. Everything was moving so quickly. My husband was going to move to Mississippi to start work and I would finish the school year and then join him.

Soon, we went back down to Mississippi to look for housing. We met up with a realtor from the church social. We saw at least ten places and nothing felt like home. We didn't want to move into an apartment and then have to move again, but time was running out. That evening, my husband and I were worn out, disappointed, tired and hungry, and decided to eat at a local spot, Old Style BBQ. A lady, truly a God-send, approached me and started talking. We told her our situation and she said we should check out the neighborhood where her family had recently moved. That evening, we ended up walking around her neighborhood. We stopped at one of the houses and the builder was sweeping. We struck up a conversation and he took us to one of the houses that didn't already have a contract on it. It seemed too nice. We prayed about it and ended up putting an offer on the house and were able to head "home" knowing we had a place waiting for us in Mississippi. We flew back to Ohio. I was starting to get a little excited now that we found "the perfect home."

One day during the transition, I was naked, wet, cold, and confused and realized I passed out in the shower in Ohio. I didn't know how all this was going to work. Everything was falling into place but I felt totally scattered and out of control. I felt like shouting, "Mayday, mayday!" Often when things seem to be falling apart, they're really falling into place.

Moving day quickly arrived and my oldest brother and his wife had a send-off dinner party with all the family. It was wonderful. As we left, I turned around and saw all my favorite people waving. Reality sank in for all of us. We were actually "leaving." I cried all the way down the driveway. I looked out the window in silence, crying the whole way as we drove to Mississippi. I looked over at my husband and saw tears coming down his face as well. We barely said a word to each other. That night in the hotel, I was still crying. I prayed that I could do this and be joyful. I didn't know why this was happening but I was being obedient. My husband prayed with me and for me on the end of the bed.

The next morning, I felt a huge relief and trusted God that everything would be okay.

Later I told my mom about it and she said that she was having her own tears. She told me she was looking in the mirror and told God she needed Him to help her because she couldn't do this on her own. The next day, we were both at peace. (*Way Maker* – Song by Michael W. Smith)

That summer, as we were settling into Olive Branch, Mississippi, I met with one of the principals and was offered a teaching job. We loved our house. We got connected with Great Commission Church with Pastors Trevor and Angie Davis, we were leading groups, and my husband eventually joined the staff as the Director of Volunteer Ministries. During this time, the vision for our Go Life Savers CPR and First Aid Training business was birthed. My parents visited every school break. The four of us enjoyed numerous Goldwing motorcycle trips together. Many of these trips included the Gulf Coast in Alabama. Life was good.

Ten years later, my husband started getting the urge to be in Florida, again. By now, I figured I already made the big move, so I was more open to the idea. Wasn't it nice of God to ease me into it?!

During our ten years in Mississippi, my husband earned his BSN nursing degree and was working at a behavioral health hospital in Memphis, TN. We took a tour of Florida and visited several hospitals that would allow him to transfer. He received several offers and chose Jupiter, Florida. It took courage to pick up and move again because I didn't hear God telling us to "GO" this time. It was more because I was following my husband.

We took a weekend to look for housing. Everything was selling before we could even make an offer. We adjusted to the fact we might need to live in an apartment first. I felt like we had been down this road before. Within the last hours of our last day, we saw this cute, clean little townhouse in a beautiful neighborhood with a water view and walking distance to everything. Two steps into the house, I grabbed the realtor's arm and said, "Write it up now!" We got it. But the owner wanted 30 days. Our Mississippi house sold so we needed the Florida house sooner, so we thought. Our realtor worked out a situation for us and we stayed near the beach for a month at Jupiter Bay Condominiums. It was like a vacation. I was able to walk to the beach every day. This was a gift of time from God.

We soon got involved in a church and fell in love with the people. My husband was working weekends at a behavioral health hospital (at that time) so I attended church alone. Go Life Savers, LLC was really starting to take off and we needed to make a decision. It took courage, but, after much prayer and consideration, we took another leap of faith and we began to work full-time on our Go Life Savers CPR business. This freed my husband up to be able to join me at church on Sunday mornings and we led the Medical Response Team. The church was a blessing to us during the time my father went to live with Jesus in 2018.

One day, a friend invited us to a Fourth of July BBQ party at another friend's house. We accepted the invitation and I immediately felt a connection with Kimberly, the hostess. She was from Ohio too, and we shared a love for horses and art. She and her husband led a Stay Positive Tiki Life Group. We ended up going almost every month. Later, she shared a vision and introduced Women World Leaders. During my time of getting to know Kimberly better, I found out she had been to Israel four times. I would **NEVER** travel that far! But, as God would have it, he was planting another seed.

We found ourselves attending worship services for several years at another church on Saturdays and started taking some classes. After 21 days of prayer and fasting, we were led to make Christ Fellowship Church our home. We started to serve and lead groups. They had been promoting a church tour to the Holy Lands in

2020. My adventurous husband said he always wanted to go to Israel. I knew we would **NEVER** do that. One thing led to another and before I knew what happened, we were signed up to go to Israel. I invited our friends, Richard and Patricia, to join us. She said they couldn't because they just booked a trip to Europe six months earlier. I told her to pray about it and see what God told her. That afternoon, she said they signed up and were renting out their house to pay for it.

Isaiah 48:17 NIV – This is what the Lord says–Redeemer, the Holy One of Israel: I am the Lord your God, who teaches you what is best for you, who directs you in the way you should go.

I know I have at least one more move. (*In my Father's house*, Who You Say I Am – Song by Hillsong Worship)

I have learned …
*My mother and I are kindred spirits.
*Life is better with a godly husband and I'd rather be with him anywhere than without him. He is a wise leader.
*Wherever you go, get connected to a church family.
*Family has a broader definition than I realized.
*Sunshine on my shoulders makes me happy.
*Time and financial freedom come with owning and operating our own business.
*It was a privilege to spend the last three months of my father's life by his side.
*Traveling to Israel with my church family was a gift I will **NEVER** forget or completely understand.
*For us, COVID-19 was a blessing. We were able to shelter-in at

our rental condo in Orange Beach, Alabama, which was another gift of time from God.

*Jesus is our true Life Saver.

In the beginning, I thought I was just visiting the state of Mississippi for the weekend and everything would go back to normal. Little did I know, saying yes to that flight would change my future, just like saying yes to God would change my final destination. (*Temporary Home* – Song by Carrie Underwood)

I realize moving isn't as big of a challenge or as courageous as some other things, but it was for me. Moving isn't always easy and rarely comfortable and most likely an inconvenient time, but God's timing is always on time.

John 10:27-28 NIV – My sheep listen to my voice; I know them, and they follow me. I give them eternal life, and they shall never perish; no one can snatch them out of my hand.

(*I know who holds tomorrow* – Song by Sangah Noona)

I'm still learning...

During the early stages of this writing adventure, I sent Kimberly a text saying, "I need to pass at this time and you can fill my spot with another writer." I figured she would accept that and replace me but she told me to pray, pray, pray before she totally took me off the list and make certain I was 100% sure. So Mark and I prayed about it and God had other plans.

When God has a plan, nothing and no one can stand in the way. He is the master pilot.

> *Psalm 40:3 NIV – He put a new song in my mouth, a hymn of praise to our God. Many will see and fear the Lord and put their trust in him.*

(*Trust and Obey* – Song by Don Moen)

> *Hebrews 13:5 – ... "NEVER will I leave you, NEVER will I forsake you."*

Let me en**courage** you: Follow the Lord where He leads you, then depend upon Him to give you more courage to take the next step...

I'm "*NEVER*" going to Africa!

Courage to overcome DOUBT

Kimberly Ann Hobbs

Doubt is an experience that all of us face at times. Even those of us who have faith in God struggle with doubt. Whenever we venture out to conquer new ground or fulfill something God has called us to do, doubt and opposition seem to come. As Mark wrote in his gospel about the father petitioning Jesus to help his son, sometimes we must simply cry out to God, "I do believe; help me overcome my unbelief."

The enemy loves to stir up unbelief and fears that are often the result of past failures. These things can haunt our minds and, more often than I am sure we realize, cause doubt in the darkness. Why do we doubt? Often, it is because the opposition wants to take your eyes off Christ. Do you ever feel the enemy attack when you know God is getting ready to do something great in your life?

Doubt enters our mind at various times. Doubt can be described as lacking confidence or being wary of something unlikely to happen. Doubt is a tool that Satan uses to make us lack confidence in God's Word and consider His mercy, grace, provision and goodness unlikely. We can't hold the devil responsible for all of our problems though; instead, we must take responsibility for our own doubts and reactions to the world's attacks.

Zachariah in the Bible was visited by an angel of the Lord telling him he would have a son (Luke 1:11-17). Zachariah doubted the word given to him because his age and his wife's age were so far beyond a possible pregnancy by worldly standards. As a result of his doubt, the angel said that Zachariah's voice would be muted until God's promise was fulfilled (Luke 1:18-20). Zachariah doubted God's ability to overcome human obstacles.

Is this you? Do you allow your human reason to overshadow your faith in God? No matter how logical our own reasons seem, God has made foolish the things of this world (1 Corinthians 1:20).

The remedy for our doubt is faith! Faith comes by hearing the Word of God (Romans 10:17). Once we understand what God has done in the past, what He promises us in the present, and what we can expect from Him in the future, then we can overcome doubt and act in faith instead. God tells us in Hebrews 11:1 that we can have confidence even in the things we cannot see because God has proven Himself faithful, true, and able. When you surrender your life to Christ, the voice of truth tells you what doubt lies to you about. Don't doubt in the darkness what God shows you in the light.

. . . .

 **Sharon Watson** was a professional television actress, spokesperson, and TV show host for more than two decades in New York City, LA, San Francisco, and Florida. She has been the principal actress in more than 50 national television commercials and has appeared on the cover of twelve national magazines.

While growing up in West Palm Beach, Sharon won nine beauty pageants, including Miss South Florida Fair and Miss Sunflavor, for which she had the honor of representing Florida Agriculture across the U.S. and Canada for a year. She graduated from University of Florida in 1980, with a degree in Journalism, and in 1985, met and married her husband, moved to New York City, and began her 20-year television career. For the past 15 years, she has been a 5-star-rated real estate agent, recognized as having impeccable integrity and exceptional Christian values.

Sharon now lives with her husband of 35 years on a small horse ranch in West Palm Beach and maintains a wonderful relationship with her only daughter, who lives in Miami.

"Til Death Do Us Part"
Sharon Watson

I met my husband one afternoon in West Palm Beach and 77 days later, we were married on top of a mountain in Colorado while on a snow ski trip. That was 35 years ago. Bob was an answer to my prayers! I truly believe that it has been my strong faith and commitment to God that has been the glue keeping our marriage alive for 35 years. It's because of my courageous steps of faith. One step at a time.

In my early 20s, I did what I wanted, when I wanted. Partied a LOT. I was not living a very Christian way of life, but I thought I was a good Christian… trying to be good, not hurting anyone. I didn't cheat, lie (do white lies count?) or steal. I did not know for a long time what a real personal relationship with God really was.

I have always strongly believed in God from a very young age. I knew and felt God was watching over me, but it wasn't until much later in my life that I really GOT IT. My relationship with God grew over time, with many trials and errors where my courageous steps of faith helped me learn and experience God.

My faith walk has been more like peeling off the layers of an onion, rather than some holy epiphany. I had to practice trusting in God a little more each day, praying for guidance, and asking Him more and more to help me through each difficult step along the way. I think I had to "learn" to be obedient first, to trust in the Lord and His Word, before I could actually commit to him. I had to put Him first, and after doing that, my faith-life finally flourished, and I could hear Him and feel Him in my life.

After graduating from college, and dating all the wrong kinds of guys, I started praying to God to bring me someone who was more like my dad, the best man I knew and a great father. One day Bob drove up and stopped me as I walked across a parking lot. As luck would have it, he had all the qualities I had been praying for. I knew he was an answer to my prayers, so I took a giant leap of faith and got married 77 days later. I believe that God brought Bob to me. He was smart, stable, sensitive, faithful and loving.

Bob encouraged me and set me on a path I never would have imagined or dreamed of for myself. He encouraged me to go to NYC and try my hand at the acting thing. If it weren't for Bob's encouragement, I would never have had a wonderful career and all the adventures traveling all over the world acting and modeling. The Lord really had some great things in store for me that I would never have dreamed for myself. *Now to him who is able to do immeasurably more than all we ask or imagine, according to his power that is at work within us.* Ephesians 3:20 NIV

Just a few years into our marriage, however, tragedy struck and threatened to shatter our little fairy tale. We were home visiting my family for Thanksgiving, having a great time, when everything came to a screeching halt. We heard a loud raucous commotion at my parents' door in the middle of the night. My oldest sister and her husband were banging on Mom and Dad's door screaming and howling that her firstborn and oldest son, Christopher (17 years old), was just killed in a car accident. It just couldn't be true! How was that possible? It was unbelievable, horrific, and made no sense. Nothing like this had ever happened to our family before. I watched and felt this tragedy practically destroy my family.

We were staying at my mom and dad's house for a couple days for Thanksgiving weekend and we ended up seeing and feeling, firsthand, the pain that this kind of tragedy and grief will inflict on a family. I heard screams from my sister that didn't sound human. She couldn't get off the bed or stop sobbing for days. To make matters worse, she actually drove up on the accident just after it happened and saw Chris's mangled car on the side of the road and the ambulance pulling away – not going to the hospital…but to the morgue.

Chris was just getting ready to graduate from high school and start his life. He loved to surf, so he and his girlfriend were heading out to the beach to get the first sunrise waves. How is it possible that Chris would be in that place, on that road, at that time with two drunk drivers on the very same road, coming from opposite directions, about to cross his path? These two women, both drunk, driving separate cars (one of whom had her children in the car), were heading home from a night out on the town when they crossed paths with Christopher and changed my family forever.

We all struggled to find any meaning. Why would God take Chris at such a young age? Some people said it was "meant to be" and that it was God's plan. I would struggle with that explanation for many years. When tragedy strikes like that, the brain tries to make some kind of sense of it. I came to understand later that our God is a good God and that that was just a horrible accident and not something God had planned or wanted. It took a lot of courage after the accident to not live in fear, to not wonder when the next tragedy would occur. It was a very hard time for all of us. *Even though I walk through the darkest valley, I will fear no evil, for you are with me; your rod and your staff, they comfort me.* – Psalm 23:4 NIV

The loss of Chris and seeing my sister's pain tore us all to pieces. It was inconceivable for my parents to see my sister going through that pain. It is not natural for your children to die before you. Our strong family faith kept us together as well as could be expected under the circumstances, but it really took a toll on my mom. She had battled Lupus her whole adult life but was doing well at the time of the accident, enjoying retirement and traveling all over. But after the accident, she ended up getting very sick and passed away at about the same time the following year. She got cancer, but I think it was the tragedy and the pain that really killed her.

So my dear sister Sandy lost her son and mother in the course of just over a year. Later in life, we had another unexpected tragedy. My sister had to bury her other son, Chad, my only other nephew. It crushed us all over again. I look at my sister today and cannot even begin to understand how she survived the grief of burying two of her three children. She will tell you that God is the only way she did it. I know that God carried us all when we could not walk ourselves. Talk about courageous steps of faith! She took that pain and put it to work for the good of humanity, working for the next few years to help start Mothers Against Drunk Drivers. She will always be an inspiration to me.

I can do all this through him who gives me strength. – *Philippians 4:13 NIV*

A few years later, I decided I wanted to have a baby. My "time clock was ticking" very loudly all of a sudden in my head. After trying unsuccessfully for nearly two years, we found out I could not have children naturally. My tubes were blocked so there was no way for me to naturally conceive. We were told that the only way we could possibly have a child was through in-vitro fertilization, which was still a relatively new technology at the time. If it had been a few years earlier, I would not have had that option at all, and even then, the probability statistics for my situation and my age were extremely low. I was on the "older" end of the spectrum to even try. I was so afraid that I might not be able to have a baby, I was anxious and stressed out, and stress is the last thing you need when you are trying in-vitro.

I prayed and decided I must put it in the Lord's hands. It was out of my control. Despite all odds, the doctor retrieved two eggs. He said there was one great-big-plump egg, and the other was just so-so, but he was going to put both back and we would have to hope for the best. Well, I have to say, my BIG PLUMP perfect egg grew into my Allie Catherine (Alley Cat, for short). She was, and is, a true miracle! I think I could write a book on how God has blessed us in so many ways with her and how grateful we are. God answered my prayers again. The layers of the onion were peeling away.

When we moved back to Florida, Bob decided to launch another company. This would be his third start-up experience and we already knew the perils. He bought the assets of a boat company and he set out to build the best little center console boats ever made. He owned the business and he was building boats. What could be better, right? I couldn't help but being excited about the prospect of the new business, moving back home to Florida, and doing it with our little miracle baby on board now. But it was also pretty scary for me, starting a new business with an infant. I just knew that it was right to support Bob in this venture. We were going to make it work.

As the months and years went by, things began to get really difficult at home and things weren't quite going the way we wanted or expected. Money got tight. All the money we had coming in had to go right back out to pay employees, buy the materials to build the boats, do marketing and sales costs, and carry us through the lag time while we were trying to get the boats sold. It got to the point where we were putting all our money into the business and not getting anything out of it.

It was getting so stressful and scary; I was in a very uncomfortable place. I was worried about the finances and being able to have the things we needed for our baby. I was not used to this. My mom and dad had very normal, stable jobs and managed their money well, so I never had to worry about money growing up, as a lot of people do. However, Bob did not see it that way. Bob's dad was an entrepreneur, and he is from a family of entrepreneurs, so he was used to the ups and downs of starting a new business and totally figured this was part of the process.

After a while, I felt like I was drowning. I was so angry and bitter about the circumstances. At times, I was so mad, it was even hard to talk to him on the phone when he was on sales trips. It was incredible to me how my life had been turned upside down so quickly, and at the same time, I had the most important thing I ever wanted. I had my miracle baby. I couldn't figure out what God wanted for us. I was crying all the time and asking why. *How did I get into these circumstances now? Why now? What am I supposed to learn from this? What do you want from me, Lord?*

> *Do not be anxious about anything, but in every situation, by prayer and petition, with thanksgiving, present your requests to God. – Philippians 4:6 NIV*

My marriage was in big trouble and I was really scared. I never thought I would be thinking about divorce. We weren't even allowed to say that word out loud in our marriage (a pact we took when we were first married).

But now, I wanted out of the situation. Out of the business and, I thought, out of the marriage. I was so mad at him I couldn't feel the love anymore. I would lie awake, crying every night, worried about how/if my daughter and I would be okay and if we would have what we needed in the event of an emergency.

I just couldn't believe that my once-happy marriage and life had taken such a frightening turn. I was in a very dark place. I had been praying for courage and guidance. I didn't realize at the time, but even then, I was taking the baby courageous steps of faith, praying about what to do next.

Right about that time, coincidentally, I heard about a Bible study starting in my area called "Bible Study Fellowship," and they were going to study The Book of John for an entire year. I grew up Catholic and didn't really know the Bible. I had never been in any kind of Bible study. I really felt like the Lord was putting it on my heart to do this class, but I was so worried about the time commitment and having to care for a toddler at the same time.

I made the decision to take the leap of faith and be obedient to the Lord. I signed up for the class. Throughout that year, I got closer and closer to the Lord. I got strength and courage I didn't know I had.

> *For this reason a man will leave his father and mother and be united to his wife, and the two will become one flesh... Therefore what God has joined together, let no one separate. – Matthew 19:5-6*

If I always really truly believed that Bob was an answer to my prayers, how could I end it because we were having difficult times? I came to realize through prayer that I could not make a life-changing decision in a time of crisis like this. The Lord said, *Wait. Be patient.* I got confirmation that I needed to be patient, hang in there, continue to pray for guidance and trust that the Lord would carry me through. I would wait until the business crisis had passed and see how I felt after this storm was over.

The boat company was eventually closed, and we moved on. God literally changed my heart and I found that love again. I looked back and was amazed at how God had changed my heart. I didn't think it was possible. Now I know anything is possible with our Lord.

We argued about money for many years of our marriage. After the boat company, I wanted my husband to have a normal 9-to-5 job and bring home a regular paycheck like other people so we could budget things and know what was coming in or not. The arguing and difference of opinions on this issue was causing strife again in the marriage.

I totally put it in the Lord's hand. I had to. I didn't want to destroy our marriage over it.

God taught me that I had to stop wanting something that wasn't going to be. Bob was never going to have a normal 9-5 job. He is an entrepreneur and will always forge his own path. I needed to learn to be grateful and be happy with what we had, to trust God to provide when we couldn't provide for ourselves, and to keep taking those courageous steps of faith when things got tough. When I really learned that lesson, it changed everything. We stopped arguing about his jobs and money. I started to see how hard he was working all the time for us and started to be more supportive and grateful.

> *Therefore I tell you, do not worry about your life, what you will eat or drink; or about your body, what you will wear. Is not life more than food, and the body more than clothes? – Matthew 6:25 NIV*

As the layers of the onion were coming off, the Lord laid something else on my heart. About twelve years ago, I felt the Lord was calling me to step up and develop a more personal and serious relationship with Him. I was obedient. That day I made a conscious decision to put Christ first in my life.

Since then, I've been involved in some sort of Bible study group most every month of the year and have been getting stronger and stronger in my faith. Reading the Bible and learning God's Word has been so rewarding and has strengthened my faith and understanding beyond what words can express. I have also been developing my prayer life and surrounding myself with Christian women for support. It has been an incredible journey. God has shown me so many things, answered so many prayers and blessed me in so many ways I just could not have imagined.

Over the 35 years of our marriage, I learned that I needed to be patient, non-judgmental and obedient. I had to learn to trust, put it in God's hands when things got tough, and trust that God would provide. God did provide. He is a wonderful and mighty God. He has changed my heart and I have learned so many lessons over the years.

I truly believe that if I had not let our Mighty Lord take the wheel when I couldn't, when going through those really hard times in our marriage, I would have thrown in the towel, given up and been divorced. That would have been the biggest tragedy of all. I can't imagine a life without Bob in it. I feel so lucky every day we are still here and healthy. We worked through all the difficulties to come out stronger on the other side, happier than ever.

Marriage is difficult and there are many ups and downs. Happy times and sad times. Seasons of hope and inspiration and darker seasons that challenge us. I'm hoping my story will help and encourage other women to find strength in their commitment to their marriage and not to give up when times are hard. God can change your heart. Be patient. Pray. Your faith and God will carry you through.

Courage to overcome
BITTERNESS
Kimberly Ann Hobbs

Does bitterness have any place in your heart? We can fool ourselves into thinking that no one will ever know the layers of anger and resentment that have a way of seeping into our emotions and causing bitterness. We can try to hide our emotions, but if they are there, they will hold us back from serving our Lord in ways we may not realize.

Bitterness is a root cause of disturbing our inner peace. How do we prevent bitterness from permeating our hearts so that we can live at peace with everyone? We want to be free from the shackles that bind us because those shackles are like a heavy tethered weight holding us back from moving about freely. The Bible says, "If it's possible, as far as it depends on you, live at peace with everyone" (Romans 12:18). God knew it wouldn't always be possible to live at peace with some people; that's why Romans 12:18 says "IF it's possible" ...But even if peace is not possible, our forgiveness of others IS possible. And what's more, God says that our forgiveness is required.

Lack of forgiveness is choosing to hold on to bitterness, which is dangerous because when our bitterness grows, it can become full-fledged resentment. To keep from reaching the point of resentment we are often required to take a courageous step away from bitterness, understanding that we are called to, in that step, move toward forgiveness.

Let's look at how Jesus forgave us. He lived a perfect life, but He was beaten, mocked, spit upon, and hung on a cross to die. John 3:16 says He loved the world so much that He died for it. That world includes you AND whoever offended you. Jesus forgives you and He forgives me. We are told to forgive others as Christ forgave us. When we have an unforgiving spirit, our eyes are no longer fixed on Christ, but instead are fixed on ourselves as we hold onto something that can cause our own demise. God knows what is going on inside each of us and inside those who have wronged us. He also knows every person we must forgive in order to remove all bitterness and be able to move forward with peace. Ask Him to search your heart and melt away any resentment you may have so that you can be free to move on from an ice-cold heart of bitterness and move into the purpose He has for your life—a purpose of serving free from all bitterness.

"Do not take revenge, my dear friends, but leave room for God's wrath, for it is written 'It is mine to avenge; I will repay' says the Lord" (Romans 12:19 NIV).

Please don't hold anger or bitterness in your heart. If your heart is burdened, give it to God, He will take care of it. Forgiveness is the key.

"I can do all things through Christ who strengthens me" (Phil.4:13 NKJV).

Michelle Redden is the founder of Mae Dae Mentoring. She is an established international life coach, mentor, and biofeedback specialist. Michelle uses her passion for growth and her love of people to assist individuals in creating new patterns in their brains and lives. She has extensive experience with personal and spiritual growth, and she uses her background in management of multimillion-dollar companies to guide clients in business development. She is married to her husband, Donald, with five stepchildren, nine grandchildren, and three fur babies. Michelle has recently launched her own website, michellemae.net, and in the near future, she hopes to expand her business by doing more speaking and writing more books. She is also a bestselling author in the book Tears to Triumph.

Be About Your Father's Business

Michelle Redden

God was at work in me long before I was aware of it. My job was my stronghold, always granting me great authority and responsibility, and it seemed as though I was always being promoted. Because of my work ethic, other companies were always wanting to hire me. God gave me a leadership gift which was apparent from the very day I started my first job. Once I got my first position, I did not apply for another one until I was 40 years old, and that was only because my husband's job moved us to Mississippi. I did not know anyone in Mississippi, nor did I have any company connections there. My Mississippi career began with me managing three branches for a plumbing/HVAC company. I worked for about a year when I was told that the company had been bought out, so there were many changes about to take place. I had gone through company buyouts before, so I had a feeling how things would go. Even so I still tried to remain in a positive state of mind.

I was driving 1.5 hours one way to work every day and working 10-hour days. So at minimum, my day was 13 to 14 hours, five days a week. At that time, my three stepchildren were teenagers. My husband's career was demanding and required travel almost every week. I was having allergy issues and was just tired all the time. I liked having a career, but I was not enjoying my work. I had never felt that way about my career before.

One day while sitting in my office I began to not feel well. I had cold sweats and felt faint. I wanted to lie down and go to sleep. My stomach started to hurt, and my left arm had shooting pain. I had had pain in my left arm for weeks, but I just brushed it off as muscle related. I remember thinking, "OK now, snap out of it!" But I just could not make my mind push through how bad I was feeling. So I told one of my employees, Stacy, and he came to sit with me. After sitting with me for about a half hour, Stacy observed I was getting worse.

He finally said, "You look awful and I really think something is wrong. I'm calling an ambulance." At that point I was so short of breath that I could not speak, so I just nodded my head yes.

My symptoms were all over the place. My heart rate would go sky high and then bottom out. It was scary for me. The ambulance came and took me to the hospital. Once they had my heart rate stable, they kept me overnight. They ran tests and said that I had a small heart attack which was caused by allergy medicine I was taking and the effects of my lifestyle.

When I followed up with the heart specialist, he said, "You seem to be doing ok now but you will need to think about your lifestyle, and you cannot take that allergy medicine again."

I said, "It's weird because I lived in Mississippi for two years before I had any allergy issues. And what's wrong with my lifestyle? What does that mean? I don't drink or do drugs." I felt like I had a good lifestyle even though I was busy, often skipped meals due to work and drank a lot of coffee. And I was only 42 years old.

He leaned into me and said in his soft Southern voice, while pointing to my heart, "Sweetie, if you don't know what is going on in there then you cannot expect me to cure you in a 20-minute office visit."

I thought, Gee, *where did I go wrong? What did I do in the past that seemed to keep me healthy?*

And now my mom's words were ringing in my head. She had told me for years that I was stressed out. I would say I didn't feel stressed out. Well, here it was, the proof that I was, in fact, stressed out. It was time to take some courageous steps of faith to safeguard my health. I thought about what I had done to try to stay healthy in the past. I used to get massages, chiropractic, and acupuncture treatments weekly. I intentionally exercised every day. Mentally, I maintained a positive attitude, which was the best I knew to do at the time. I took an inventory of my surroundings and realized I did not have the necessary resources available to me in my current city. As I focused on what these activities had done for me physically, I realized they all created a frequency change in the body. So I started researching normal ranges for frequencies of the heart and different organs. Then I began to acquire methods of creating those frequencies. I came across three machines which all had different capabilities related to frequency balancing. I compared them and bought the one best for my needs. In the meantime, I took one of the most courageous steps that I would take on this healing journey: I quit my job. I knew deep inside it was time – time to start my own business. This was the kick in the pants I needed to change direction in my life. I always knew I would have my own business at some point, I just did not know what that business would be. I can remember sitting at my kitchen table trying to brainstorm ideas. Unbeknownst to me, that was not necessary. God already had a plan and purpose for my life that He began laying out before me.

Once my imagination was stimulated, Mae Dae was born in 2012. I called my brand "Michelle Mae" and my Quantum Biofeedback business "Mae Dae Mentoring". It is spelled differently but it reminded me of the distress call 'May Day!' I didn't realize at that moment how fitting it would become.

Even though I knew I was headed in the right direction, I was still disconnected from God. My belief system was a hodgepodge of ideas. I wanted a relationship with God, but I did not want any rules. So I applied whatever parts of any religion that would let me create my own belief system. God would have a lot of work to do in me and he would have a lot of ungodly beliefs to set me free from.

I was exhausted and had no support. Other emotions started building up within me that I couldn't identify. I felt alone, not only in this new venture, but with events of my past that I hadn't realized were still imprisoning me. In hindsight, I can see how the darkness introduced small lies to my mind over and over again until I believed them. The devil repeated them until they became strongholds in my life. Once I was aligned with the darkness, oppression overcame me.

Because I had not forgiven myself for a past abortion, which is described in detail in my previous story included in the anthology, *Tears To Triumph: Releasing Pain to Receive God's Restoration*, I felt unworthy of having my own business and helping other people be restored to wholeness. Other issues compounded this oppression, including the realization that being adopted had been affecting my self-worth my entire life despite the fact that I had a wonderful upbringing with my adoptive family.

And the lie that had steered my professional life to that point: "If you don't work a lot of hours at your job then you're irresponsible, lazy and unworthy of promotion."

Heck, there are even books written by so-called experts that say you should be the first to get to work in the morning and the last to leave at night. That is not the truth. It will give people the impression that you're dedicated, but it does not mean that you are really even working. Please don't misunderstand me and think I am saying that a career does not require many invested hours; however, there is so much more to life than a career and we should never sacrifice the life that God has called us to live by becoming trapped in a career that we have begun to idolize.

God did break this stronghold in my life, and now uses my work to convert businesses for His Kingdom.

But how I came to the Lord is its own story. I was not attending church. I didn't have godly mentors. I felt a stirring but didn't understand Him at all; and as I said, I had pieced together my own brand of faith. One day, while I was on an acupuncturist's table full of pressure point needles, God manifested Himself before me in a cloud descending from the ceiling. He was holding my son, whom I never held on this earth, on His right shoulder as a father holds his child. He drew me upwards to Him and we all merged together as One. I felt the forgiveness from Him and from my son envelop me and I could feel the healing and self-forgiveness within me.

It took me close to a year of reflecting daily on how good God is and how He wants to forgive us of all our sins, no matter what they are. One day, as I was driving down the highway running errands, I heard a voice say, "Today's the day."

"OK, I'll play along. Today's the day for what?"

"Today is the day that you will accept my Son Jesus as Lord and Savior."

"I don't know how to do that."

"Turn the radio on."

I pushed the button.

There was a man on the radio, and he said, "If you want to accept Jesus as your Lord and Savior..."

Romans 10:9 NLT – "If you openly declare Jesus is Lord and believe in your heart that God raised Him from the dead, you will be saved."

From that pivotal moment, God started the process of delivering me from all the lies, strongholds and oppression that Satan had inflicted on me. My belief system was an assortment of many different opinions. I did not understand that facts sometimes are not truths and that even the truth can be easily manipulated. For example, the world tells me I'm ill-equipped, uneducated, unworthy, and don't meet the world's criteria of attractiveness. According to the world, my upbringing dictates my status in life. But actually, Truth reveals my identity in Christ. I am chosen, holy and dearly loved (Colossians 3:12); I am anointed (1 John 2:27); and I am a conqueror (Romans 8:37).

I began reading the Bible voraciously because I hungered for His Truth. This has been an ongoing process and God continues to show me how to accept his healing and promises. He has called and equipped me and I am always being educated through his Word. I am set apart and sanctified by Him daily. He has given me a crown of beauty for my ashes (Isaiah 61:3).

"But God, being rich in mercy, because of the great love with which he loved us, even when we were dead in our trespasses, made us alive together with Christ—by grace you have been saved" (Ephesians 2:4-5 ESV).

Following God's call courageously, I began to help others walk through this same process of finding their value and worth in Christ alone. It seemed to me that my past mistakes were going to disqualify me from my destiny. Through His Word, God assured me that that would never happen. Instead, He took my past and actually used it to promote the Kingdom of God. Who better to help guide people through a healing than a person who has been experiencing God's healing herself? My testimonies continue to give hope and encouragement to others. God has given me such an inner knowing that this is exactly what I was created to do. I did wrestle with the idea that God really was my provider. He had to strip me of the idea that I had to have an employer in order to receive a paycheck. As I studied in the Bible, I learned that God doesn't possess a quality, God is what we have come to know as a quality. For example, God is Love. He doesn't just exhibit the qualities of love. He is Love! And well, it's the same thing with being the Provider. God doesn't just provide for us, He Himself is our provision. After all, one of God's names is Jehovah Jireh, the Lord will provide (Genesis 22:14).

At first my business grew slowly, and the enemy would use this to lie to me daily, telling me that I was not as successful as when I had a job. He used my husband to pressure me to get another job in management so I could bring home $100,000 a year. My husband really could not understand why I wouldn't use the experience I had to get another high-paying position. I knew what I knew. I had to stay on this path for the Lord. I repeated scripture over and over again in order to stay focused and continue to walk courageously. For months, at least a couple of times a week, God would have me read the entire book of Nehemiah in one sitting. I was praying to trust that He was my Provider, and through this process God was building my faith. It took courageous steps of faith to trust God to build my business. I didn't see it as clearly then as I do now.

One day, I heard of an acquaintance who had died. This person was young, had been alone for long periods of time, and had drunk herself to death. It saddened my heart a great deal to think about the details of what led her to that end. And while I was sobbing for her, I became so angry at the devil and I told God, "I hate Satan! Am I allowed to feel that way?"

He said, "Yes. That is righteous anger, and you can harness that to produce good for the Kingdom of God. Because the bottom line is, I only need my workers to say 'yes.' There are many industries that the devil has control of and I need my people to take them back. The devil is the one to blame for that person's death. He was able to convince her that death was the only option to stop the emotional pain."

I prayed that night, "God, help me reach the people You want me to help, so when a person is referred to me or finds my information online, I know it is a divine appointment." Because I prayed that prayer, I know that when someone comes to me it is God himself connecting us for the purpose of inner healing and guidance. With God all things are possible (Matthew 19:26).

I was faithful in stepping courageously where God called, and now have a few individual businesses. I do faith-based biofeedback therapy, life coaching, accountability coaching, speaking, and I am also a best-selling author. This has all happened through trusting God and surrendering my insecurities to Him in every area of my life.

Has God been calling you to a new beginning? If so, pray for God to give you the faith and courage to be about your Father's business.

For God has not given us a spirit of fear but of power, love, and of a sound mind (2 Timothy 1:7 NKJV).

Courage to overcome
INSECURITY
Kimberly Ann Hobbs

There are many causes of insecurity, but chief among them is our failure to fully trust God. Jeremiah 17:7-8 NKJV teaches us "Blessed is the man who trusts in the Lord, and whose hope is in the Lord, for he shall be like a tree planted by the waters, which spreads out its roots by the river, and will not fear when he comes, but its leaves will be green, and will not be anxious in the year of drought, nor will it cease from yielding fruit."

God made us to love Him and to love others. One of the main issues of insecurity is being self-conscious. Self-consciousness is when you are focused on self. When we are focused on ourselves, we are not loving God and loving others or showing them to be more worthy. Philippians 2:3 tells us to do nothing from selfish ambition or conceit, but in humility count others more significant then ourselves.

Another cause of insecurity is relying on wealth and posses-sions instead of God. The world encourages us to strive and to be Number One in what we do. When we are insecure, it reveals that we long for justification before people rather than before God. God, who richly provides everything for us to enjoy (1Timothy

6:17), wants us to trust Him.

God loves you just the way you are. He created you with all your beauty and attributes. Insecurities can come when we are preoccupied with the securities of this world. We will never obtain it all.

Our righteousness is what pleases the Lord; unfortunately, many of us get hung up on having a better reputation with people than with God. We become overly obsessive at times when we are longing for the Facebook likes or the accolades from our career to boost our worthiness. We forsake the righteousness of Christ that actually makes us worthy (Romans 6:16-17).

It takes courage to surrender insecurities. Just as the Apostle Paul said, "I count everything as lost because of the surpassing worth of knowing Christ Jesus my Lord" (Philippians 3:7-8 ESV).

Let us not doubt what security we have in Christ, giving Satan the win. God is in control and His sovereignty extends to anyone who believes. True security will come when you recognize that God will supply every need of yours according to His riches and glory in Jesus Christ (Philippians 4:19). With courage, overcome insecurity and never forget God's promise to keep those in perfect peace whose minds are steadfast, because they trust in you (Isaiah 26:3).

• •

Adriana Laine was born and raised in Jupiter, FL. She loves to travel and has been to multiple countries leading mission's teams to spread the gospel. She is a sister of Alpha Delta Pi sorority and a third-year pre-medical student at the University of Florida. She plans to attend medical school in the Fall of 2022 to pursue a career in pediatric surgery (Lord-willing!) She is also the president of the UF Women World Leaders chapter, the first tiara group started on a college campus. In her spare time, she likes to read, sing, cook vegan food, spend time with friends and go on adventures.

Christ is in Control

Adriana Laine

As children, we are often told, "You can be anything you want when you grow up." We are encouraged to dream big, to work hard, to stay focused and to shape our lives accordingly. Students are praised for their laser focus on the future and are instructed to open every door that holds opportunity or experience.

These approaches and perspectives on life are faulty when it comes to living for Jesus. Although fine in theory, as Christians, and especially as women, we are called to lean on Christ with every bone in our bodies. We must submit to Him in every possible way, seeking His will for our lives instead of our own. And this is where my conflict arose.

My name is Adriana Laine. I am a 20-year-old college student who used to seek what so many others do – knowledge, respect, a successful career, a well-rounded resume. Now, two years into my college experience, my rose-colored glasses have come off. Today, the only thing I seek is Christ. He is enough for me, sustaining me in every area of my life. And by seeking Christ, all these things have been given to me as well.

> *Not only so, but we also glory in our sufferings, because we know that suffering produces perseverance; perseverance, character; and character, hope. And hope does not put us to shame, because God's love has been poured out into our hearts through the Holy Spirit, who has been given to us. You see, at just the right time, when we were still powerless, Christ died for the ungodly.*
> Romans 5:3-6 NIV

As a freshman, I began my undergraduate experience with much excitement. There were so many opportunities to chase, so many incredible people to meet, so much knowledge to be gained. Living on campus, my life became completely centered around me. What career path would I choose? What leadership experiences would I gain? What sorority would I join? Everyone around me said, "College is the one time in your life you can be selfish." And so that's what I did. My time, my thoughts, my money – everything was for my glory, not God's. And the worst part was that I did not even realize there was anything wrong. I went with the status quo.

I enjoyed the freedom. The world was my oyster. I was smart, young, brave, and competent. I sought approval from myself and from the world around me, but not once did I look up. I had it all going for me – if I worked hard, I thought that I could earn it all.

But slowly, as time passed, I started to realize that the great friendships, the fun activities, and the good grades were no longer bringing me the satisfaction they did initially. My faith was starting to grow very stagnant.

> *I am the vine; you are the branches. If you abide in me and I in you, you will bear much fruit; apart from me you can do nothing.*
> John 15:5 NIV

I was born and raised a Christian, blessed to be raised in a home full of love, support, and discipline. All throughout high school I served and sought the Lord, and I gained a passion for missions from my experiences abroad. My faith and my relationship with Jesus have always been fundamental to my life and to who I am as a person. I have walked closely with Him ever since I can remember.

Arriving at university, I attempted to stay as close to Christ as I could. I did my daily devotionals, spending time in prayer and praying for others. But I had an attitude of selfishness. In retrospect, my attitude was more "What can God do for me?" than "What can I do for God?" I had so many good and promising opportunities come my way, and I became entangled in the world. My faith grew dull, and I lost my fire and passion for a few months.

> *Whoever finds their life will lose it, and whoever loses their life for my sake will find it.*
> Matthew 10:39 NIV

My life was in my hands. I was in control. I believed that, being a Christian for so long, the Lord had just put me on autopilot until my next opportunity. I did not lean on Him. I did not spend time in worship. I had not found a local church; I did not even have a real Christian community, despite my prayers and petitions. But my faith was still strong, right? God would want me to be investing in myself.

I have a friend who always says, "When there's distance between you and God, only one of you has moved. Guess who it is that walked?"

I realized that although I was living by Christian ideals, I was not living by Christ. Those first few months I spent glorifying myself instead of God made me develop this unrealistic and inaccurate perception of who Jesus was. I began to believe that, by investing in myself, I was investing in His future for me. I sought to make Him proud of who I was, of my accomplishments, my titles, my friendships, my popularity with others. I thought that He had given me these things so that I could be a servant to the world. But Christ calls us to serve Him, not the world and not ourselves.

> *Do not offer any part of yourself to sin as an instrument of wickedness, but rather offer yourselves to God as those who have been brought from death to life; and offer EVERY PART of yourself to Him as an instrument of righteousness. For sin shall no longer be your master, because you are not under the law, but under grace.*
> Romans 6:13-14 NIV

As can be expected, I started to make mistakes. I made friendships with people who would often tempt me to sin, and by choosing to refuse I began to feel isolated and alone. I did terribly on my first college exam, and I remember calling my mom and crying to her in the courtyard at midnight, thinking, *Why me? I work so hard; I don't understand why I'm doing so terribly.* I struggled with so many things including the sin of comparison. Pursuing a degree in medicine, the atmosphere for undergraduate students is incredibly cutthroat, and I lacked the support and community that I had growing up. It was just like they always said: a whole different ball game. I was no longer living in a bubble of shelter and love.

> *And so we know and rely on the love God has for us. God is love. Whoever lives in love lives in God, and God in them.*
> 1 John 5:16 NIV

I now had friends, coworkers, and professors who would loudly declare their disdain for Christianity. I saw people who claimed to know Christ living sin-ridden lives. I had so many friends fall prey to drinking, pre-marital sex, comparison, cheating, lying, coveting, and just plain selfishness. This world that was once chock full of opportunity was now crowded with oppression, hate, disrespect for the Lord and a clear lack of empathy.

There is no love on a college campus but that of Christ. The more I began to realize this, the more I began to process how lost those around me truly were – and how lost I had become by living there. I slowly grew stronger in my faith and began to fight against the temptations and lies of the enemy. I chose to clothe myself with righteousness, to guard my heart, and to begin seeing my campus as a mission field. I had the opportunity, in March of 2019, to spend my 19th birthday and spring break in Guatemala with some of my sorority sisters and other college students distributing water filters to those in need, while also sharing the gospel.

> *But I tell you, love your enemies and pray for those who perse-*
> *cute you.*
> Matthew 5:44 NIV

This trip was a pivotal moment for me, as I realized the fault in my mindset. I led Guatemalans to Christ and built beautiful, life-long friendships with the most extraordinary brothers and sisters in Christ. But most importantly, I was humbled enough to listen for that still, small voice of the Lord.

Jesus loves me for who I am, not for who I will become. He loves me despite my flaws, not because of my perfection. He doesn't want me to impress Him with my grades, my accomplishments on this earth, or my works. He wants ME. Sister, He wants you too.

> *I praise you because I am fearfully and wonderfully made; your*
> *works are wonderful, I know that full well.*
> Psalm 139:14 NIV

The rest of my freshman year was a slow and steady path toward knowing Jesus deeper and more personally. I began to welcome Him into every area of my life, giving Him full control. One by one, He tore down the walls I had built up around myself, and He did so with grace, compassion, patience and understanding. I had to trust Him, and I had to give up my own life, just as Jesus gave His for us. I learned that, above all else, my relationship with Jesus is the most important relationship I will ever invest in.

It was a relief to me. The Lord, in His perfect and holy way, had delivered me by reminding me of His sacrifice on the cross. He died to take away my feelings of inadequacy, my shame, my selfish nature. He humbled himself to serve us so that we can serve others. I grew to realize that I no longer wanted what those around me did – success, perfect grades, an amazing resume, and a future secured by earthly wealth. What I want is Jesus. His plans are so much greater than ours; He is the perfect teacher, the loving father, the supportive friend.

> *Now to Him who is able to do exceedingly abundantly above all that we ask or think, according to the power worketh in us.*
> Ephesians 3:20 KJV

My sophomore year was a challenging one, but I continued to walk courageously with Jesus by my side. I faced many battles, spiritually, emotionally, and physically. I was diagnosed with a painful disease. I got my first C in a class. I faced harassment in my work environment because of my faith. I struggled with mental health challenges. But the battles I faced my second year pale in comparison to the love God has for us. And if I had to do it over again, I would choose the battles with Jesus by my side rather than the blessings without Him.

I live my life for Christ and Christ alone. I desire to live in His dwelling, sharing His love and courageously serving others until I meet Him face to face. I once lived of the world; I still live in the world, but I am not of it. I am consumed with the beauty that is our perfect father. Sister, I pray that you, too, will be consumed with Christ. Choose to submit. Surrender. Give God control, walk courageously, and find heavenly peace.

What, then, shall we say to these things? If God is for us, who can be against us?
Romans 8:31 NKJV

. . . .

Courage to overcome CONTROL
Kimberly Ann Hobbs

Many of us struggle with multiple things in our lives, such as worry, anger, and depression, but how many of us struggle with the desire for control?

All the way back to the Garden of Eden we see Adam and Eve struggle with control. God said to Adam and Eve, "You must not eat from the tree of knowledge of good and evil." What did Satan do? Satan discredited God by accusing Him of withholding good from His children. He told Eve she shouldn't trust God to define good and evil for her; she needed to be able to do it for herself. Then she would have control.

Today, in our pride we still crave control. I struggled with this and realized it is part of the curse of sin that is ongoing. I don't believe I'm alone in this struggle, as many women have the desire to be in control.

We think being in control will make our lives better. We want to decide ourselves what is best. But one day, when we wake up to what God says, we see that life does not revolve around us, our thoughts and our desires, as we once believed. Think about the enemy of our souls and how he desires to save your hearts. He tells you that control will give you peace, safety, power, comfort, respect and much more.

We do not know what is best for us. Only God in His infinite wisdom, sovereignty and love deems what is best for us.

Dying to a desire for control is not easy. It takes courage to admit this to God and yourself. It's a time between you and Him to truly recognize you are not God and you are not all-knowing, or even able to make every decision in your life.

Trusting God for your circumstances, relationships and choices takes extreme courage. Overcoming your own will and surrendering to His will can help you to become confident—confident in knowing that His plan is the best plan. This will bring Him glory and give Him the ability to fulfill His purpose in you. Even though you think you have the best plan for your life and try to control it, God will confirm that you don't.

"For I know that good itself does not dwell in me, that is, in my sinful nature. For I have the desire to do what is good, but I cannot carry it out" (Romans 7:18 NIV).

As you surrender control to God, remember to pray and seek Him first before making any decision, and be comforted knowing what he says in Isaiah 55:8-9 NIV: "'For my thoughts are not your thoughts, neither are your ways my ways,' declares the Lord. 'As the heavens are higher than the earth, so are my ways higher than your ways and my thoughts than your thoughts.'"

Pray about relinquishing all control to God, be assured that He knows what He is doing, and watch as the big things you seek to control become little in the hands of God.

• •

Connie Thornton, the daughter of a World War II veteran, was born in Guatemala City. She has two wonderful children and a niece, whom she loves like a daughter, and is the proud grandmother of four.

Connie began her career in the hospitality industry. After earning her Bachelor of Fine Arts and Interior Design, she worked 23 years in the residential building and interior design industry, rising to the level of Owner and President of Mila Design Group. Currently, she works in financial services helping people become financially independent.

When she was 17, Guatemala was hit with a devastating earthquake, which ignited Connie's love for volunteering. Years later, she created J and M Especially for Kids, a non-profit organization helping children from low income families achieve high grades.

Blessed with a happy spirit, a compassionate heart and exceptional family values, God has always graciously used Connie to help others.

Taking Care of My 100-year-old Mother

Connie Thornton

There are two things that I have always understood: that God is with me and that taking care of my mom was part of God's plan for my life. My mom has always been a happy and very responsible person – a wonderful daughter, sister, wife, mother, grandmother and great-grandmother. But as you will see, her life has been filled with rugged terrain and missteps – and God called me to be her courageous hiking companion. Every hiking trail is rated for difficulty – and it seems the trail that my mom and I would walk together was rated for the "experienced" hiker. Praise God that we had Him, our experienced guide, as we walked the path laid out before us.

The first real difficulty that we encountered together was the passing of my grandmother when I was 14 years old. That was the first time I had lost a loved one, and I was devastated. Some of my grandmother's final words to me were, "TAKE CARE OF YOUR MOM." As we sat together alone in her room, she warned me that she was not going to be able to make it to my 15th birthday, which was just two weeks away. Not realizing the seriousness of the situation, I told her not to worry because she was going to be with me for a long time. I was wrong. Even as we spoke, she fell on the floor, having been struck with a heart attack. My grandmother passed away as I watched in horror – her words echoing in my ears.

The pain in my heart was unbearable and attending my grand-mother's funeral was heartbreaking. My mother blamed my aunt, my sister, and me for the death of my beloved grandmother. She blamed everyone that she could. My mother has always had a strong and demanding personality. She always looks for someone to blame for everything that happens. This was so unfair to all of us, but especially to my aunt, who loved my grandmother very much and had spent all her life taking care of her. The respect, admiration and gratitude that my aunt showed was remarkable – she was a true example to me. Looking back, I know that God put my aunt in my life to teach me things that my own mother was not capable of teaching me. *Blessed are those who find wisdom, those who gain understanding, for she is more profitable than silver and yields better returns than gold.* – Proverbs 3:13-14 NIV

A few days after the funeral, I did not know how to ease my pain, so I decided to go back to the room where my grandmother had passed and I asked God that if she was with Him to please give me a sign. I needed to know, but not knowing what to expect, I just waited and waited. After a while, the curtains started to move for no reason at all. I knew that was a sign from God telling me that she was okay, that she was with him in heaven. At that moment, all my pain went away and I was at peace. *Peace I leave with you; my peace I give you. I do not give to you as the world gives. Do not let your hearts be troubled and do not be afraid.* – John 14:27 NIV

Years later, I got married and had two wonderful children, but unfortunately the marriage did not work out. After my divorce, my mother and father moved in with us. They were my support system and the best grandparents for the children. Our home was filled with love. My father was everything to me. He was my best friend and the man of the house. In his later years, he was diagnosed with emphysema, and my sister, who was a nurse, took care of him. She loved taking care of him because he was such a good patient. The emphysema took its toll and eventually the day came when he would enter the hospital for the last time. The Holy Spirit gave me the wisdom to spend time with my dad, and the Lord provided for this to happen. I was able to take a leave of absence from work and we took time with each other, talking and remembering the good times. One thing that he told me was that he was sorry to leave me alone with my mom – that he knew it was not going to be easy to deal with her temper. He also gave instructions to me: "TAKE CARE OF YOUR MOM." I told him that my sister and I were going to take care of her, that he had nothing to worry about, that he could go to heaven in peace. My father believed in God and he had asked Him for His forgiveness.

For my mom, losing my father was very hard. I stayed true to my word and was there for her. *When you make a vow to God, do not delay to fulfill it. – Ecclesiastes 5:4 NIV*

The path continued to be rocky for our family. The day of my father's funeral, my sister told me that she was feeling very sick. A few weeks later, she was diagnosed with multiple sclerosis (MS). After fighting MS for two years, my courageous sister was diagnosed with breast cancer. For the next year, my mom, my niece, the kids and I took care of her, even as we were still grieving the loss of my father. My sister lost her battle with cancer three years after my father passed away, at 42 years old. I can say that 1998 was the worst year of my life.

My family was devastated. At night, I listened as my mom screamed and blamed God for taking my sister from her at such a young age. My mom was just lost, confused, and very sad. The grieving process was long and painful. But my God was always there for me. He gave me the strength and courage that I needed to get through the hard times and be strong for the children and my mother. *Be determined and confident. Do not be afraid of them... Your God the LORD himself, will be with you; he will not fail you or abandoned you.* – Deuteronomy 31:6 GNT

As the years have progressed, we have faced more uphill trails together. My mother had a hip replacement, which was a success, but caused pain down the road. She also began losing her hearing as she grew older. After she was involved in a small accident at 90 years old, my son and I had to ask her to stop driving. God gave her a spirit of submission and blessed us with the quick sale of her car.

We also faced a long period of financial difficulties. We struggled, but somehow God always saw us through. In September 2013, I began a new job and felt as if we were finally hitting our stride.

Six months into my new job, the path turned rocky again. As my mom was visiting my aunt in Guatemala, she had a bad fall. My brother was able to go to Guatemala to stay with her that first weekend, but we quickly discovered that one weekend was not enough time, as my mom's health had started to deteriorate very quickly. She was diagnosed as having had a stroke. As a result, she didn't recognize family, and because of her disorientation, she was screaming and insulting the hospital staff. I knew I needed to go to Guatemala to be with her.

I explained the situation to my boss, but because I had been working for the company for less than a year, I was told that they couldn't hold my job for me. I decided that if that was the price I had to pay, I would pay it, because my mom was more important than my job. I arrived just in time, as the doctor had overdosed her with sedatives in an effort to calm her down, which resulted in severe symptoms including disorientation and lethargy. I brought her home and assured her that I was there just to help her get better, that she was going to get this sickness out of her body. I slept in her room and stayed with her day and night. Her physical recovery was fast, and it was remarkable that in just ten days she was her old self. She actually did not remember what happened at all.

Instead of being appreciative, however, my mother reacted in anger. She was upset with everyone and constantly complained. Among other things, she was upset that I left my job and was there with her. After all, SHE had never asked me to come. I got very upset at the time. I was simply walking the trail with her – something that God had called me to do. And it wasn't without sacrifice on my part. But God graciously helped me to understand that she just did not know how to react. Friends and family helped explain to her what had happened, expressing the fact that we had experienced a miracle in her healing. Even the doctors were surprised. She was, after all, 94 years old at the time.

I prayed to God day and night for her recovery and that I would get my job back. God granted me both miracles. Fifteen days later, I left my mom at the house with my aunt and three wonderful care-givers whom God had so clearly sent, and I went back home and was so blessed to be able to return to my job. *Before they call I will answer; while they are still speaking I will hear.* – Isaiah 65:24 NIV

Two years later, in 2016, my mother and I began the last leg of our hike together with the passing of my mom's younger sister, my Tia Mila. Tia Mila, 94 at the time, had stopped eating as her body was shutting down due to natural causes. I was cautioned by the doctors that, because of the close connection that the sisters had, this could have devastating consequences for my mother. As long as I could remember, my mom and her sister had a codependent relationship. While my mom felt responsible for her and "took care of her," she also abused and mistreated her on an emotional level. This was upsetting to me, even as a child, but I always chose to focus on and learn from the grace and forgiveness that my aunt modeled for me in their relationship.

Tia Mila, whom I loved very much, passed away on July 12, 2016 in Guatemala. During and after the funeral, my mom started to blame me and everyone else for my aunt's death. It seemed that it was her way of coping with her feelings. We all were very sad at the time, it was understandable to have crazy emotions, and everyone deals with pain differently. After a few weeks, I had to go back to work and my mom came to live with me full time. This was the time that my grandmother and my father warned me about.

When we arrived back in Florida, my mother and I struggled to find our new routine. She was not doing well emotionally, and we were both grieving. As we continued to walk the path that God put before us, I kept thinking about how my mom had emotionally abused my aunt all her life and I began to get very upset at her. I prayed to God to help me with those negative feelings and to take those thoughts away that I knew weren't healthy. But even as I prayed, my mom began insulting and treating me like she had treated my aunt.

God, our Guide who never fails us, gave me wisdom and courage to take the steps I needed to take. I first hired a caregiver to stay with my mom while I went to work, but that did not work out very well. Not discouraged, I next decided to take my mom every morning to a senior daycare center on my way to work. That was great – for a few weeks. Then my mom started to give me excuses for not wanting to go. There were days she just would not get in the car – it was not easy. Sometimes I had to take her to work with me, go to a meeting, and then go back to drop her off at the senior daycare center.

Next, I decided to try a rotation: three days at the senior daycare and two days with a caregiver at home. After a few months of this schedule, she was not happy, and I was very tired all the time. I had no days off and I was spending a lot of money for a solution that didn't seem to be working. And deep in my spirit, I felt that I should be the one taking care of her – but that was impossible with my job.

I continued to ask God for help because I really did not have the answer. I knew that this trail was impossible to walk without His help.

I started making changes, beginning with having a heart-to-heart conversation with my mom. It was not easy, but it had to happen, and God gave me the courage. She had to understand that I was not my aunt, and that I was not going to allow her to abuse me or disrespect me like she had abused and disrespected her. I was not sure why she was behaving like that toward me, but it had to change, because with her abusive attitude, I wasn't going to be able to take care of her. I also told her that she had to stop blaming God for the deaths of our family members.

She apologized to me and, to my surprise, she never abused or disrespected me again.

A few months later, I was let go from my job. I was so happy that I told my boss, "Thank you very much." I knew that God had a plan for me. I was not sure what it was, but I just trusted Him.

By the grace of God, I was able to manage everything.

Four years later, I continue to take care of my mom. She now goes to the senior daycare only when she wants, and we travel and visit family and friends together. I get some time off, the bills get paid, and my mom gets the best care that I can provide for her. My daughter and the boys visit often; friends come over for lunch and dinner. My niece and her family are living with us now and they have a wonderful four-year-old son we enjoy every day. My son and brother visit sometimes and sometimes we go and spend time at their homes. Everyone helps as much as they can.

I've learned that age is just a number. Physically, she is a 100-year-old person, and despite the fact that she has to deal with pain in her body all the time and the changes of getting old, her mind is as sharp as you can expect. Her mind travels faster than her body can. She was always a very independent woman and just cannot be independent anymore. "If I could just walk, I would help you clean," she says. "I would go to work and help you."

My mother is a remarkable woman. She is always ready to go and is a person to be admired. She has a deep love for life, and always tells you that she has a lot more to give and to do. God has given her this life and she plans to live it to the fullest.

Throughout this journey, I have learned that when you are a caregiver, it is difficult to not lose yourself. The one you care for depends on you for everything, just like a baby, but with the mind of an adult who has his or her own ideas. It is important to keep the balance. This is not an easy path, but it has to be done. Scripture tells us to "honor your father and mother" (Exodus 20:12) – and His Spirit within us will tell us the same.

My mother and I began this hike together. First, she carried me in her arms when I was a child, then we walked with each other, and now I do a lot of the carrying as I help her with her final footsteps. But all along, it has been God who has guided our path, who has helped us climb those steep rocks, and who has given us the glorious views along the way. Holding close to Him has allowed me to make the climb. I have always held to the first chapter of Luke, when the disciples asked Jesus how they should pray. There have been times when I did not even know how to pray – but I always knew the words that Jesus taught. And those words have helped me scale the mountain!

Our Father, who art in heaven,

Hallowed be Thy name, Thy kingdom come; Thy will be done on earth as it is in heaven.

Give us this day our daily bread, and forgive us our trespasses as we forgive those who trespass against us; and lead us not into temptation, but deliver us from evil.

(Luke 11:2-4)

Courage to Overcome Abuse

Julie Jenkins

God loves you and He never intended for you to be abused. The world, as God created it, was good. Perfect. But when man began to sin, that perfection was thrown into disarray. The very ground was cursed, and individuals were set against each other. The resulting abuse of one individual toward another is a sin which only the devil takes joy in.

So what do we do when we encounter abuse in our lives? The answer can be confusing, because in the Bible God speaks of love and forgiveness and turning the other cheek. But let me say it again: God does not want you to be abused! As a Christian woman, when faced with abuse you are called to stand strong in the Spirit with wisdom and steadfast love.

The first thing to know is that love is patient and kind (1 Cor 13:4), and if the "love" directed at you is anything other than patient and kind, it is corrupted by sin. Second, know that this corruption of love doesn't surprise God. We are told in 2 Timothy, *There will be terrible times in the last days. People will be...abusive... Have nothing to do with them* (3:1-2,5).

Standing strong in the Spirit with wisdom and steadfast love includes asking God what He wants you to learn in the situation. Please don't misunderstand, abuse is NOT the fault of the abused, but God can use all things to teach us and to bring us closer to Him. James 1:19-20 NIV teaches us, *Everyone should be quick to listen, slow to speak and slow to become angry, because human anger does not bring about the righteousness that God desires.* Notice that it says to be slow to speak and slow to become angry – we are not instructed to be silent and complacent, but rather kind: *Do not answer a fool according to his folly, or you will be like him yourself* (Proverbs 26:4 NIV).

Standing strong in the Spirit with wisdom and steadfast love includes knowing when to walk away and to seek help – from your church (Matthew 18:15-17) or from law enforcement if appropriate (Romans 13:1).

Standing strong in wisdom includes praying and taking refuge in God.

The Lord is a stronghold for the oppressed, a stronghold in the time of trouble. (Psalm 9:9)

He heals the brokenhearted and binds up their wounds. (Psalm 147:3)

The prayer of a righteous man is powerful and effective. (James 5:16)

It is not our place to judge others, but it is our responsibility to protect ourselves – God's holy temple. If you are being abused, please go to God first, go to a trusted pastor or Christian friend second – enlisting the help of local authorities when necessary – and stand strong in the presence of the Spirit of God with wisdom and steadfast love as you walk away.

. . . .

Michelle Lieberman Is the mother of three grown children and two teenage daughters, the mother-in-law of two, and a grandmother to her one-year-old granddaughter.

She was born and raised in a suburb of Cleveland, Ohio where she now lives with her husband and two teen daughters.

Michelle has worked in the medical field for a large healthcare system in Cleveland for the last twenty-five years in various nursing departments. Currently she is working in pain management in medical insurance utilization management and medical review.

She is an advocate for mental health awareness, specifically that of women's mood disorders.

She loves spending time in prayer and meditation, as well as reading and studying scripture.

Her other passion is spending time with her family, including weekly Sunday dinners together.

She is excited to pursue her next endeavor in the future, which is to write childrens' spiritually-based books.

Having the Courage
to Change
Michelle Lieberman

Each new day is a gift and fresh start. I cannot proceed without coming to you, Lord, and asking you to take it all on you! I am helpless without you! Only by your love and grace can I get through each day! I need you and I know I need to show you my love and honor every day. I love you and I know you will take care of every single worry. Faith is your gift to us.

When we pray, we don't physically hear God talk to us, but by our faith we know He is there and showing us Himself and His love. <u>That is faith!</u> You just know it that much and that strong! Faith has to be that strong in <u>all</u> circumstances.

I wrote the above paragraphs six years ago on an index card. I read it multiple times a day for months. At the time I was going through one of the most difficult times of my life. During my adult life, I've had episodes of major depression that were debilitating. With two of these episodes, I was hospitalized for two weeks, just as my mother had been, and her mother before her. Unfortunately, this is a condition that runs in my family.

Throughout my life, my actions and poor choices during these episodes caused people I loved so much pain. If I was the cause of their pain, I reasoned, I should not be allowed to ever be happy, even though these episodes were not really the results of my choices. Some were situational episodes and other were physiological. My episodes of postpartum depression were mainly caused by huge hormonal fluctuations after giving birth. I also had other risk factors for depression, like my family history. What hindered me was that I was so immature in my relationship with God that I didn't realize I could courageously come to Him, even in these times of affliction.

My mother was Catholic, and my father was Protestant. My mother took my siblings and me to church. I remember many times seeing her kneeling by her bed to pray before she went to sleep. My grandmother taught me well-known prayers such as the "Our Father" and the "Hail Mary". My mother did a good job at making religion a part of our lives.

When I was around eight years old, my family was introduced to a different type of worship by my sister. I am so thankful for her. She was a born-again Christian, having given her life to Christ, which brought the opportunity to me to begin learning things in a different manner. We began attending a Baptist church. This is where I began to learn about the Bible and its stories, how to communicate with God through my own prayers, and how to receive Jesus into my heart.

My father gradually began attending church with us and fully enjoyed church services. He was learning also. Earlier in his life, he was a hard-working man with vices of drinking and heavy smoking. He eventually gave his life to God in his mid-fifties. This was life-changing for him. He had an extremely strong faith and love for the Trinity. He didn't just read the Bible, he studied it. He memorized verses. He prayed in supplication.

My first bouts of major depression occurred after the births of both my first and second children. After my oldest child was born, I had a case of depression that was more severe than the least severe form of postpartum depression known as the "baby blues," but thankfully, it was not long-lasting. I prayed for relief, but not in fervent prayer. I know my family prayed. I began to feel better a few weeks after the episode started, thankfully.

The second episode was worse than the one before, which caught me off guard because I didn't know I was at high risk of recurrence with my second child. After my daughter's birth, I was doing so well for months – I thought I was in the clear. Thirty years ago, depression wasn't really talked about, therefore, no one knew that I could be affected again. To this day, psychiatry is the least studied of all the body systems. Four months went by when I started to feel peculiar, but not enough to concern me at that time. Day by day it gradually worsened, hitting me hard and lasting close to a year and a half. With this episode, I began having obsessive thoughts and feeling despair. I could not stop my obsessive thoughts no matter what I tried.

My family always knew what was going on in my head just by the blank, flat look on my face. Lack of concentration was a big problem because I could not stay focused. Somehow, I managed to work during this episode, but it took everything in me. At least I thought it was me getting myself to stay on task. I didn't know enough to understand that I had this wondrous, faithful, loving Creator of everything and anything there is everywhere. That was another aspect of my episodes – before I had full and total understanding of what this was, I didn't let the Lord have it all. I would pray about it and read some comforting Bible verses, but that was the extent of it. Family members prayed for me all the time. I, however, did not pray or make my requests in total supplication. There was no way I could ever ask for help. God is the ultimate being of the greatest magnitude. I was this little speck of life-form on earth. There were so many other bigger problems that people from all walks of life had. In my fleshly mind, I thought that I could not go to God because I didn't deserve His help in any of my concerning matters. Of course, I would pray for other people, but that was about them and not me, so it was the right thing to do.

I started looking for ways to distract myself, thinking that if I was distracted enough, I would not be thinking the troubling thoughts but instead would experience relief. That false relief can come in many forms, which helped my depression, but did so much damage to my marriage. I am unable to go into the details in this chapter but suffice it to say that my marriage ended. I caused so much pain to the people who loved me the most. God was still with me, but I wasn't letting Him heal me. I tried on my own to fix it all in ways that wasted precious time and energy. My life was not settled for several years.

All praise to God, I did remarry, leaving behind that hurtful period. Later, however, the depression would resurface.

When my father was 81, he was diagnosed with mesothelioma, a form of terminal cancer. He was not a candidate for surgery and only minimal amounts of chemotherapy drugs could be used in his treatment due to his age and condition at that time. In a matter of nine months he got weaker and sicker every day. He went from an otherwise healthy 190-pound man to 106 pounds at the time of his death. During that time, we knew that although he may have been scared, he brought his fear to the Lord. We later found pages of Bible verses he had written down and read that were comforting to him while he was getting sicker. We know he died knowing he was going to Heaven and would be embraced by our Heavenly Father. He rested assured that all of God's promises would be kept. He knew he had been forgiven for his past transgressions. He would never be alone because he knew that he lived with the Holy Spirit. It was harder for us watching him painfully slip away. He was a great, strong, faithful man of God.

When he passed away, his death hit me so hard that I barely functioned. I did the minimum home duties. I would cry and go to sleep. My children watched me cry just as I had watched my mother cry during her episodes of major depression 40 years earlier. The only thing that mattered was that my father died. He had wonderful individual relationships and bonds with each of us kids. I felt mine was extra special because I was born on his birthday. He always said that I was his best birthday present ever. There would be no more birthday celebrations together, no advice or guidance. No more of a human father's love and devotion to his children. Only memories were left.

Months went by. My marriage was affected because I had barely any interaction with my husband. I didn't feel like being a good wife. I was selfish and only thought of myself. I was able to care for my children because they were so young and I knew they needed me, though what they got of me was not my best. I was consumed with sadness. My husband began thinking I did not love him anymore. Looking back, I could not blame him. Our interactions mainly consisted of hello and goodbye. He tried to make me happy, to cheer me up and make me laugh. He loved me and he wanted me to feel better. That didn't matter. Two years had come and gone. Our marriage had deteriorated. We were living separate lives. We also worked opposite night shifts and weekends so childcare never had to be a concern. That in itself caused problems in our marriage. The weak spots in our bond became huge gaps. By no coincidence, the enemy used this opportunity to do even more damage in different ways. That's what he does. Our marriage was dead.

In all this time, I did not take advantage of the personal relationship I had with the Holy Spirit because I ignored Him too. The Holy Spirit grieved due to the broken bond I caused between Him and me. There were nights I would go to my bedroom with thoughts of hating my life. I was definitely not suicidal. I just hated my life.

There was a day that came when I realized that I did not want to be apart from my husband. I loved him too much. I loved what we had even though there were issues. I told him how I felt. He reluctantly agreed to try to save our marriage. He didn't think things would be better – that it was too late to try. I began to become aware of the presence of the Holy Spirit even though He had never ever left me. He was always there, but I chose to not acknowledge Him. He always gives us the freedom to choose. He is saddened so much when we choose to not go to Him. Although a human father would be saddened by a severed relationship with his child, the magnitude of grief caused by our separation from God, our Heavenly Father, is so much greater.

It was so natural to feel afraid. We are born with our fleshly brains which are limited in so many ways. We want to know there will not be a sad ending. We'll do anything to avoid emotional pain. Putting our faith in God seems like too much work and not reliable. I forget that God sees all things. I was only able to see things from my small vantage point. God already has seen and known the other side of things even before any of us we were born.

> *"For you created my inmost being; you knit me together in my mother's womb." – Psalm 139:13 NIV*

Shortly after this time of beginning to reconcile, there was a day that I went to the cemetery to visit my father's grave. I was desperately seeking a sign from God. I stood there and what I felt in my soul was a voice telling me to get my life together. It was God. He was telling me to stop the sadness and start fixing my life. From that day, I fought hard for my marriage. I was terrified of failure and more sadness consuming me.

My anxiety levels were over the top. I would wake up each morning and the mind-chatter would start. For a split second upon waking, I felt normal and happy. Then it all came flooding back to me: the feeling of dread, anxiety, fear and immense sadness. Physically, it was something I could feel in the pit of my stomach. It was unsettling. I was grinding my teeth during my sleep. I was experiencing abdominal pain. My intestines felt like they were in one big knot. I wore a mouthguard for my teeth, and I took medication for the pain, which helped somewhat. My body was in self-preservation mode. Anxious thoughts were always there. They created a cycle of horrible feelings that nothing could seem to break except for my favorite go-to: sleep. Sleep was my one escape, if I could shut my mind off long enough to even get to sleep.

Why was I trying to manage all of these things on my own? I would talk to friends, which helped during the time of the actual conversations. When the conversation ended, however, the cycle started up again, ruminating and obsessing over things I had no control over.

That is when I wrote those words on my little index card. I could not fix any of the brokenness on my own. I had to submit to Him with complete faith and trust. He helped me to remember that He wanted me to come to Him with anything. This was the beginning of a new start. God brought a dead marriage back to life and made it better and stronger than before.

God has a plan for each of our lives. We want to know and understand it, but we don't always get to. Our miniscule minds are not even remotely able to comprehend God's plan for us.

"For my thoughts are not your thoughts, nor are your ways my ways," says the Lord." Isaiah 55:8-9 NKJV

It wasn't until I had a full understanding of God's love that I found peace in my life. I had to stop being afraid and have the courage to let go of the hard things so the Trinity could do all its work in my life. Until that happened, I would not let myself be forgiven, nor would I forgive others who had hurt me.

The devil began to attack me with a fear of aging and death. I hated the fear. Although I knew that upon physical death, the Christian's soul rises to heaven to be with God forever so I did not need to fear death, that knowledge alone did not calm me. My thoughts would race – I knew I was going to Heaven...or was I? Uncertainty became the new obsession. But God continued to reach out to me.

"Peace I leave with you; my peace I give you to you. I do not give to you as the worlds gives. Do not let your heart be troubled and do not be afraid." – John 14:27 NIV

I began listening to Joyce Meyer broadcasts, reading her books and daily devotionals. Through her teaching, I was finally able to comprehend God's love. This sparked such a passion and interest in me that I wanted to learn more, read more, study more of the Word. I had never had the desire to read the Bible in an effective way. Now I did. I finally had the powerful connection that would free me from everything that had hold of me. It was then that I fell in love with the Lord. I was taught that He wants us to come to Him so badly. There is no prayer or request that is too big or too small. He is God! God is love, the truest, deepest kind of love. He will never leave us to fend for ourselves. All we have to do is go to Him. That's it! It is something so complex but yet so simple. He makes it simple because of His love for us. When He sent his Son to save us, He made it perfect. It does not even make sense to not want something this wonderful in your life. Everyone needs to know this kind of love before any more time is wasted. I thank God endlessly for bringing Joyce Meyer into my life to be a vessel to me. There are more vessels out there for us. Another person I admire is Hannah Keeley. I also have been blessed to be reconnected with a childhood friend from 35 years ago. Nothing is a coincidence with God. Because of my loving friend Kimberly Hobbs, I was introduced to Women World Leaders.

As long as we're physically alive on this earth, there are always going to be difficult times and things we have to go through. There will be sadness and pain. I am not sure what else God is preparing me for. I do know that I have the courage to face anything because I am now armed with faith like never before. I am still a work in progress, but I am in the best place spiritually that I ever have been, and I love it.

In addition to all this, take up the shield of faith, with which you can extinguish all the flaming arrows of the evil one. — Ephesians 6:16 NIV

Courage to Overcome Guilt

Julie Jenkins

I drove my car out of the driveway and looked at the sun shining from behind a beautiful white cloud – it was the first time I truly understood the words "silver lining." I marveled at the sight through my side window as the perfectly filtered morning light created a heavenly aura. And then I turned the corner – and all I could see as that beautiful light came in through my front window was a very dirty windshield.

As we learn more and more about the perfect nature of God and see His beauty more clearly, His perfection shines a bright light on our own filth. The dichotomy is striking. And emotions arise as we become aware of the darkness of our own sin.

The devil, in his never-ending attempt to derail us, will tempt us with feelings of guilt and shame.

But through the maturity we gain in our Christian walk, God shows us the darkness of our sin, not so that we will experience paralyzing guilt, but so that we will recognize the impossibility of overcoming the sin on our own and turn from that sin to Him in full dependence on His ability to cleanse us. Through this process, we get a glimpse of the heavenly aura as we witness God's glorious redemption in our own lives.

God promises over and over in Scripture that He is a God of love, forgiveness, and grace.

I – yes, I alone – will blot out your sins for my own sake and will never think of them again. -Isaiah 43:25 NLT

So now there is no condemnation for those who belong to Christ Jesus. Romans 8:1 NLT

If we confess our sins, he is faithful and just to forgive us our sins and to cleanse us from all unrighteousness. – 1 John 1:9 ESV

I will cleanse them of their sins against me and forgive all their sins of rebellion. – Jeremiah 33:8 NLT

And I will forgive their wickedness, and I will never again remember their sins. – Hebrews 8:12 NLT

Not only does God promise to clean our windshield, He forgets that it was ever dirty in the first place! Do you see how giving your sin to God for forgiveness allows you the joy of seeing His beauty and love?! Satan leads our flesh to sin and then attempts to crucify us with guilt. BUT GOD takes our sin, gently washes it away, and leaves us a glorious view of Himself. Now THAT is a silver lining we can shout about! Let us praise God by telling the devil, *You intended to harm me, but God intended it for good* (Genesis 50:20 NIV).

· ·

Jessica Morneault is Photographer located in Palm Beach Gardens, FL. She volunteers at the Women World Leaders meetings throughout the year and at special events. She has grown to love this group of ladies and has been inspired by their faith, willingness to grow and help others. Jessica is currently serving on the Board of Love's Calling International Inc. – a Non-Profit Christian fundraising organization for youth who are called to missions. She has a heart of compassion and wants to encourage women to live with purpose and to seek out peace over their past. It is also her desire to reach others for Christ by sharing her story. Jessica is a wife, mother to her son and two step-daughters.

Getting to a Place of Peace
Jessica Morneault

I was born in New Jersey and moved to Florida in the first year
of my life. I am the youngest of three children and was a little
surprise that came 13 years after my brother, the middle child. My
childhood memories in our home were very happy. My parents
spoiled me since I was the baby and gave me a lot of love and
attention. Although there was a large age gap between me and my
siblings, we all had a close relationship. I remember my mother
and father took me everywhere, so I was mostly in the presence
of adults. My times with other children were few. That resulted in
me feeling pretty awkward when I started school. I couldn't relate
to kids my age and kept to myself. I was picked on in elementary
school because I was shy, mostly by girls who could be quite mean.
Early on, most of my friends were boys for that same reason. By
the time I was eight years old, I met two girls who were sisters
that lived in my neighborhood. They invited me to church, where
I learned about God, memorized verses and got involved in the
youth group. Later I joined the choir. Prior to that, the only time
I remembered attending church was when I went to a Catholic
church a couple of times while I was visiting my grandmother.
So this time with my new friends was really my first introduction
to God. I was blessed to attend church with them until I was 18
years old and to accept Christ as my Savior when I was twelve. I

will share later how my inner dialogue as a child shaped who I became.

Like many teenagers, I found myself attending church less and less as the years went by. I had my own agenda and it didn't necessarily line up with what God intended for me. I dated a lot during those years and found myself jumping from relationship to relationship. I had some really great guys in my life, but somehow I would find myself feeing unfulfilled. In my twenties, I found someone I was head-over-heels for. I was truly in love and he was crazy about me! We had some wonderful times, but went through some struggles together as well. In 1992, we were living in Miami when Hurricane Andrew hit. We lost our home and were forced to live in a hotel for six months after that. "Steve" had some personal things going on with his side of the family around the same time. I didn't realize it then, but he actually was going through a period of depression. Being young, I was not familiar with depression. He became withdrawn, and I perceived that behavior as a lack of interest, which made me question if he still even loved me anymore. In my own insecurity, I decided it was best for me to move on. Almost immediately, I regretted my decision and was disappointed in myself for making that decision, but there was no going back. It was over. I started to analyze why my relationships were not working out. After taking a hard look at this pattern of mine, which I now call relationship sabotage, I determined that each time I was not getting the right amount of attention or feeling loved, I walked away. I was also afraid to be alone. Upon introspection, there were several times when I had hurt many people – including families of those I loved and my own family. As I approached 25 years old, I had a light-bulb moment. I began to realize that because I had received so much love and attention from my family as a child, I set those same expectations for anyone who entered my life as an adult. I was always looking for someone to fill me up.

Having this new understanding, I intended to approach life differently going forward. My next relationship was with a man who was very charming and funny. His job allowed us to attend a lot of events. Every other night I was out somewhere new. I was desperate to get over the most recent breakup and I thought that keeping busy would help me move past it. I could see the new man in my life thrived on having a good time, which often led him to drink in excess. Time showed me that he would become a different person when he drank. He would belittle me, curse at me, and publicly embarrass me. Being down on myself, I was convinced that the treatment I was getting was what I deserved for all the past hurts that I had caused. Slowly, after about six months, I finally started to regain my self-respect. I tried to end the relationship, but he begged me to stay and promised me that he would stop drinking. He was very convincing, and I thought maybe there was hope that he would keep his promise. I agreed to give our relationship another try and the drinking ceased almost immediately.

Over the next year, the man I placed my hope in began quitting jobs for no apparent reason. His reasoning was that he either didn't like the job, didn't like a co-worker, or didn't like the boss. He would quit from one day to the next. Since we were living together, I found myself scrambling to pay the bills and stay above water financially. I wasn't sleeping, and the feeling of insecurity was overwhelming. Suddenly, there was a new twist. Because I had not been feeling well physically, I went to the doctor and found out I was pregnant. This was a surprise, to say the least! Years earlier, I had been diagnosed with medical issues and told that I would need to go through fertility treatments when I was ready to have a baby. The man in my life was thrilled with the news and said that he was going to make the necessary changes to make this relationship work. He was employed consistently over the next nine months, and then my son was born.

We had gotten engaged by this time and I decided that I wanted to stay home with our child. I was able to do this until he was three years old. At that point, we finally married and I started working part-time again. Unfortunately, history started to repeat itself. My husband started to be in and out of jobs once again. He also started taking pills for anxiety, which seemed to take the place of the drinking that had occurred in years past. He took much more medication than he was prescribed and he was always trying to get more. I could see it was a problem. I knew we were just a couple of months away from not being able to pay the mortgage and I was doing all I could to hold on to my credit. I convinced him to sell the house, and it sold in four days.

During this same time my father had lost an ongoing battle with cancer, which was so heartbreaking. My mother was in the process of moving to Titusville, Florida and she asked us to go with her. I thought this could be a fresh start for all of us. We could keep my mom company and we looked forward to buying a house in the surrounding area a few months later. A week after my father passed away we moved to the new location. Only a couple of days had passed when we got the word that my sister was diagnosed with breast cancer. My world was spinning and I just wanted it all to stop! My sister was close by, so my mother and I were able to spend time with her. My husband had mentioned that he wanted to visit his family up north so he took a trip to see them. After about two weeks, I opened my bank account online to pay some bills, and I could not believe my eyes. Five hundred dollars a day was being withdrawn. I rushed to the phone and called my husband. He admitted that he had been gambling. I was understandably angry and threatened to close the account. He apologized, said he had been feeling depressed, and had been gambling to escape. He assured me he was done, but this was far from the truth. The next day he took out a cashier's check from our account for twenty thousand dollars! He had taken more than thirty thousand dollars in all, which was most of the proceeds from our house sale. I reached out to him and told him not to bother ever coming back.

My husband refused to accept this rejection from me and returned to Florida. He cried, pleaded and made me feel guilty for wanting a divorce. He told me that I would be the reason my son had divorced parents. He promised to make things right. Within a couple of days he was off to a job interview in Boca Raton, Florida. He got the position and said he was putting a down payment on an apartment. My brother was just moving to Titusville and agreed to stay with my mother as I ventured back down south. I arrived in Boca with my son and found a job quickly. A short two weeks later my husband quit his job yet again. I was physically sick at that point. I thought, *If I lose my health, I will no longer be able to care for my son.* Certainly, I could do a better job on my own. My son, seven years old by then, had been sick with a cold, so he stayed home from school with his dad. I went to the office but called my husband soon after I arrived. I told him it was over 100% and said we would discuss the details later. At the end of the day I finished up at work and went home. I entered the apartment and it was quiet, too quiet. I walked into my son's room, where I noticed the closet was wide open. I could see it was empty; all his clothes were gone. I felt sick. I checked his drawers, but they were empty as well. I proceeded down the hallway. There was empty space on the walls where all the pictures of my son once hung. My heart sank and I felt desperate. I ran to the phone and immediately called the police to file a missing person's report. He had taken my child!

I had to take the courageous step of faith as I decided to do whatever it took to get my son back. I had hit rock bottom, and even though I couldn't see it then, God was still there. I urge you to take a courageous step of faith BEFORE you ever get to this point to save yourself from heartache.

The next day I hired an attorney who then hired a private investigator. One day started to run into the next as I couldn't sleep. I remember selling my jewelry and furniture to pay legal fees and to survive. I lived on ramen noodles and slowly parted with everything I owned, even my bed. Only a couch remained. I was at my ultimate low and thought I would never stop crying. I was devastated and no one could help me or console me, but I would never give up.

I started to walk each day as I was trying to process everything. I knew it had been a long time, but I found myself seeking out God and I began to pray. I asked for forgiveness for the way I had lived my life, for those I hurt, and for distancing Him as my Savior. Day after day I talked to Jesus. I was really alone for the first time in my life and He was all I had. Down deep inside I knew He was always there and that He was just waiting on me. I had been trying to fill myself up through other people since I was a child and through most of my adult life. It was finally crystal clear to me that God was the only one that could fill me up. I remember taking courage to step out in faith and released everything to him. At that moment, the words "It is well with my soul" came quickly to my mind. I was out of money, and I didn't know how things were going to pull together, but I had faith. I knew in my heart that was enough.

It took two and a half months and a court order before my son was returned to me. When I saw his face, it was the most precious thing I had ever seen. I slept in his bed the first two nights.

We were back together and I held on to him like never before. I imagined how traumatic this must have been for him and praised God for carrying us through all this. I reflected on how painful it was and how I finally had gotten to a place of peace. I had never thought for a moment that I wouldn't see my son again.

After a couple of years my life finally settled down. I remarried in 2007 to my husband Bob – my love and my best friend who accepts me for who I am. We started attending church regularly as a family and about six months later my husband and son were baptized in the ocean. It was beautiful! My son is now 23 years old and is an amazing gift. We have an extremely close relationship, probably closer than most. God has taught me so much during these periods of my life. I even forgave my ex-husband many years ago. The Bible says in John 16:33, we all will face many hurts and trials on this earth. It can feel unbearable at times. God does not promise to remove those things, but he does promise to carry you through them.

You may be living through something that I can't even imagine. I want to encourage you that if you don't know the love of God and are trying to manage on your own, there is another option. You do not have to go through your troubles alone. He heals the broken-hearted and binds their wounds (Psalm 147:3 NIV). God sent his only son to take on the sin of the world and Jesus died on the cross taking on this burden. The Bible says that if anyone believes in Him, they shall not perish but will have everlasting life (John 3:16). If you pray and ask for forgiveness, He will wash your sin away and be there for you as a father is for their child. None of us have lived perfect lives, but we are forgiven and we are loved. The eternal God is your refuge, and underneath are the everlasting arms (Deuteronomy 33:27 NIV).

Father God, I thank you for how you have moved in my life, for your provision, guidance and the strength you gave me to walk courageously. I pray that the person reading this would take the steps to walk courageously and allow you to be their strength. May they understand that this life is only temporary, that we will one day be reunited with you in heaven in complete serenity. Amen!

Courage to Overcome Desperation

Julie Jenkins

Living in desperation is living in a situation so bad that it feels impossible to deal with. I pray that you are not there, but if you are, I have a word for you: HOPE! Hope isn't just a word that we as Christians write on the front of Christmas cards; hope is the truth we live. Hope is Jesus.

While we were but sinners, Jesus came into the world to set us free. You've heard it said that when one door closes, another opens. I can go one step further – Jesus is the door to hope, and that door will never close.

The English version of the word hope means a feeling of expectation, or a desire for something to happen. But hope in the Bible is quite different.

In the Old Testament the word yāhal is used in places like Psalm 31:24, *Be strong and take heart, all you who hope (yāhal) in the Lord.* This word goes far beyond the meaning of desiring that something should happen, but instead means waiting with expectant anticipation for something that will happen. Have you ever been in a situation where you couldn't sleep at night because you were just so excited about what was going to happen the next day? The energy coursing through you was almost palpable – you *knew* something exciting was around the corner. That is the kind of hope that the Bible speaks of when we hope in the Lord – it is a confident expectation of something on the way; we just have to be patient. *But hope that is seen is no hope at all. Who hopes for what they already have? But if we hope for what we do not yet have, we wait for it patiently* (Romans 8:24-25 NIV).

As Christians, what are we hoping for? What are we confidently expecting? The Bible tells us that we can count on God's unfailing love (Psalm 147:11), joy (Proverbs 10:28), strength (Isaiah 40:31), an inheritance in heaven (1 Peter 1:3-5), power (Ephesians 1:19), endurance (1 Thessalonians 1:3), and eternal life (Galatians 6:8). The list goes on and on. When you are feeling at your end, search the word 'hope' in your Bible and just bask in the glory of all that God has promised is waiting for you!

We don't have to live in desperation; we can live confidently in the hope of our Lord Jesus Christ! *Let us hold unswervingly to the hope we profess, for he who promised is faithful* (Hebrews 10:23 NIV).

Amen and amen!

• •

Traci Brown has a passion to see broken and hurting people healed and renewed. Her heart is to use her life's struggles to encourage others in their faith. She desires more of God, sharing His love wherever she may go.

Traci loves to cook, garden and being with her family whenever she gets the chance.

She married her high school sweetheart, Grady Brown, in 1990. God blessed them with two children, Brittany Joy and Tannie. Brittany went to be with the Lord in 1999, but her story is a testimony of God's love.

Traci and Grady currently serve together at their church in Mathews, VA, where Grady is the Worship Pastor. Traci sings and plays drums alongside him on the Worship Team. They are the founders of Britjoy Ministries. Through this ministry, they spread the love of Christ through music and His Word.

Living Above Dystonia and Fear
Traci Brown

"What do you mean I have dystonia?" Finally, this thing I'd been living with had a name.

What seemed like a lifetime before this, when I was in my early twenties and after years of dealing with uncooperative muscles, a neurologist had tested me and concluded that my symptoms were all in my head – that I was just imagining them. I felt so alone. Why would I possibly make up something that led to such fear and embarrassment? Nonetheless, the doctor prescribed me medicine to help my nerves, but it just made things worse. After a while, I stopped taking the medicine and went on with my life, praying and hoping the affliction that had ruled my life would go away eventually.

I first noticed my symptoms when I was in the fifth grade. Without any conscious signal from my brain, my arm would curl under and pull into my torso. It had a mind of its own. At just ten years old, I had no control over my body. If I got up too quickly, my arm would twitch and draw in. A spasm would ripple through my bicep. And it wasn't just my arm that was affected. At times my leg jerked, and I couldn't walk correctly. Or my face became distorted as if I was suffering a stroke. Sometimes I'd awaken with bruises that had seemingly appeared in the middle of the night. There were times when both sides of my body would jerk and spasm.

There were some warning signs that I began to notice before a "spell" would come on. I would get a sensation in my toes which would warn me to stop and wait for the symptoms to pass. I learned to clench my toes and move my feet front to back to keep the spell from coming on. Sitting down and waiting for the spell to pass or grabbing my arm to keep it from involuntarily moving were some of the preventative methods I developed to handle each episode. It was a constant battle. Most of the time, the spell would still come on. And I would beg God to make them stop.

My disability became my obsession. I constantly worried every second of every day.

In my mid-forties, I was able to receive treatment, finally. But before the diagnosis, I was walking in a state of confusion and trying to figure out where I fit it. I feared so many things. I wanted to be part of different activities, but the fear of a spell would always haunt me. I didn't have many friends because I stayed to myself. The fear of what others thought of me and this disability scared me to the core. I didn't know how anyone would act or how they'd treat me once they knew. At times, I'd even cry myself to sleep. Why did I have to deal with this? Maybe I should have had more trust in people.

There were many times when I longed to participate in different activities, but dystonia halted my ambition. On one occasion, I signed up to compete in the Miss Phoebus Pageant. At the first meeting, I stood up when my name was called, and a spell immediately took over. Feeling embarrassed, I ran out of the building, abandoning that dream. From then on, I was afraid to go in front of people and would avoid any activity that required me to do so.

As a senior in high school, I was to receive the distinguished Office Services of the Year Award. It was an honor. But my joy was dampened because I was concerned about accepting the award, knowing in my heart that I could not walk across a stage. As I prepared for the ceremony, thoughts of my past experiences continued to surface, and I was gripped by anxiety. The night of the event, Grady—my boyfriend at the time, now my husband—worked to keep me calm.

"And the award goes to Traci Walker." Nervousness forced me up too quickly. On stage, I accepted the award, and almost immediately shaking consumed my whole being. My arms swung wildly, and my legs didn't cooperate. I ended up walking into the curtain. Grady ran up and ushered me outside.

I was devastated and cried, unable to bear what people must be saying.

My parents and siblings were there to see me receive the award. My eight-year-old brother, Trevor, said to my parents, "Traci is the worst break dancer I've ever seen!" He had no idea what was going on. In a few short years he, too, would begin to see the signs of the disease in his body. "Why didn't you tell us you had this?" my parents said. They never knew what I had been dealing with.

They recognized the symptoms as those my father battled with. He too never told anyone until he was married. I always feared what people thought of me. I was laughed at so much as a child, I did not need another thing to prompt my peers to make fun of me. So I kept it to myself. Grady – and now my family – were the only ones who knew.

Unlike most high school seniors, I dreaded graduation. Walking across the stage to receive my diploma wasn't worth the anxiety. My government teacher knew I was scared, and when graduation day came, he was there for me. As I made my way across the stage, he walked behind a row of teachers, calling out, "You can do this!"

I received more than my diploma that day. I stepped off the stage full of pride and confidence. I could do anything! I had not let fear hold me back. God used my teacher to encourage and stretch me.

No matter what I went through or how I got through each moment of fear with the dystonia, I would still move on to the next thing and be worried and scared of the outcome. My life was a constant battle of what was to come. When it was time to walk down the aisle at my wedding, I again let fear grip me. My dad was by my side, yet I still let it consume me. Why did I let fear and worry of this and how others will react rule my life? I knew I should be living my life for the Lord and enjoying it, yet I let fear of people and the fear of my disability overtake my mind.

At twenty-one and married, I was ready to get my driver's license. Grady wanted me to take a driver's class because of the dystonia. No problems arose during the lessons. But during the actual driving test, my muscles refused to comply. I couldn't hide it.

"You handled yourself well," the instructor said. I was so excited! I passed and could now drive my very own car.

Even after I successfully passed my drivers' test, fear still gripped me when I got behind the wheel, especially when several cars seemed to crowd around my vehicle. The high speeds and busy roads gave me terrible anxiety. Bridges were the hardest for me. To focus myself, I'd blare Christian music and repeat "Jesus, Jesus, Jesus" until I got to the other side. It became a ritual. That was the only way I could do it. Calling on Jesus always helped calm my anxiety and gave me the power to work through a situation that I otherwise would not have been able to.

> *Joshua 1:9 NIV says, "Be strong and courageous. Do not be afraid; do not be discouraged, for the Lord your God will be with you wherever you go." God was always right there with me, all the way.*

I had a Caesarean section with my first child Brittany, and afterward I was heavily medicated when the familiar signs of an imminent spell appeared. Alone in my hospital room, I held my newborn tightly, praying the whole time that she would be safe. I was so worried that I would drop her because I could not control my arms. I'm so blessed that God was there for me then as well.

As a young mom, fear invaded my life on a deeper level as now my concern was not just about me, but also about my family. There were many times at home with my daughter when I would wonder what her life would be like. I worried that she would have to live with dystonia, and I allowed that fear to overcome me as well. I never wanted my children to experience what I had to live with. In *Tears to Triumph* I wrote a chapter about Brittany. Although she never dealt with these issues, she died at an early age. I had shared about my fear of losing her as well, because of her heart condition. Fear is like a disease. If we don't take care of it and remove it from our lives, it will consume us, and we can become trapped in our own lives. The only way to stop letting fear rule us is to let God rule and reign in our lives. To deal with my own fear, I prayed. I spent time with God, but that wasn't enough. I had to learn to let God take over—to trust and believe that He would take control. That is my advice for you, too, if you are facing fear. Psalm 56:3-4 says, "When I am afraid, I put my trust in you. In God, whose word I praise—in God I trust and am not afraid. What can mere mortals do to me?"

Years later, when my husband and I noticed the familiar, abnormal jerking and twitching in our son's motions one day as he walked away from the car, we were crushed. We had prayed he would live free of dystonia. Unfortunately, we found out it is hereditary. He now would have to live a life with the same disease that had struck fear into me for so many years.

Tannie became so fearful of experiencing an episode that he didn't want to go anywhere. If we traveled, he wanted to stay in the hotel. He didn't want to go into restaurants or be around a lot of people. It seemed that fear took hold of him as well.

Dystonia changed his life as he knew it. When we were visiting my husband during a business trip to Pennsylvania, Tannie stood in the middle of the convention center like a statue and wouldn't move. He was too scared. I got so upset with him. I should have understood right away. But I just wanted him to obey. There I was again, worried about what people might think. I had to get hold of this fear! Once I realized that I wasn't helping the situation, I helped him to relax, and we were able to get to the car. It had taken me a while to learn to deal with this disease. Tannie wasn't there yet.

Fear can paralyze us.

We must move!

God created us to live! We are not to stand still.

> *"For in Him we live and move and have our being." – Acts 17:28 NIV*

We exist because God created us for a purpose—and He uses us just as we are. My son was having a difficult time and I needed to demonstrate understanding. He is at a place now where he can do many things and is finding his purpose. Medicine helps him, but at times he forgets to take it and may have a spell. Despite this, he has learned to keep moving. He's a brave young man. Through prayer, God has helped him to rise above his disease and his fear and do things that he never thought possible. Just like me, God has helped us both learn how to live above the dystonia.

One of the purposes for which God created me is to worship Him. Singing in church – worshipping my Heavenly Father – is one of my favorite things to do. But being on stage is stressful. The many faces staring up at me, the fear of a spell taking over, and the potential embarrassment used to make me so nervous. But God made a way. I learned to go barefoot to help with the sensation in my toes. Something about having my feet feel the floor helps. The Holy Spirit showed me that I'd made an idol of this condition. I let dystonia rule me. So, I pressed in and leaned into God. I wanted to be a vessel for His glory, to be used by Him for His purpose. He helped me establish a new habit. Every service before stepping onto the stage, I prayed that God would help me look past the dystonia and focus only on Him. I wanted to worship God and Him alone. Praise the Lord! I've never had an episode while on stage leading worship.

Years later, it was my brother who found a good neurologist who listened and understood what was going on. This was when we found out the name of our disability: dystonia, a neurological disorder. The doctor and the information she offered were answers to our prayers. Anxiety, panic attacks, fear, and hiding the truth were all common reactions to this type of dystonia, which is related to Parkinson's disease. When I learned I was a candidate for medication, I hugged the doctors. What a relief! But, despite the relief that the medication gave me, my fear did not completely subside.

The prescription I take keeps me from having any spells. But because I lived with dystonia so long, I would still let fear consume me and I would be scared while driving. Because of my fears, I would not drive on the interstate or on long trips for fear of having a spell. I wanted to be safe and I didn't want to put anyone else in harm's way. My doctor has informed me that I can drive without any problems, but I would still let my fears overwhelm me.

Once when my husband needed help making a delivery in another town across a bridge – the longest and highest one I ever drove, no side rails, just big cement blocks – I thought I was going to have a panic attack. My son went with me. But I still prayed, and

I was able to get through it. It wasn't the bridge itself, but the fear overwhelming me that kept me from doing things or following through with tasks. Because I take medicine, I have now been able to drive to Florida, over numerous bridges, on the interstate and I've become more fixed on God and not letting my fears rule me. I can now say that I drive with confidence. Not so much because of the medicine, but because God has given me peace, free of fear and with confidence.

Isaiah 43:1 NKJV says, "Fear not, for I have redeemed you; I have called you by your name; You are mine." God commands us not to fear! 'Fear not' is used in the Bible 80 times. We must remember that we fight against a power that wants us to fail. Staying fearful is a big part of that failure.

Fear appears in many forms: anxiety, lack of faith, doubt and worry. When these feelings rear up, we need to go to God in prayer and let Him take over. There have been many times I would rather hide in my room than face the challenges of my life. We cannot do that. We are here for a reason. We are to live the life that God has given us.

How can we be victorious if we allow fear to overcome us? By drawing near to God and letting Him be in control we can walk through fear that the devil sent to stop us in our tracks.

God has taught me many things through dystonia. God has shown me how to be confident in Him, have peace, and how to trust others. He has blessed me with an awesome husband who has been there as I walked this journey. Grady is a huge blessing. Early on in our relationship he was always watching out for me. Whenever he was around and a spell would come on, he would put his arm around me and keep my arms from flying all over the place. I know God sent him to me. Grady has helped me see past my fears and helped me do and be part of things I never thought possible.

In the past, I allowed fear to overcome me and prevent me from doing things. God helped me push through it all and be brave. Fear is a distraction to all that God wants to do in and through me. We are not to be held back by fear. God wants us to have a life free from it. He is always with me. I can do all things through Him.

Courage to Overcome Anxiety

Julie Jenkins

A feeling of anxiety can hit us out of the blue when we are least expecting it or can build up over time when we are not attending to it. Anxiety is a feeling of nervousness or worry, often about something we have little control over. Left unaddressed, anxiety can be crippling! But you don't have to be stricken with a severe anxiety disorder to understand the debilitating effects that arise from this emotion.

In His Word, God attacks anxiety head-on – and so should we! In Philippians 4:6-7 NIV Paul teaches, *Do not be anxious about anything, but in everything, by prayer and petition, with thanksgiving, present your requests to God. And the peace of God, which transcends all understanding, will guard your hearts and your minds in Christ Jesus.*

It is easy to think "Don't be anxious" – but the key to leaving anxiety behind is replacing it with something else. Paul teaches us to replace it with prayer, petition, and thanksgiving. And in doing so, we will receive the peace of God – a peace that is beyond what our human minds can understand! And that peace will GUARD both our hearts and our minds.

The devil wants control of your heart and your mind! As a Christian, the Holy Spirit has marked you with a seal as a daughter, a princess, of the one, true King; and God has kingdom-work for you to do here on this earth! But the devil, even though he knows he has no claim on your life, will do his very best to make you uncomfortable and unproductive. If I wanted to make someone uncomfortable, I would take away her peace. And if I wanted to make someone unproductive, I would take away her focus. Anxiety is the devil's attempt to attack our hearts by taking away our peace and making us uncomfortable, and to attack our minds by taking away our focus and making us unproductive.

So how do we guard against anxiety before it hits us? If the antidote is prayer, petition and thanksgiving, the prevention is focusing on God daily! Paul follows the instruction above with this: *"Whatever is true, whatever is noble, whatever is right, whatever is pure, whatever is lovely, whatever is admirable – if anything is excellent or praiseworthy – think about such things"* (v.8). And then he takes it one step further: *"Whatever you have learned or received or heard from me, or seen in me – put into practice"* (v.9). Ladies – God is teaching you through the pages of this book! Lean into Him! Put into practice all that He has given you! And allow His peace to guard your heart and mind!

. . . .

Lois Daley has walked with Jesus over 50 yrs. She is a Bible teacher, speaker, published author and prayer fanatic.

Being the daughter and first born of two powerfully effective Bible scholars and teachers, she was saturated in Bible knowledge from an early age. Besides her academic degrees in Aviation and Business, Lois graduated from Emmaus Bible School.

She has led ministries at church throughout her life and has spent many years writing Bible study sessions, poetry, and creating materials for both children and adults. Her other passions include music, gardening, and football.

Lois is married with three adult children and a grand kitty. Her commitment to Christ and her family is demonstrated in her unconditional love of righteousness and an intentional, what-ever-it-takes attitude.

Her life verse, "For to me to live is Christ, and to die is gain," can be seen in her tender, unbashful conversations, prayer and/or singing about God anywhere.

Lois spends a lot of time on her knees and cherishes adding your name to her list for daily intercession.

God's Purpose Prevails
Lois Daley

Often, students set career aspirations for their lives. I was fascinated with air travel. Although it was pertinent that I learn how to pilot an aircraft, I knew that with my myopia, being a pilot as a career was out of the question. So I leaned my strengths into airline management.

I left my home country and immigrated to the United States, where I pursued my degree in Aviation Business Administration with the goal of being in Administration at an airport. Plans were going well. I was near the end of my studies. I had the privilege of interning at Miami International Airport under the direction of its president.

Life's schedule was falling in place.

My dreams were materializing. I got my Valentine wedding and was completing projects that would catapult me into my career. But a hurdle popped up a couple months after the matrimonial bliss. At first, I thought I had a stomach virus, but the vomiting and cramping was going on too long. After a week of this misery, my husband took me to my doctor at Baptist Hospital.

Upon examination, the doctor ordered a blood test. Based on his stoic attitude when he returned, I could not tell what the results of my tests were. Then the bombshell dropped! To our astonishment, I did not have a virus, no ailment.

"You are going to be a mommy!" he exclaimed.

I sat speechless. There were no plans for children. I could not even face my new spouse. We had just started marriage only a couple of months ago. I was faithfully taking my 'birth control' pills each night. How could this be? The mental conversations kept racing through my mind. My gynecological system was never right. I had spent many years with hemorrhaging and a menstrual flow that went on for extended weeks. The introduction of the 'birth control' pill had helped that situation somewhat, but never in a million years would I have expected it to do the reverse of its intended purpose.

Anyway, the doctor continued, "You may want to take life easy and cut out most of your daily activities." He ordered me to quit my job, do less schoolwork and lie in bed.

This cannot be happening, plus I am the main bread earner! I yelled in my thoughts.

At this point I was not at all pleased. I stared at the doctor with an expressionless face. My husband sat in silence. This was definitely not the plan!

The heavy silence came home with us.

The next few days were strange, but we became accustomed to the idea that we were going to be parents, whether we had planned it or not. The nausea and vomiting continued every day, day and night. The medicine that I was given was ineffective. I argued with God about this. I knew the Bible well and verses such as Romans 8:28 KJV, "And we know that all things work together for good to those who love God, to those who are called according to His purpose," and Isaiah 55:8, which tells us that God's ways are not like my way, neither is my way like His. The memory of these verses did not console me. I was physically, mentally, and emotionally miserable and overwhelmed. I wanted to have my mother close by, but the miles across the ocean fostered more despair.

The days crawled on. I still tried working on my aviation assignments, banging the keys of my typewriter, especially when I was alone at home. I was working on projects that I only had a couple of weeks to compete.

Life had a different idea.

I was about eight weeks pregnant. My husband and I went to bed. A few hours into our sleep, a wet sensation hit my back. Annoyed, I nudged hubby and complained that he had spilled his water in the bed. He reluctantly rolled over and defended his glass of water. Without even opening his eyes he teased me for urinating in the bed as an adult. That thirty second discourse was not fun. Apparently, I would have to handle the matter. Upon turning on the light, to my surprise it was not urine, but blood. The sheets were covered with an enormous red pond. I began crying. I was so tired of this. I was emotionally exhausted in addition to being physically weary.

We rushed off to the emergency room at the hospital. After the usual emergency room admitting procedures and initial healthcare preliminaries, the doctor examined me and solemnly said that I had a miscarriage. He explained that with the amount of hemorrhaging that I had, there was no way for the fetus to have survived. I was trapped in an emotional maze. A part of me was happy and relieved. I could get back on track with my educational and career plans, yet I surprised myself that a big part of me was devastated.

So the doctor said that he would have to perform a Dilation and Curettage procedure (D & C), to clear the uterus lining of any residual tissue. Suddenly, he spun around and decided to do an ultrasound first. Those days, ultrasounds were not as commonly used as they are today. The nurse prepped me, and I was taken away on my gurney to get the ultrasound. The cold gel was pressed on my abdomen. The technician said nothing. I said nothing. After that was completed, I was taken back to the room in the emergency department. The obstetrician came in and told me to look at the lit gray screen on the wall. I saw nothing besides light and dark shades and a little fuzz. Then he pointed to a tiny white dot that seemed as though it couldn't keep still.

"Well, Mrs. Daley," he said, "I cannot explain this, but that's your baby," tracing his fingers alongside the small white comet track. "That's an active fighter you have in there, or you are the fighter!" he exclaimed.

The OB doctor continued to make it clear that something in his gut prompted him to do the ultrasound, and he reiterated that the volume and intensity of the bleeding should have eliminated the fetus. He went on to explain that I would have to be on bedrest in the hospital for a while and even when discharged, it was imperative for me to rest at home in order to have any possibility of carrying the baby close to full term. The message was clear. The fact that I was still hemorrhaging was of great concern. What was very clear to me was the confusion in my soul.

All the possibilities that I could face had drawbacks. How would I manage? How would we manage? I had a good job which paid most of our bills.

What other perils will I go through with this pregnancy? I wondered.

Because of the excessive hemorrhaging, I had the option to abort. I was scared! The easy choice would have been to eliminate the emotional mayhem, physical peril and the career disruption. Despite this, after hearing the doctor's words about terminating the pregnancy, without hesitation, I loudly snapped at him, "Absolutely not!"

Tears trickled down my cheeks. I was totally confused. I needed a moment to be alone. So I asked everyone to leave for a few minutes. I had no one to comfort me besides the man who was planning a childless, happy marriage. But at that time, I didn't even want his attention.

God was dealing with me. I could feel His presence. I heard His voice. The room seemed to transform from a hospital room to a place where I was going to make a decision to honor and accept my miracle, my child, my new path with God. I was in a cloud of spiritual freefall. I wrestled with my desired future vision versus the present battle that I was facing.

That day God made clear to me that He was going to take care of me. Although I could not envision what my future would look like, although I feared the process and hospital bills, God's promise to be with me overrode the fear. He also kicked me off the abortion fence. Back then I felt that there were bad circumstances that would open the door for women to choose an abortion. He rebuked me for my attitude and scorched the pessimism in me about His creation that was in my womb. Whatever the situation, He was going to be with me. He reminded me that He is God, the Creator, my provider, the miracle worker who is more than capable of handling my situation. I need not fear.

At the end of that day, I was referred to an obstetrician who cared for women with 'high risk' pregnancies, at a different hospital. That created another problem. The new hospital was far from my home.

Without family close by, a husband working long hours, and not many friends, the days and nights spent on bedrest were lonely. Sometimes I had to console myself with reading or reciting verses from the Bible. Often, I would comfort my heart with songs. I sang songs I knew from church, school and the radio. I even sang some impromptu compositions, usually with lyrics mixed with salty tears and crazy laughter that expressed my emotions.

Through those times, God had to carry me. One day while resting in the hospital, there was no heartbeat indicated on the baby monitor. I screamed so hard that the nurses could not calm me down. I was about 27 weeks pregnant. Fear raised its ugly head. I had fallen in love with this child. How could I come so far and lose the fight? Would God railroad my life like this?

Within a minute, the doctor turned me on my side and manipulated the baby. The monitor started its beating again. Relieved, tired, yet angry and alone, I laid in bed, determined to birth a strong, normal baby.

A couple weeks later I was sent home. Hope embraced.

Finances were low, but my husband and I forged through with meager living, something we had never experienced. There were silent nights and deep sighs, until another trip back to the hospital. The pain was intense, the same old drama. As usual when things settled down, I was discharged.

Elated to be out of the hospital, I decided to give myself a treat. I went for lunch with an old coworker and then shopping. This must have caused too much stress on my body, as down came fluid while I was putting on makeup in Burdines department store. Of course, history repeats itself: I thought it was urine. When abdominal cramps started, I felt it must be constipation. My legs started to buckle under me. Gingerly, I made it to the car, went to Carvels for ice cream (the solution to all problems), and then home, driving very slowly.

Bravery was my flag to fly, so all night I grinned and bore the accelerating pain on the toilet seat. If things did not improve the next day, I would take a laxative.

Early next morning, the phone rang and my girlfriend, Cheryl, told me that she dreamed that I had had the baby. As we chatted of how unprepared I was for that, and the lovely baby furniture and things I had seen the day before, extensive hemorrhaging began.

I was fed up!

That Thursday morning, I wailed and screamed all the way back to the hospital.

When we got to the emergency room, the attendance was speedy. The doctor said I was in labor and contractions were less than a minute apart.

"I have a least six more weeks. I am just constipated and, of course, hemorrhaging!" I insisted. But the medical geniuses ignored my diagnosis.

I learned that what had happened the day before was actually my 'water breaking' – the assumed 'urine' running down my leg in Burdines was actually amniotic fluid. I felt deceived, as in Lamaze prenatal classes the facilitator talked about the gush that would take place.

Unfortunately, the baby was not in any hurry to be born and dilation was not happening. I had a fever of 103.5 and my blood pressure was very high. All this was due to the amniotic fluid and membrane which had a premature exit.

God gave me a gift in the midst of this mayhem. I was the only pregnant patient in that hospital for two days. I had the attention of all the obstetricians and their staff. As a teaching hospital, 'Lois' case study' was recorded on the schedule. I was hooked up to machines which monitored the baby and my vital signs. Friday morning, the baby went into distress and needed oxygen. The wait would take all day, until both our lives were in danger and, with or without the fever, a Caesarean section was ordered. At one point my husband was forcibly put out of the room. I was in a daze through most of this, too weak to even talk.

My husband called me the following day to find out about our new daughter, Samantha. He had gone home to rest after the all-night ordeal. He told me that while the doctors and nurses were hustling through the hallways to get me to the operating room, they noticed movement in my abdomen. Right there, the baby popped out her head! Immediately after delivery, she was taken to the neonatal nursery. At first, I thought he was dreaming or something and explained to him that I was still pregnant. I could still see my enormous belly. He was adamant that I had given birth at 12:40 that morning. I called for a nurse, who confirmed that I had a 'bundle of joy' wrapped in pink in the nursery, but I would not be able to see her until the pediatrician gave permission.

I asked her why my tummy was still distended. She called for a doctor, who explained that my uterus was infected. Until the fever was eliminated, infection gone and blood pressure back to normal, I could not see the baby.

I was extremely upset!

The next few days were difficult for me. I shed tears as I cried out to God. One day my friend Carol came with ginger tea (a go-to cure from grandmother) for me. We decided that she would be putting ice in my clothes to get rid of the fever. It was hilarious.

Finally, on Samantha's eight day of life, I got a peek at her through the viewing window. Tears streamed down my cheeks as I saw her long, thin body with tubes attached and eye patches on.

We spent a couple more weeks apart as we both recuperated in our separate chambers. Unfortunately, I was discharged without my daughter.

God's Word and music were my go-to cushions. I clung to the book of Psalms and my favorite donuts. Even in my disappointment, the Lord showed me His favor. He gave me time to get the crib and many baby things that I did not have. He orchestrated my mother's schedule so that she would be available to return from Israel when Samantha came home.

The day the pediatrician called me and said I could come for the baby, I did cartwheels in my heart. I do not recall how fast my husband and I drove to the hospital, but after stepping through the hospital doors, I hurried to the nursery as fast as I could go. This was the first time holding her. The joy that God erupted in my soul stretched an immoveable smile on my face. The anxiety, mixed feelings, and unpleasant moments, though not forgotten, were insignificant to the beauty that the Creator had formed.

As the years have passed and I evaluate that adventure, I have seen the blessings that my firstborn daughter has brought to my life. She has given me many proud moments through her academic years and with her involvement in sports. Besides her achievements, she has been my hairstylist, pedicurist, and logical daughter. There are times we discuss the Scriptures with an intensity that thrills my soul. The Lord has used Sam (as we lovingly call her) to show me magnificent ways in which He would prove Himself faithful to me. Throughout Sam's academic years I was privileged to be home with her and her siblings. Challenges of various types came, but each time, God's presence, protection and provision were beyond my imagination. His Word is true as He told Joshua in Joshua 1:9 – "I do not have to fear, but to have courage; because He is with me," and Hebrew 13:5 – "He will never fail, leave or forsake me." Isaiah 41:10 tells me that as I choose to be brave, that I should not be dismayed for "I AM" is my God. He says, "He will strengthen me and help me. He will uphold me with His right hand."

Through it all I gained courage to face the unpredictable, faith that is stretchable beyond measurements and trust in a God who is bigger than my visions.

Courage to Overcome Addiction

Julie Jenkins

Addiction is a force that overcomes your mind allowing, on one hand, an escape from the reality of life, and on the other hand, a sapping of satisfaction from any activity that does not involve the addiction. Overcoming addiction involves seeing the truth that the addiction itself will never satisfy but will only lead to a desire for more and more, which will never be enough. Addiction is a lie wrapped up in pretty paper of promise. If I can just lose five more pounds, buy that one shirt, eat that one candy bar, watch that one show, take that one pill, have that one drink…THEN I will be happy.

The tragedy of an addiction is that the thought of 'one more' will overtake our minds and keep us from doing, becoming, and enjoying all that God has for us.

The grip of addiction is the claw of the devil. We are made to worship, love, and honor God. The devil comes at us with addiction, pulling our focus from God to an idol.

To overcome addiction, we must first recognize its deadly grip and admit our shortcoming, realizing that our battle is not against flesh and blood but against the spiritual forces of evil and destruction (Ephesians 6:12) – this is no time to blame or condemn yourself! God knows our flaws and our propensity to sin, but He loves us and offers us His mercy and forgiveness!

Second, we must sever our tie with the focus of our addiction – rip the claws of the devil away! This is not going to be easy and cannot be done without the strength of the Holy Spirit and the wisdom and guidance of a godly friend, minister, or even professional specializing in the given addiction. *If someone is caught in a sin, you who are spiritual should restore him gently… Carry each other's burdens, and in this way you will fulfill the law of Christ. (Galatians 6:1-2)*

Third, we must cling to God! When an addiction is ripped from our spirit, a hole is left, and that hole must be filled immediately with God, or the devil will swoop right in to fill the void with something else destructive. In Philippians 4:8-9 NIV, Paul gives us practical advice, warning and encouragement, all wrapped into one: *"Whatever is true, whatever is noble, whatever is right, whatever is pure, whatever is lovely, whatever is admirable – if anything is excellent or praiseworthy – think about such things. Whatever you have learned or received or heard from me, or seen in me – put it into practice. And the peace of God will be with you."*

Aren't we all craving the peace of God? Our soul longs for it! If you are fighting an addiction, don't fight it alone! If you need a place to turn, please contact us at womenworldleaders.com – we are not professionals, but we can point you to someone who is. We are all in this together!

. . . .

Claire Ellen Portmann is wife to Brian, Mama to Kimberly, daughter to Janet, and little sister to Larry. With a heart on fire for Jesus, she is running the race for the Glory of the Kingdom of God.

Claire and Brian have worked for over a decade, breeding and raising English Cream Golden Retrievers for families all over the United States but knew in their hearts they wanted to leave a legacy showcasing God's faithfulness. With that in mind they took what God had blessed them with and trained their first therapy dog, "Finn." Finn and the rest of their growing team now go out to bring the Gospel of Jesus Christ to the lost and broken of this world.

Claire also focuses her time volunteering at her church, teaching Sunday school, and she also belongs to the outreach team of Women World Leaders. Claire, Brian, and their Ocean Golden Pups live in Jupiter, Florida.

A Time to Trust
Claire Portmann

One morning, about eighteen months ago, God clearly spoke to me while I was journaling. The following Sunday, when I began to share with a friend at church, there was more to the message than when I wrote it days before. What I heard was, "Daughter, I love your servant's heart and how you selflessly care for others." What was added was one sentence that would change my life: "However, when you don't care for yourself, you dishonor me." What?! I was baffled. My friend, who has walked with the Lord almost her entire life, is someone I seek wisdom from. Her words will stick in my mind forever: "I think you need to meditate on this and ask the Lord for clarity." So I did.

In my quiet times that followed, I kept hearing the Lord say, "Clean your house." I didn't know what that meant. Where was I to start? I started with a list but gravitated immediately to a focus on my health. My health has never been great. I assumed it was due to being born a preemie. I was about five years old before I caught up physically. I wouldn't walk until I was about two and a half, eye-hand coordination was an issue, and the big one, digestion. It would take me on a long journey of more than 18 months to discover hidden truths about my health as well as lies I had believed about myself personally to find true healing and freedom.

I began by looking into allergy testing as well as meeting with a friend from church, Jess Royston, who is a health coach specializing in "Gut Health." We went through tests and nutrition protocols. Despite our work together, there was no improvement and I was frustrated. After spending more than 50 years with stomach issues, I figured this was what God had been referring to when He told me to care for myself. Oh, how I wanted this to be so, but it wasn't. I wanted to look at the iceberg but not at what lay below. I knew that I had buried things in my soul, but what good could come of going through what can't be undone? I would find out, but it would be painful. So painful that I had run from it for a very long time, but you can never outrun God. He wanted to knock down the walls I had built up around me. I thought those walls protected me, but they didn't. They imprisoned me in dysfunctional relationships that were unfulfilling, difficult, and didn't serve God or myself. To understand this better, I had to go back.

When I was growing up in Sunday school, Norma Gaebelein assigned each student a Bible verse to memorize and would reward us with a Bible with our names embossed in gold on the front. My verse was *Jeremiah 31:3 AMP – The Lord appeared to me from ages past, saying, "I have loved you with an everlasting love; Therefore with loving kindness have I drawn you and continued My faithfulness to you." Miss* Norma knew how much I needed to know that I was loved.

Our home was chaotic. When I was about three my father began living with another woman Monday through Friday and would come home on weekends. Eventually this broke my mother in such a way that I don't believe she ever really recovered from it. In the body that my once-vibrant mother inhabited was a distant, disconnected woman who no longer had an intimate relationship with her children. She went to work, started to date and eventually went to college. This created a situation of three children who were often left alone, and violence became the norm. Mom was in denial, and she was unable to deal with it, so my brother Larry and I were on our own to defend ourselves from an older brother who physically abused both of us and sexually abused me for years. With no parenting, there were deep wounds that never healed which I dragged into my adulthood. I felt alone and afraid most of the time, and had no one to tell, as the shame was too great. This skewed view of the world left me defensive and afraid of real closeness, fearing someone might find out how messed up I was.

As "the girl" in my family, my life was difficult as I managed one family crisis after another. Those two words would redefine my self-image into an image of something ugly that nobody would want. As early as I could recall, my maternal grandmother told me that as "the girl," it was my job to take care of the family. My grandmother would also become my tormentor for many years after she and my grandfather moved into our home. She brutally shamed me in any way she could and held me accountable as the caregiver for my mother. Mom, after enduring many years of having a "weekend husband," filed for legal separation from my father. This enraged my father, who wanted to know why my mom would want to end such a happy marriage. My father began calling late at night threatening my mom. This led to many sleepless nights as I listened to Mom cry, and then I would go to her room telling her that I had had a nightmare so that I, a seven-year-old, could do *my job of comforting her. The job that I never intended to hold was the beginning of a role that would fill my entire life.*

The value that my family placed on me was limited to how I could care for and what I could do for them, which led to years of an unfulfilled need for recognition of my worth as an individual. As a result, I learned to ignore my own needs, which cost me my friends and even my first marriage as I continued to manage my family's many issues. The snowball effect was that I turned to rage in order to make my own opinions heard. I had turned into my grandmother, becoming the tormentor to my loved ones.

As I continued to focus on God's word to me to "clean your house," I opened my eyes to what was going on in my marriage, and the fact is that things had become so bad between my husband and me that I wondered if we would make it. I believed that God was telling me that there were situations in my home that I needed to address to care for myself – in His power and with His guidance. No longer did I need to be the little girl holding the family together; instead, I needed to rely on Him.

God began a process of healing me and my marriage through having me take courageous steps of faith. After a series of events in which God was trying to get my attention, including outbursts of anger on my part, my first step was spending more time with the Lord. I began by getting up at 5:30 each morning to go to the beach and watch the sunrise. It was difficult at first, but I found I was sleeping better every night and actually began to look forward to morning, which was a new experience for me. During this time, God kept focusing me back to the same scripture: **Ezekiel 36:26 NIV – I will give you a new heart and put a new spirit in you; I will remove from you your heart of stone and give you a heart of flesh.**

One place where God brought this scripture to my attention was in a movie called *The Case for Christ. In it, the wife of an atheist reporter prays this verse over her husband. My thought was that praying this verse might fix Brian. The funny thing, though, is that when you focus on scripture, there is always a moment of clarity. That clarity was that I* *needed to look in the mirror and pray the same scripture over and over, but not for Brian, for myself.*

As I prayed, the change I hoped for didn't occur. Instead, things seemed to get worse – I knew it was time to take another courageous step, as Brian and I were struggling like never before. I asked another Woman World Leader about how she had overcome a similar struggle. That conversation led me to Breakwater Coaching, and Cindy and David Southworth. Of course, my first hope was that they could fix Brian so that we could be happy.

Brian and I began marriage coaching with Cindy and David, and through that I was given the opportunity to attend the 9th BreakThrough Retreat at Breakwater Coaching with 12 other women – yet another step that took courage. During the retreat, we shared our stories of pain, brokenness, and the sincere desire for our lives to have meaning and heal. We laughed, cried, and even giggled, and we all grew. We grew in the knowledge of not just who we were, but more importantly, whose we were.

Romans 8:15 ESV – For you did not receive the spirit of slavery to fall back in fear, but you have received the spirit of adoption as sons by whom we cry, "Abba, Father!" The Spirit himself bears witness with our spirit that we are children of God and fellow heirs with Christ, provided we suffer with him in order that we may also be glorified with him.

On my drive home, I felt lighter – like weights I had been carrying had been lifted off my shoulders. Despite the soaring that I felt in my spirit on the way home, within 48 hours the devil had convinced me that the retreat had been a waste of time. But God wasn't finished. My next step was working through a program for adults who were abused as children called "The Wounded Heart." As I was guided every week for months through this program by my wonderful mentor Cheryl Roberson, I began to see what lay beneath all my pain. The battle wasn't over, but I didn›t feel shame like I once had, and that was huge. During that time, our marriage still struggled, and I knew it would take both of us embracing the process and using the tools we had been given. It would take yet another courageous step to dig up the ugly, buried pain and its consequences throughout my life. That would be the turning point to my healing.

Brian and I breed English Cream Golden Retrievers for a living. Besides puppies, we have nine dogs under our roof and another 12 in foster care that will join the breeding program as they age in. The workload to keep the house clean is overwhelming, and I take on the brunt of it. I was under the impression that when our girls were finished breeding, they would be re-homed to a family or couple who would dote on them the rest of their days. When we discussed this, Brian used the word 'betrayal' to describe how he felt about letting any of the girls go, and I was devastated. I was overwhelmed, feeling that my husband was picking the dogs over me. This hurt was amplified by the fact that months earlier I had been diagnosed as allergic to dog dander, and I felt then that my husband put the dogs' wellbeing above mine, leading to the most painful time in our marriage. I was crushed. But that would be the thing that would lead me closer to healing. God was crushing me to mold me into who I was supposed to be.

When I didn't know where to turn, God intervened. A friend called and she immediately knew that something was seriously wrong. I broke down and told her everything. She listened and then asked me if I would consider speaking with a dear friend of hers who was a therapist, and I agreed.

I saw the therapist the next day, and after two hours of sharing my story, she said these words: "Claire, I believe you have what is called Complex Childhood Trauma-Induced PTSD." She then asked me a series of questions about my physical responses to stressful situations and the answers confirmed her suspicions. Ironically, my physical therapist had mentioned something similar in regard to my physical stance, which she described as one of prepared anticipation of fight or flight. So now what was I to do with this breakthrough? Learning a new normal can be easy for some, but for me it meant throwing out every natural reaction – I had developed the attitude that I had to fight to be right.

The biggest hurdle for me in our marriage was the dogs. Besides the allergies and the continual cleaning and care, having nine dogs puts any owner on a leash: no vacations, and no going out very late or too far. I was weary. So what now? Brian essentially wanted to let the dogs dictate our lives, and he wasn't going to budge. Without my "go to" of fighting back, I was powerless. BUT GOD WASN'T! It was the very first time I actually totally surrendered something to God without picking that thing that I set before the cross up, over and over again.

2 Corinthians 12:9 ESV – And he said to me, My grace is sufficient for you, my power is made perfect in WEAKNESS.

Finally, the light bulb lit up! I had to take one more courageous step and completely surrender. I had to let God in to take care of things that I couldn't. I had met with the therapist twice that week and I had shared with her about the use of the word betrayal, and she asked, "How are you going to deal with it?" That night I simply asked Brian one question: "Do you expect us to live with nine dogs until they die off one by one?" I got my answer, which was no answer, and I cried myself to sleep.

The following morning, we met with friends of ours who also breed Goldens. While I was in with our girl and one of their boys, Brian was out with Pam and their other male. When I came out, as we were discussing pedigrees, Pam mentioned re-homing, and I thought I would burst into tears. She said Brian had some pretty strong thoughts on it. I agreed with her, saying, "Yes, I know. I'll be that crazy woman with 25 dogs until I die." I was being sarcastic, a defense mechanism I used, as opposed to allowing her to see how utterly desperate I was. Immediately, she said, "But he's OK with it now." WHAT? God is so good! I just had to let go and trust Him! I couldn't believe it, so I waited until we were on our way home, when Brian confirmed to me that he understood and he would be ok with re-homing the girls. You see, once I really set the situation before the cross, and stopped picking it up again and again, I fully surrendered to God. When I laid my weakness before Him, He met me with overflowing grace and deliverance in less than 12 hours. I was blown away and felt such peace. My micro-managing God never worked. I had to learn a new way and that way was fully relying on Him.

I met with my therapist the following Monday and the first thing she said to me was, "You look great; what happened?" I shared what had transpired. Then she spoke to me about putting my faith in God instead of myself and my ability to manipulate the situation to get what I wanted. She also acknowledged that God had answered my prayer. The key was changing a behavior with God's help, and not my own. I had to hold onto *Psalm 46:1-2 KJV: God is our refuge and strength, a very present help in trouble. Therefore we will not fear, though the earth be removed, and though the mountains be carried into the midst of the sea; Though the waters thereof roar and be troubled, though the mountains shake with swelling thereof.*

Then, v.10, my favorite reminder: Be still and know that I am God.

I had to get to my lowest and finally, all I could do was look up, and there He was once again, loving me right where I was. He was waiting for me, no judgment, just love and peace, and giving me wisdom to courageously step where He called.

Matthew 11:28-30 NIV – Come to me, all you who are weary and heavy burdened, and I will give you rest. Take my yoke upon you and learn from me, for I am gentle and humble in heart, and you will find rest for your souls. For my yoke is easy and my burden is light.

It is now 18 months after that life-changing word from the Lord, and my perspective has shifted, my house is clean, and I am learning to take care of myself as much as I have always taken care of others. I honor who I am as God made me. I am not defined by what happened to me, but by what God did for me. As far as Brian and I are concerned, we aren't perfect, but we are better than we ever have been. There were so many wonderful people who sowed important seeds into both of us that are now blooming. We both are in therapy, walking our own journeys toward healing, and I know that with God's help we will get to a way better place than where we started. The best IS yet to come, and for the first time in my life, I look forward to tomorrow with anticipation of what it might bring. What a precious gift from God.

Courage to Overcome Jealousy

Julie Jenkins

Jealousy cannot be described without a whole host of other words that probably make your skin crawl: insecurity, fear, inadequacy, resentment, helplessness, and even anger. It is that awful feeling that we aren't enough, but someone else is.

It's clear that jealousy has been around as long as the human race has been: Eve wanted to be like God, that's why she ate the apple; and Cain was jealous of God's favor on Abel, that is why he killed his own brother. In the book of Galatians, Paul warns Christians about jealousy: "Since we are living by the Spirit, let us follow the Spirit's leading in every part of our lives. Let us not become conceited, or provoke one another, or be jealous of one another" (Galatians 5:24-25 NLT).

These facts may lead us to ask – if jealousy comes so naturally and has been around since the beginning of time, what chance do I have against it?

One word comes to mind when I think of how to combat jealousy: trust! Before the world was born, God knew YOU! He knew when you would live on this earth, who your parents and friends would be, and, more importantly, He knew the purpose that you would fulfil for the glory of His Kingdom. And He created and gifted you perfectly to fulfill that role!! Do you trust that? Do you trust Him?

God has told us, "I will never fail you. I will never abandon you" (Hebrews 13:5 NLT). Ours is the God who "laid the earth's foundation on the seas and built it on the ocean depths" (Psalm 24:2 NLT). And this same God who laid the foundations of the earth and promised to never fail us is one who "works in different ways, but is the same God who does the work in all of us" (1 Cor 12:6 NLT).

Our jealousy will fade when we look away from ourselves and look at God, when we see ourselves as part of His perfect plan, and when we trust in the fact that we were woven together by our Father who saw us before we were born, recorded every day of our lives in His book, and laid out every moment of our lives before a single day had passed! (Psalm 139:15-16)

Let us trust that our God made and gifted us perfectly and let us praise Him with the prophet Isaiah, saying, "O Lord, I will honor and praise your name, for you are my God. You do such wonderful things! You planned them long ago, and now you have accomplished them" (Isaiah 25:1 NLT).

. . . .

Jessi Melton lives in Boca Raton, Florida with her son Jackson and is the owner of a successful telecommunications company and former candidate for US Congress. Born in West Virginia and raised in North Carolina, she earned a bachelor's degree from East Carolina University in Business Administration.

Jessi has always enjoyed being physically active, participating as an adult in kickboxing, Brazilian Jujitsu, and becoming the 2013 Florida State Bodybuilding Champion and first place winner of 'Soldier Rush' – a three-mile women's obstacle course race.

Jessi's greatest passion is sharing the message and the freedom of Jesus Christ. She has been passionately evangelizing and leading Sisterhood Bible studies for the past four years.

Additionally, she leads a ministry helping women and single mothers maximize their own career potential; and works with young girls struggling with self-love, body image, eating disorders and addiction. After her 2020 congressional run, she launched the 'American Jessi' brand aimed at giving young girls and women a positive, godly role model in the 21st century.

The Battle is Already Won, So Be Bold

Jessi Melton

The battle is already won. It only took me 30 years to discover that truth, and I endured numerous battles without the hope of that knowledge. Eventually, I learned that as Christians, we can take bold, courageous steps of faith as we tap not into our own power, but the almighty power of our Creator.

After years of trying to do things my own way, I finally decided I'd had enough. Enough heartbreak, enough confusion, enough distraction, enough headaches, enough wasted time, and enough pain. For thirty years, I pushed through life, often relying on my own strength. Many would say I had it all together, but I knew I was falling short of my full potential. Don't get me wrong, I was pretty strong for a five-foot, two-inch freckle-faced girl from West Virginia, but after becoming a single mother, enduring failed relationship after failed relationship, and watching my son suffer through the consequences of my worldly decisions, I finally decided I'd had enough. If I wanted different results, I was going to have to start doing things differently.

Coming from a broken home, I lost my way for many of my teenage and young adult years. All I knew how to do was to live as the world lived; anything founded on godly principles was a foreign concept. At age 22 I became a mother, and at age 23, I became a single mom. By the grace of God alone, on my son's second birthday I graduated from college with a Bachelor's degree in business and moved to Florida to begin a new life for my son and me.

For years, I squeezed by on my own strength, never allowing anyone to see the struggles I faced behind closed doors, never allowing myself to be seen as a victim of my circumstances. I was a single mom with an extremely energetic young toddler. I had no air conditioning in my car and worked at a local radio station selling advertising door-to-door in the South Florida heat. I lived in a low-income part of town and experienced bed bugs and home break-ins on more than one occasion.

Because of my tenacity and will to achieve, I advanced through my field and broke into the telecommunications business, rapidly scoring promotions like a child climbing a jungle gym. Regardless of how I struggled financially, I excelled in my career by always exceeding expectations, dressing for the job I wanted, cultivating business relationships, and adding value to my employer by perpetually growing my own skillset. I endured many battles along the way, suffering persecution from colleagues who detested my lighthearted spirit and ambition. Despite the obstacles and opposition, I became successful in my field at a very young age. Along the way, at age 26 and while working for a large publicly traded tower company, I found Christ. But it wasn't until age 30 that I began to truly understand the nature of God and how to tap into the power of His word.

In those "between years," I was still living half in the world, and half in the word of God. While I treated others with love and

compassion, I was still caught up in the bondage of doing relationships "the world's way." The world tells us it's abnormal to save yourself for marriage, it tells us to move in together out of convenience, it tells us that traditional family values are outdated. The world says it's ok to buy a home together, have sex, play house and have children – even if you aren't committed through marriage. The world tells us marriage is no more than "just a ring" or "a piece of paper." In my twenties, I was either single and achieving life-long goals, or in a relationship with my ambition on hold. I found myself either passionately cultivating a relationship with the Lord and building a successful career, or allowing myself to fall into a worldly relationship with a partner drawn to the light of Christ in me, only to dim my light, pull me back, fall apart, and find myself heartbroken and emaciated. After getting over one relationship, I'd be single again for several years, grow closer to God, be drawn into companionship again, lose myself, endure a painful breakup, and repeat the cycle of pain and heartbreak.

Finally, after making the same mistakes too many times, and dragging my son through the consequences of my worldly decisions, I knew it was time for me to grow up and resolve this setback once and for all. I was finished with losing myself, finished with heartbreak and pain, and determined to stop making the mistake that was holding me back from everything God had for me.

I was determined to do life God's way.

As I spent time with God asking Him to guide my path, He reminded me of the unique way He created me. From a young age, the desires of my heart gave me a deep love for people, an aversion for injustice, and a desire to lift others up. My heart longs to help those whom others have discounted, and I've always felt the instinct to stand against a bully.

Since grade school, I've had a passion for the way our country is led, or what some might call politics. As an American, I have a passionate love for my country and cherish the fact that it is a nation where a girl like me could go from being a single mom without two dimes to rub together to being a successful business owner through hard work and tenacity.

As I grew in my Christian walk, I realized that God has a way of inserting desires within us that are inextricably tied to our purpose here on Earth. Each one of us has a divine purpose, a purpose that, when coupled with the power of Christ and walking in obedience to Him, will take our legacies to unimaginable heights; or as God puts it in 1 Corinthians 2:9, "No eye has seen, nor has any ear heard, nor has any mind imagined the things that God has in store for those who love him and are called according to His purpose."

The year I turned 30 I was single and wholeheartedly following Christ. I had found freedom from my own hang-ups and was determined to serve God to my fullest potential. Around that same time, the Lord began to press a wild idea on my heart. He asked me to run for the United States Congress.

I wrestled with the idea, asking God, "Are you sure this is what you want me to do? Should I wait until my son is a little bit older? Am I hearing you correctly? Is this really you?!" I almost talked myself out of it a couple of times but time and again, God pressed it on my heart.

I knew that America needed female leaders to call our sisters out of the poverty I was once in, out of oppression, and to show our girls that we are more than conquerors, regardless of our circumstances. I knew that we needed women to set Godly examples to our youth and to our country as a whole.

I needed to seek God for confirmation before I took the courageous step of faith to run for office. So I began fasting and reading
the Old Testament (I had already finished the New Testament
years prior). Repeatedly, I stumbled upon Scripture that essentially
told me "just as you have been set free from your bondage, it's time
for you to help to set others free. Through your life battles, I have
tempered you for such a time as this."

As I turned to the Scripture, I found that my hesitation and doubt
were always met with God's life-speaking words. God had called
the Israelites to engage in battle with nations that were bigger,
stronger and that outnumbered the Israelites, but God promised
that He would go before the Israelites and fight for them. Moses
was an example of an ordinary man who, when asked by God to
lead the Israelites out of slavery, questioned God and his own ade-
quacy for such a job. But God quickly reminded Moses of who
God was.

For me, I had found myself questioning God in the same way
Moses questioned Him. Are you sure you want *me*? But then God
reminded me who God was.

Because he continuously sought after the Lord and turned to Him
for guidance, Moses, a man with a stutter, was able to lead the
Israelites out of slavery and through great battles to victory. In
Exodus 17:10, when the Israelites were attacked by the Amalekites,
Moses sent Joshua out to fight while Moses stood atop a hill with
Aaron and Hur nearby. As long as Moses held up his hands [in
worship of God], the Israelites were winning, but whenever he
lowered his hands, the Amalekites were winning. When Moses'
hands grew tired, they took a stone and put it under him and he
sat on it. When his arms grew tired, Aaron and Hur held his hands

up so that his hands remained steady until sunset. So Joshua overcame the Amalekite army, by the power of God and with the help of his friends.

As I embarked on this battle, I've found myself weary and apprehensive of my own boldness. But sure enough, at just the right times (and not a minute too soon) God sent an Aaron and a Hur to hold my hands up for me. He has sent me single mothers, cancer survivors, and spiritual warriors committed to the success of our mission to help me hold my hands up when my faith grows weary. God is always so faithful, even when we are weak.

Being a Christian doesn't absolve us of our inadequacies, but when we remember who we are in the Lord, our weakness is made strong in the Lord's strength. Like Moses, at times I have felt doubt or inadequacy, then I focus on God's promises, not my own emotions. Human emotions are fleeting, but the Word of the Lord is unchanging. As humans, it's normal to feel unmotivated, tired, even doubtful or anxious, but if we allow ourselves to submit to these human emotions, then our life will be a rollercoaster of misdirection. In Jeremiah 17:5 God tells us, "Cursed is the one who trusts in man, who draws strength from mere flesh…they will not see prosperity when it comes…But blessed is the one who trusts in the Lord, whose confidence is in him. They will be like a tree planted by the water that sends out its root by the stream. It does not fear when heat comes; its leaves are always green. It has no worries in a year of drought and never fails to bear fruit." It's a part of our humanity to battle with doubt, or to be overrun by feelings of uncertainty, thinking, "There's no way I can do this," but because we are children of God, we are called to be bold in HIS strength, not in our own.

Knowing who our Father is allows us to be bold and courageous not in ourselves, but in His unchanging, ever-faithful strength.

Take David, for example: He was a shepherd, the youngest of eight brothers, a common young boy. A Philistine named Goliath, who was over nine feet tall and had been a warrior since he was young, had been taunting the Israelites daily, challenging any one Israelite to a battle, which could change the course of history forever. King Saul and his men were terrified. Despite the fact that David's own brothers scoffed at him and he himself was not a warrior, David courageously stepped into battle with total faith in God's abilities and understanding that the Philistines had defied the Lord. David understood that God works through those who boldly and whole-heartedly follow Him and give Him the glory. Goliath came to the fight with 125-pound armor and a sword; David defeated him with a stone and God.

Once I began to understand this, and I found commonality between David and myself, I started to realize that through David's story, God was speaking to me. As God's representative, I can trust in His power as I stand against injustice and for the discounted, those whom He had placed on my heart so many years ago.

In Deuteronomy, scripture tells us over and over again of God's strength and reminds us of the ways he fights for us. "The Lord your God himself will cross over ahead of you. HE will destroy these nations before you and you will take possession of their land" (Deuteronomy 31:3). Notice the scripture tells us what God will do, not what we will do. "The Lord himself goes before you and will be with you; he will never leave you nor forsake you. Do not be afraid; do not be discouraged" (Deuteronomy 31:8). "Because he loved you, he has brought you out of Egypt with his great strength, to drive out before you nations greater and stronger than you and to bring you into their land to give it to you for your inheritance" (Deuteronomy 4: 37). God's got our back.

Of course, throughout this race I've battled with my humanity. The race has been a rollercoaster of ups and downs, plowing and bearing fruit. Doubt and complete faithfulness. When I've grown tired and weak, I'm reminded of King David, the young man who defeated Goliath and went on to lead the Israelites into years of abundance. He told God, "I will exalt you." David's heart was truly committed to honoring the will of God and I know that as long as my heart is committed to God's will, I will experience victory as well, and therefore can and should remain bold in my actions and convictions.

Over time, as David was pursued by his enemies, which at times included even his own family, God sent David warriors. At times when David was feeling weak, God stepped in by sending him angels to protect him. When I read this, I was reminded of God's promises and sure enough, God has always sent me the warriors I've needed: single moms, cancer survivors, survivors of political battles, victors of persecution. He has sent everything I have needed to courageously continue this race. He promised to give me warriors, and warriors of the spirit is exactly what God has given me.

The battles I fought in my younger years, trying to make a life for my son and climb out of poverty, strengthened my faith and prepared me to be courageous and bold in such a time as this. God has always been faithful to me, even when I have not been faithful to Him. I believe that God tempers us. He lovingly prepares us for the increasing intensity of the battles we will face. We have a choice to allow these battles to strengthen our faith in God and courageously step into all He has called us to, or to turn our back on Him and attempt to fight our own battles.

"Consider it pure joy, my brothers and sisters, whenever you face trials of many kinds, because the testing of your faith produces perseverance. Let perseverance finish its work so that you may be mature and complete, not lacking anything." – James 1:2 NIV

One thing in this life is certain, you will have trials, but know that Christ has overcome the world. So in the midst of our doubt, in the center of our trials, at rock bottom, remember that the battle is already won, and we are simply being strengthened and transformed more into His likeness, giving us the ability to be bolder and accomplish even more of what no human eye has ever seen or man's ear has heard.

If He brings you to it, He will carry you through it. Throughout this process, one thing has never changed: When my race has reached a level where we've outgrown our manpower, or lost someone who seemed irreplaceable, God has shown up, every single time. And that's how I know this mission is His, not my own. I am a vessel for his mission and I pray often asking God to use me, to find me worthy, to purify me and give me strength to purify myself so that I can be used as a worthy vessel in this great mission He has chosen me for.

He who began a good work in you will carry it on to completion until the day of Christ Jesus. In Deuteronomy and Exodus, God only asked that Moses and the Israelites trust Him, and step into the land that He had prepared for them. He promised to fight for them, and that is also His promise to us.

Courage is not the absence of fear, but the resolve to press forward, even in the presence of fear. So be bold. Step into the desires God has placed on your heart, no matter how outrageous or farfetched they may seem, because every David needs a Goliath.

Courage to Overcome Selfishness

Julie Jenkins

Our world is riddled by selfishness. If we are honest, we look at everything FIRST through the lens of self. *How will I be affected? What does this mean to me? What is my cost or gain?* The Bible warns us of godlessness in the last days: "People will be lovers of self" (2 Timothy 3:2 ESV), and yet, we are also taught "Let no one seek his own good, but the good of his neighbor" (1 Cor 10:24 ESV).

We all have a different lens through which we look at the world. Each individual lens is made up of tangibles and intangibles. Where we live, our socio-economic status, the color of our skin, our past experiences and our present responsibilities all color how we see things and what we stand for. What would the world look like if we looked through someone else's lens? What would the world look like if we looked through God's lens?

Our first step in the battle against selfishness is admitting that the lens we see the world through is very limited. Only God is omnipresent (everywhere) and omniscient (all-knowing) – so only God has the perfect lens. Only His lens is unsmeared, unclouded, and untinged.

A second step in the battle against selfishness is recognizing that not only is MY lens not clear, neither is anyone else's. This is a slippery slope that could easily lead to a spirit of judgment, but regarded with grace, will lead to a place of compassion and forgiveness. When we can acknowledge that another has been hurt, scarred, or marked by circumstances that we don't see and can't understand, we begin the process of seeing outside ourselves.

When I was a kid, we used to "borrow" each other's eyeglasses so that we could see how they looked on us. The problem was, when I put on my friend's glasses, the prescription in her lenses would not allow me to see my own face in the mirror clearly. It is impossible, this side of heaven, for us to TRULY see things the way someone else does, but that shouldn't stop us from trying!

Stepping out of our zone of self requires asking others difficult questions in love, and, more importantly, listening with an open mind and an open heart. It requires going to God and asking Him to open our hearts, as only He can, and then intentionally putting our own agenda aside and allowing Him to break down the walls that we have built up, brick-by-brick, over our own lifetimes. Those walls both keep in our own points of view and keep out those of our neighbors. Only with the wisdom of God will we be able to see through a clear lens, and only by His grace and forgiveness will we be able to love our neighbor as ourselves.

. . . .

Candice Daniel is a wife to Eddie, mom to Aiden, Alec, Anderson, and Alessia, and one Angel baby. She is a Momprenuer – part owner of three very successful companies and a District Leader for her own Financial Services Business. She enjoys educating others on taking control of their finances, equipping them with the tools they need to succeed!

Candice's passion is encouraging and inspiring women to use their God-given gifts and talents to courageously walk out their calling and purpose in life. Her heart's desire is to know Him more and to share the love of Christ with the world! God is still writing her story, but she hopes to inspire others through her testimony, life trials and tribulations; to continue to have faith, and to know that with Christ all things are possible.

She is a Tiara Leader with Women World Leaders. She has volunteered with the church for many years and is a huge advocate working to stop Human Trafficking.

She enjoys spending quality time with her family and friends and connecting with others.

Walking in Obedience
Candice Daniel

If there's one thing I've learned in my life, it's to never ever tell God what you won't do. Not only will God take you to the exact thing that you say you won't do, He will also take you through it!! But I can guarantee that you will come out on the other side in awe and wonder of just how amazing He is. His plans and the journey of your life will most definitely be filled with twists and turns. I can say with complete confidence that although trials and tribulations – as well as the victories – are unknown, God will use the outcome and destination as part of His perfect plan for your life.

> *Your eyes saw my unformed body; all the days ordained for me were written in your book before one of them came to be. – Psalms 139:16 NIV*

> *Before I formed you in the womb, I knew you... – Jeremiah 1:5 NKJV*

When I was young, I was the "good girl." I was described as the child who would never disobey, the child who would never ever do anything outside of what was expected of her. I was never the one who followed the crowd – when others broke the rules, I enforced them! The need to be right, however, led me to self-righteousness – I began craving control and wanted to fight for my right to live my own truth.

Despite the fact I that I spent my adolescence rebelling against my parents, I found myself always coming back to my faith. I got saved at 13. I decided to put my faith in God. I had a deep passion and longing for unconditional love and acceptance, something I never experienced or knew until I found HIM!

When we are saved, though we immediately become God's child, the process of sanctification, becoming more like God, is slower. Despite my faith, I was defiant and was still determined to fix things in my own strength, I was reckless and reluctant to believe that He could and would work all things for my good. I would pray the right prayers, say and do what I thought to be all the right things, but there was still a small piece of me that just wouldn't relinquish control.

Being obedient requires relinquishing control to God. Although I thought I was being obedient, I later came to realize that I was living my will, not the will of God – and I wanted and desired to live in God's will for my life. So it was a constant battle of trying to work things out the way I wanted them, all the while being far from God's plans and purpose for me and my life.

As I was growing in my faith I prayed, believing that if I prayed and had faith, God would answer my prayers the way that I wanted them to be answered. I mean, God has always been faithful, and it seemed certain to me that if I was in the Word and doing the right things, He would surely bless me the way I wanted to be blessed. He had never given me any reason at all to doubt His love for me. After all He is a good, good father! But sometimes being obedient to God's way means taking courageous steps that we otherwise wouldn't. For me, this lesson came in the painful aftermath of my first marriage.

The relationship between me and my first husband was very manipulative. For three years I ignored signs and symptoms as I overlooked and tolerated worldly behaviors, allowing myself to become numb to the evil realities around me. As my life-long mentor and many other prayer warriors prayed over me and spoke truth into me, God gave me the strength and courage to get out of a very toxic marriage. I was hurt and in a dark place. I had lost myself in that relationship. But getting out of that marriage was not the most courageous step I had to take.

Our faithful God called me to courageous obedience when He dropped in my spirit the command to forgive my ex-husband and release the anger and hurt that I had toward him. I questioned God, but finally was obedient and did what He commanded. The result of that forgiveness was that I was freed from the feelings of failure, guilt, and shame that had consumed my entire being. It was very hard to obey the prompting from the Holy Spirit to forgive, love, and pray for someone who had hurt me so badly. But God knew best, and that was His way of protecting me and teaching me – allowing me to be able to love another one day.

I'm so grateful that God gave me the strength not only to walk away from that marriage, but to walk away in a spirit of forgiveness.

We can always trust that God wants nothing but the very best for us and will stop at nothing to reveal every single inch and piece of the depths of His heart and love for us.

But stubbornness had a strong hold on me, and right when I thought I was back in the will of God, I again began to make choices and react out of emotion rather than truth. And I slid back into the snare of the enemy's trap, back into a prideful and selfish lifestyle.

I began dating my high school sweetheart again, after years of being apart. We were living in sin, and I became pregnant out of wedlock with my oldest son. I was devastated and full of fear and shame. I had broken up with my son's father just weeks before I found out I was pregnant, and I wrestled with the idea of just not telling him and raising the baby on my own.

But God knew I had come from parents that divorced when I was two and a half, and He knew how much I desired not to raise my children in a broken household and family. Looking back, I had grown – I prayed and asked God to show me what to do rather than asking Him to fix it. God gave me the courage to call my now-husband and tell him I was pregnant. He was on the other side of the world fighting for our country, and in his absence, God worked on my heart. When he returned, we got back together, and although we struggled, God ultimately allowed us to grow together and build a strong relationship.

Out of obedience to God and the Word, we got married.

Behold, to obey is better than sacrifice…- 1 Samuel 15:22 NKJV

> *Now it shall come to pass, if you diligently obey the voice of the Lord your God, to observe carefully all His commandments which I command you today, that the Lord your God will set you high above all nations of the earth. And all these blessings shall come upon you and overtake you, because you obey the voice of the Lord your God. – Deuteronomy 28:1-2 NKJV*

God has indeed blessed our marriage, but the struggles in this life are real, and we continue to walk courageously though the storms of life.

I'm struggling, as I write, to find the courage to dig deep to allow myself to be vulnerable and transparent enough to even attempt to share the indescribable and incomprehensible love that God has displayed to me. I am struggling to hold back the tears and stifle the thoughts of doubt in my mind. Swallowing the lump in my throat and breathing through the pains in my chest, I struggle to silence the noise from the enemy. This is not easy, comfortable, or anything that I really ever wanted to do. God has a way of pushing you out of your comfort zone and giving you a supernatural strength and courage to do things you never thought you could.

On my second son's first birthday, I had a miscarriage. I had many friends who had experienced the pain and loss of an angel baby, but I could never relate until I was faced with that same devastation. You never know how strong you are until you're placed in a situation where strong is the only thing you can be.

Going through that loss at the time seemed unfair, even cruel. As I courageously faced that day, I prayed to God to give me the strength and courage to walk through the physical pain that my body was experiencing with a smile on my face – I didn't want it to affect my son's birthday celebration. I needed to be strong and not act in my emotions so that I could be fully present in the moment. I couldn't let the enemy steal my joy. It's so hard to trust that God's got you and is working all things for your good in the midst what feels like your entire world falling apart. I tried courageously to cling to His Word and remember that He is the giver of life, even while the life that had been growing inside me was being taken away from this world all too soon. There are no words to describe how I felt that day.

I remember returning home and sitting on the edge of my garden tub with a flood of mixed emotions. I felt betrayed by God. I felt alone and that no one could possibly even begin to understand what I was going through. Then, as quickly as the doubts and thoughts filled my mind, I started to receive a flood of text and voice messages filled with genuine, heartfelt prayers and condolences from hundreds and hundreds of women all over the world. I immediately felt a peace that surpassed all my own understanding. My husband asked me, "Are you ok? What can I do?" I replied, "I am at peace and I know that God will restore all that He has taken away."

I'm so grateful that God is faithful to give us no more than what He knows we can handle. You see, I truly believe that if we trust and obey God in the hard times, He will restore all that is lost. I thank God every day for the blessings that He gives, and even the ones that He takes away. Proving my faith that His timing is perfect, He blessed me almost a year later with twins—His glory, our story. He only has our best interest at heart. It's just who He is.

My husband and I have been married for eight years now, and there have been other trials and tribulations along the way, but God is faithful and through the storms and valleys, He has always given us the strength and courage to continue to fight for our marriage. God is still working in our favor, and writing our story, but I have no doubt that the very best is yet to come!

It wasn't until the last two years that I finally acknowledged and completely surrendered to God's unconditional love. Perhaps that is the most important thing that walking courageously has taught me. I have finally allowed Him to take full control and fight my battles for me, and God has brought me to the end of myself and even beyond—so much further than I could have ever imagined. God is writing my story and testimony every single day. And because I've learned to stand on the Word and His promises, and to walk according to His will and not my own, I can claim and believe that God will completely heal, restore, and grant salvation to my husband. That will be my greatest blessing. In Jesus name, Amen!

His Truth is real. The evidence has been clearly displayed throughout my entire life. God has seen and knows the innermost parts of me. At times I've run my own race instead of the Lord's race, but He patiently stood by, allowing me to fail time and time again. He continued to pursue me and come after me with a reckless love every single time I went astray. There were times when I knew that I was deliberately disobedient and doing things in my own strength. Even though He heard my every thought and saw my every action as I turned away from Him, taking for granted His love, mercy, and kindness, His love remained. What love is this, that you gave your only son, to be ridiculed, despised, beaten, and even crucified for a sinner like me! That kind of love, that kind of mercy and grace, cannot be comprehended in the natural. It can only be comprehended through the act of the unconditional love of an omnipotent God.

Love is patient, love is kind... - I Corinthians 13:4-8 NKJV

That is this incredible love that I am writing about.

Many nights I sat in my closet in the dark, crying out in desperation for answers, for peace from thoughts and whispers that tormented my mind. When darkness had fallen and I sat in my pool of self-pity and shame, you were right there beside me, God. Your arms wrapped around me, your hands wiped my tears away, and your love pierced through the hardened walls of my heart. Your words whispered and rang true through the Holy Spirit, clear and precise in my mind, "You are not alone! I'm here, and we will win this fight, together. You were made for so much more! Pick up your head, my child. I am yours, and you are mine, and no one or nothing will ever take me from your side." When you have that burning in the core of you, and that knowing with zero doubt that you are called, favored, and loved, any and all weapons that the enemy may be using to form against you are driven away.

What a wonderful Savior you are, God! I wonder how many times you watched and longed for me to just let go. How painful it must have been for you to watch me, your beloved daughter, weather the storms and suffer the consequences of my own disobedient actions. Yet you comforted, protected, and loved me anyway because you knew that through this, I could grow to know you more. The fact that you could watch and allow me to make mistake after mistake and walk through the hurt as I walked through the storms, and yet you still reached down and wrapped your arms around me and told me that you love me anyway. One can't wrap their mind around that kind of love. I am still so in awe of you.

For years and years, I have shared your love, compassion, and kindness with every single person that I've met. When prompted I've never questioned any opportunity to spread the gospel with anyone you've placed in my path.

> *Even as scripture states, "Go into all the world and preach the gospel to every creature..." – Mark 16:15 NKJV.*

I've never had any problem with being obedient in that area of my life. When I have obeyed and acted in obedience, you have always blessed me and rewarded me with favor. The times I haven't, I have sown seeds and reaped the consequences of my disobedience.

You knew, Father God, that I would come to this point, to this time, to finally reach complete surrender. And for the first time in my life, I truly am walking in complete and utter obedience to my Heavenly Father!

God's ways are not our ways. His plans are so much better than ours. He revealed Himself to me in a real, tangible way. He rid me of myself and stripped me of my selfish pride. I am free from the bondage of disobedience that the enemy has had on me. No longer am I a slave to the ties that have bound me in shame and doubt. No longer does the enemy have a hold on me. I am free. There is no boundary between me and my Heavenly Father anymore. This was the plan for my story all along.

Thank you, Jesus! Thank you for never giving up on me. I am grateful. I am blessed beyond measure. Thank you for loving a sinner like me and saving your child, your daughter, again and again. You are my God, and I am your child, and nothing will ever take me from your side.

. . . .

Courage to overcome
UNFORGIVENESS
Kimberly Ann Hobbs

Unforgiveness in your heart is like having poison in your veins. It can lead you to death if you do not seek the antidote. Forgiving people who hurt us is extremely hard to do. You can feel pain from what they have caused you, making it difficult to release true forgiveness. Trying to take control or revenge on a specific person will only further complicate the destruction of yourself. God clearly says in His Word, "'Vengeance is mine; I will repay' says the Lord" (Romans 12:19 ESV).

No one is claiming it is easy to forgive a wrong that comes against us; however, you can help yourself to counteract the poison by courageously moving forward into forgiving anyone who has offended you.

If we trust God and choose to forgive, God will take care of the rest. By doing this you are taking an action in the form of obedience by forgiving. it is your "seed" of obedience to God's Word. God is faithful and honors his Word and is faithful to bring a harvest in one way or another. Do not allow your unforgiveness to hinder your faith from working, creating a barrier. Confess it and go to the person immediately – do not wait and allow bitterness to brew.

"Therefore I tell you, whatever you ask for in prayer, believe that you've received it, and it will be yours. And when you stand praying, if you hold anything against anyone, forgive him, so that your father in heaven may forgive your sins" (Matthew 11:24-25 NIV). Your communication with God needs to flow freely, and if sin resides from unforgiveness, communication with God becomes blocked.

Don't give the devil any foothold or advantage over you because if he wins in this battle, it can become a strong hold over your life. Unforgiveness is poison!

We cannot forgive without the power of the Holy Spirit. Humble yourself and read John 20:22-23. Jesus breathed on the disciples and said, "Receive the Holy Spirit!" In the very next verse He said, "If you forgive anyone his sins they are forgiven. If you do not forgive them, they are not forgiven."

God's Word clearly tells us throughout to forgive and be forgiven. Get rid of all the poison that comes from unforgiveness, bitterness and resentment.

Courage to repent of unforgiveness will wash away the spiritual filthiness by draining the poison of death that stops life. As you are obedient to wash in the POWER of God's word and offer forgiveness to your offender, forgive in Jesus' name. This will bring refreshment to your soul and restore communication with the God who loves you most. Your life will become alive as the burden of sin is lifted and you are able to move about freely without the weight of resentment, restoring all communication with your Creator as you confess your sin.

 **Melissa C. Dyer** is a writer and podcaster who has lots to say about courage. She believes that all women need encouragement and a Champion in their corner. Her first book, *Learning to Roar*, released in September of 2020. Melissa knows first-hand how easy it is to fall into a pit of discouragement. Helping women understand how to cultivate courage in their everyday ordinary life and climb out of the pit, is her passion. Melissa resides in sunny South Florida with her husband, two teenage children, and two fur babies.

You can keep in touch with Melissa on Instagram @MelissaCDyer_ on Facebook @MelissaDyerWriter on her website www.MelissaCDyer.com and listen to her weekly on her podcast www.TheCostIsCourage.com (available on all podcast platforms)

Into the Fire

Melissa C. Dyer

I pulled up a stool in her kitchen and leaned my elbows on the edge of the granite bar. She was slathering some peanut butter and jelly between a few pieces of wheat bread for us. We were hungry. She wasn't just a spiritual leader in my life, she was also a bit of a mother figure—not quite old enough to be my mother, but close. We were still getting to know one another, so she began asking me questions about my childhood.

Looking back now, I realize how vague I was when narrating my painful story to her. I used statements like "my childhood was bad" or "messed up." I was doing my best to live out the standard of honoring my mother and father, which is a command. However, I didn't recognize that by generalizing my experience and squelching my pain, attempting to cover the abuse I experienced, I had fed its power over me. Emotionally, I had a stronghold left unconquered.

I may never be called to run into a burning building, but I know for certain what it is to be called into a fire. That may be why the story of Moses and the burning bush resonates with me so. It's the fire where he encounters God. Thankfully, with God, we don't burn in the fire.

God called me into a fire to provide the emotional healing that only my Heavenly Father could. The fire wasn't a punishment; it was a gift. But like all gifts that God wants to give His children, we must be open to receiving them. And often they look very different than what we would expect, much the same way Moses first encounters God. At the end of Exodus Chapter 2, we learn that God takes notice of the afflictions of the Israelites by the hand of the Egyptians and their Pharaoh, their god. Moses, minding his own business, having run from that same danger decades before, has settled into his complacent life in the desert, separated from His people and His God. But God decides to break through and speak to Moses.

Exodus 3:2-4 (HCSB): The Angel of the LORD appeared to him in a flame of fire within a bush. As Moses looked, he saw that the bush was on fire but was not consumed. So Moses thought: I must go over and look at this remarkable sight. Why isn't the bush burning up? When the LORD saw that he had gone over to look, God called out to him from the bush, "Moses, Moses!" "Here I am," he answered.

And just like Moses, God called me into a fire.

My fire was a phone call. It came not long after my conversation with the woman who had been making us lunch that day. The phone call was an interruption of my own complacent life in the desert. The caller relaying the information, without the slightest acknowledgment of the trauma their words were inflicting, detailed the following: My younger sister had been arrested and jailed as a result of her addiction. Her young children were now being brought into the state care system, and my mother's deception, enabling, and destructive codependency was now fully exposed. The graphic retelling of these circumstances by the voice over the phone immediately pulled me back into my broken childhood. The fullness of the pain I had suppressed for years flooded back, nearly overtaking me. Flickers of memories reminding me of the bondage I had experienced growing up. My childhood captivity. All the dangers I had fled from years before. Now burning so hot, I had to pay attention. There was a fire.

It was right there in my own story where God decided to break through, inviting me into a trial where He had plans to give me the gift of His presence and bring me needed healing that I had put off for so long. Of course, I didn't know this at the time. When the crisis hit, all I wanted to do was run away. Again. Flee for my safety. Keep that deep emotional wound buried. But something else prevailed. It was my faith. That supernatural deposit that I received from God nearly 20 years earlier was taking the lead. Yes, when Jesus stepped in and freed me from the sin that enslaved me, my sin, I was free. Free spiritually, that is. But looking back, I was never emotionally free from the pain. It was time for my faith to take a step that required courage. With all the faithfulness I had experienced in my life with God to this point, I had to trust that He would show Himself faithful to me again, even in this.

It wasn't me that had the courage to step into the pain; it was Christ in me—a work of the Holy Spirit. Over the years I've faced many crossroads. Intersections where it didn't matter which direction I looked, all there was to see ahead was a healthy dose of hard. This too was one of those crossroads. And I've come to accept the "hard way" over time. But pain, on the other hand, I avoid at all costs. Still, I chose to trust that with God all things are possible. So I took a courageous step into the pain.

In Isaiah 43:2, God gives us this promise: "I will be with you when you pass through the waters, and when you pass through the rivers, they will not overwhelm you. You will not be scorched when you walk through the fire, and the flame will not burn you." And this promise He fulfilled for me; I can attest. As I walked through the fire, I was not burned by the flame.

There were days, then weeks, then months, and finally, even years of fiery experiences I had to walk through as a result of that initial phone call. Visits with foster parents, visits with my sister in detox centers, shuttling little people back and forth, kept bound in other people's chaos. Not able to straighten out their mess. Pleading with my mother and sister to get the help they so desperately needed. All the while reliving my childhood trauma over and over again. This was the very pattern of life I had been so vague about whenever I shared my story: instability in every realm of life, moving frequently, random men being brought into our home, alcohol, drugs, and on many occasions being left unattended for hours on end. These were the harsh accounts of my childhood circumstances which escalated when my sister was born. Learning to be overly responsible and high functioning amidst the chaos became a new kind of rearing I was subjected to. At the age of 12, I became my sister's full-time daycare provider.

I recall that summer she was born. Friends would go to the neighborhood pool, have sleepovers, walk to nearby shopping. I, on the other hand, spent all day indoors, alone, with the demands of caring for an infant thrust upon me. And that was the final nail in the coffin of my childhood. First, my mother robbed me of my years of innocence by exposing me to her morally impure lifestyle, and then she demanded I share in her responsibilities as a mother. Childhood cut short. It was only the very brief and infrequent visits with my father that gave me air to breathe. Of course, these were untraditional in their own respect, but they were freeing nonetheless. For as long as I can remember, the only thing that I desired growing up was to flee. To break free from the hideousness of the home life that held me captive.

That's what made stepping back into the chaos so painful for me. It felt like walking back into my own captivity. I had often wished that the care system would save me from the chaos. That's how bad it truly was. I know so many wonderful families who foster or adopt children, who make a real difference in the lives of those born into broken homes. I even prayed for a new beginning for my sister's children. I had hoped that somehow, someone would get rescued out of our family chaos; if not me or my sister, possibly them. But that's not what God did when He called me into the fire. He didn't go back and rewrite my story by changing someone else's; that would have left me untouched by His love. He desired to see me healed of my pain.

Often that's how we receive the Christian message – we think we can receive healing by helping others who have experienced the same hurts we have. But that's not my experience with God. He's shown me time and time again that it is His presence in my life that brings the healing. Healed and freed people are what the world needs. And we become healed and free by experiencing God for ourselves.

All He asks is that I trust Him and follow His lead.

Hebrews 12:28b-29 says, "By it, (referring to God's unshakable kingdom that we receive through grace) we may serve God accept-ably, with reverence and awe, for our God is a consuming fire."

When we read that God is a consuming fire in scripture, it speaks to His jealous love to be number one in our lives. He wants the first position, first priority, and the glory that comes with being first. The glory He deserves. God does the work to heal us. Not a program. Not a ministry. Not another Christian. God does the healing work of salvation and restoration. And He does it as we are in His presence.

Although my childhood wasn't saved and my sister's addiction snatched her away too soon, and even though those precious little people are still entangled in their grandmother's chaos, God was still present through it all. And He did bring about the healing that I needed. Yes, the journey has been insufferably long for me. Far longer than I had ever imagined when I took that very first small step into the fire. However, I've learned that these cross-roads, these trials in our life, serve a greater purpose. As much as I squirm, beg, and even throw tantrums over the hard choices I've faced, all has not been wasted.

Instead, I've been given perspective.

Now, when I find myself at a crossroad where every direction seems difficult, I've learned to look through a different lens – to look for the way that requires courage. Even though the path that requires courage is sure to end in more pain and hurt, that is where I know I will also find healing, strength, wisdom and God's love. That is the road of transformation.

Looking back at this particular crossroad, God was with me every step of the way. He was there when I sat through hours and hours of state care classes (which were a requirement) to be more involved with my sister's children, and I heard Him whisper, "Melissa, I know you suffered this same abuse as a child. I am so sorry. I love you." In that brief whisper, He acknowledged my pain. Gave my pain a voice. God validated the emotional and psychological abuse that was so insidiously covered up by my mother. He was there when I was pressed to give an account of my home life as a child. As I completed documents and was questioned in court, being demanded to give an unfiltered account of the lack of parenting and nurturing I should have benefitted from in my early years. Forced to relive my pain. I never would have understood that my physical freedom as an adult, which I had longed for as a child, would not be enough to heal me. Deep down inside, I was still in bondage to those childhood wounds. But God was there. He allowed me to experience these events, bringing my pain to the surface so He could break through the emotional stronghold that had tethered me to my past.

Yes, when I received Jesus as my salvation, I was free. Free from my bondage to sin. My sin. And there was proof of that in my life. Fruit. I had a healthy marriage. I am a good parent to my own children. Not perfect. But good. In many areas of my life, I was healed and changed. Generational curses have been broken. But God doesn't want us to be healed and free in many areas of our life – He wants us to be healed in ALL areas of our life. That's why I love Matthew 19:26, "With God ALL things are possible." As long as we commit to take courageous steps of faith WITH God, ALL things are possible. He wants to transform every area of our life. Every area where we've been hurt. Every area we've messed up. In every area we need hope. But our part is to take courageous steps with Him. To trust Him. To allow Him to lead us into the fires and broken parts of our stories so He can do His work in us. We must make the choice that requires courage because these are the crossroads that lead us to transformation.

As for my story, yes, I wish it had a fairy tale ending. But it doesn't. Fairy tales are not real. But God is. He works in our reality right where we need Him. And I needed healing. And that's how it glorifies God. Even though He called me into a fire, I was not burned. Instead, I was healed. God promised His presence would be with me and He fulfilled that promise to me, showing that He is faithful and can be trusted. God promises His presence will be with you too, and He wants to prove Himself faithful to you. But you need to trust Him. Take a courageous step of faith into the fire when He calls your name.

Today, I'm able to live more freely than I've ever lived before, without the invisible shackles that had held me back for so long. The inability to use my words, my voice, to speak up for myself was an emotional stronghold binding me to the childhood version of myself. For too long I was blind to the way I had allowed my mother to have power over me. She continued to devalue me and had made every attempt to ensnare me in her chaos as an adult. Until God called me into the fire. Still today I pray for her. I pray that she will turn and take her own courageous steps toward healing. But she will need to take her *own* steps, and so do you. If you know that there is something in your life that is separating you from intimacy with your Heavenly Father, be brave and take a step of courage with Him. He is always waiting for us to turn from the things that separate us from His presence and healing power.

And what about unresolved hurt and pain? Would you recognize God in a fire? My fire wasn't a literal burning bush, but I knew the trial was a fire. I recognized God's presence in the situation because I had grown in my knowledge of who He is and how He has revealed Himself in scripture. I had taken a million baby steps over the years to grow my faith. Daily reading my Bible. Quiet days full of prayer and solitude. Hours of singing songs to Him in worship. And surrounding myself with His people. These practices prepared me to follow Him where I did not want to go and gave me encouragement on the journey. The Holy Spirit reminded me of a verse, or a hymn, or spoke through a friend to provide assurance that God was present in these chaotic circumstances, consistently leading me from one little fire to another. But I was able to encounter His peace daily as I sought Him out myself. If I had relied on the circumstances to change, had waited for all the details to come together just as I'd prayed, if I had kept watch only for my happy ending, then I would have missed what God had planned. He planned to refine my faith.

In 1 Peter we are told, "You rejoice in this, though now for a short time you have had to struggle in various trials so that the genuineness of your faith—more valuable than gold, which perishes though refined by fire—may result in praise, glory, and honor at the revelation of Jesus Christ. You love Him, though you have not seen Him. And though not seeing Him now, you believe in Him and rejoice with inexpressible and glorious joy, because you are receiving the goal of your faith, the salvation of your souls" (1 Peter 1:6-9). A faith that depends on happy endings and pots of gold at the end of rainbows is not a faith authored by God, but man-made. And that kind of faith has no power to save our souls.

If you are enduring a fiery trial right now, have courage; cling to God on the journey. He has the power to burn through every stronghold that keeps you from Him. And please don't trade a true and enduring faith for anything that will perish. Instead, be brave and choose to walk through your fiery trials with God. Follow where He leads and seek Him daily. This is how to take courageous steps of faith. Let Him prove His faithful presence to be with you no matter how hot life gets, because with Him, all things are possible.

. . . .

Courage to Overcome Captivity

Julie Jenkins

Captivity. Imprisonment. Confinement. Slavery. Bondage.

None of these are pretty words. The very thought makes our breath catch and our pulse race. And yet the thing that holds us each captive more than anything else is something of our own choosing – our own sin.

Have you ever watched a "scary" movie and rolled your eyes at the predictable outcome, thinking, *Of course she is going to get caught by the bad guy – she is not making a smart decision – she should know better. Just turn the light on and don't go out in the dark!?* And yet, don't we often make wrong decisions when we should know better? Don't we often put our foot right in the devil's trap?

Scripture teaches us the way to freedom. 1 Thessalonians 4 and 5 are just two chapters that we can meditate on to help us 'turn the light on' to keep from walking through the dark into the devil's trap. I picture a string of lights with each tiny bulb encompassing words of wisdom that light the path of our lives: Live in a way that pleases God, remember what you were taught, be holy, stay away from sexual sin, never harm or cheat a fellow believer, mind your own business, work with your hands, be on your guard, stay alert and clearheaded, honor your leaders, warn those who are lazy, encourage the timid, give tender care to the weak, be patient, always try to do good to each other, be joyful, never stop praying, be thankful, hold onto what is good.

These rays of light are given to us not as a list of rules, but as a means of keeping ourselves free from the snare of the devil, thereby giving us freedom.

We are also taught the way to freedom through the Holy Spirit's guidance. I heard it once said, "Don't devalue the voice of the Holy Spirit by calling it your conscience." That still small voice that guides your path is the voice of God! Don't dismiss it! "How gracious he (the Lord) will be when you cry for help! As soon as he hears, he will answer you...Whether you turn to the right or to the left, your ears will hear a voice behind you, saying, 'This is the way; walk in it'" (Isaiah 30:19,21).

Sister, we don't have to walk in the dark! We can steer clear of the devil's trap! Turn on the light and follow God's voice to freedom!

. . . .

Afterword

May the scriptures in this book linger as you hold on to "ferocious faith" governed from your seat of authority in Jesus Christ. May you be more passionate in your calling in Him, taking your own courageous steps of faith toward what you believe. Be a voice of love of hope and of truth.

God has given each of us our own story. Your story matters. Pray over your story, write it down, and then consider sharing it. Do not be one who allows doubts and destruction to sow rivers of unbelief within you. Have courage with faith. Write down your message inside your heart and be known as someone who stands boldly on the Word of God and on unshakable, solid ground. Do not back down and do not be swept away. It is time to come out of hiding and seek God's heart for your beautiful purpose. The time is now. God has a role birthed in you and it is your choice to step out in courage with faith to be heard in the nations within this earth.

The enemy believes he could stop you, but God says "NO."

"God is your mighty defender, perfect and just in all His ways; Your God is faithful and true; He does what is right and fair."
– Deuteronomy 32:4 GNB

Remember, you can do all things through Christ who strengthens you, but you must take the first courageous step of faith and move from the place you are. You can do this! Step out in faith, remembering ... "With God all things are possible." – Matthew 19:26 NKJV

If God has moved within you through reading this book, prompting you through the power of the Holy Spirit to be courageous and share your story, we want to hear from you. Please reach out to us at womenworldleaders.com and let us know. We can help you get your story to the world. May God do exceedingly, abundantly beyond what we can ever imagine according to the power at work within us.